CW00494756

OFFROAD ADVENTURE CYCLING

50 ROUTES IN ENGLAND FOR THE MOUNTAIN BIKER

Jeremy Evans

The Crowood Press

First published in 1990 by
The Crowood Press
Ramsbury
Marlborough
Wiltshire SN8 2HE

British Library Cataloguing in Publication Data

Evans, Jeremy
Off-road adventure cycling: 50 routes in England for the mountain biker.
1. England. Description and travel
I. Title
914.204858

ISBN 1 85223 368 0

Acknowledgements
Thanks to Roger Tushingham of Tushingham and Lester Noble of Orange Mountain Bikes who helped with rides in Yorkshire and the Lake District. Lester also designed my trusty bikes – a Tushingham B52 and the Clockwork Orange which superseded it. Ian Leonard, Ben Oakely, and James and Jane Ellis were among those who accompanied me on rides in the south. Thanks to them, and to Lesley and Bryony who invariably formed the support team.

Picture Credits
All maps and all black and white photographs supplied by the author.

Typeset by Keyboard Services, Luton, Beds
Printed by Butler & Tanner Ltd, Frome

Contents

	Introduction	5
	DARTMOOR	
1	Castle Drogo	12
2	Burrator	15
3	Holne and Scorriton	18
4	Challacombe Down	22
5	Postbridge	24
6	Lustleigh Cleave	29
7	Cosdon Beacon	32
	EXMOOR	
8	Doone Country	36
9	Exford to Simonsbath	40
10	Dunkery Beacon	43
	DORSET AND THE PURBECKS	
11	Blandford	47
12	Chaldon Down	51
13	Maiden Castle and Hardy's Monument	54
14	Bloxworth	58
15	Nine Barrow Down	62
16	Winterborne Kingston	66
17	St Alban's Head	70
18	Poxwell and White Horse Hill	74
	THE ISLE OF WIGHT	
19	The Shepherds Trail	80
20	The Hamstead Trail	85
21	The Tennyson Trail	88
22	Niton to Luccombe Down	92
	SUSSEX AND THE SOUTH DOWNS	
23	Wey South Path	97
24	Watergate Hanger	101
25	Kingley Vale	104
26	Stane Street	108
27	Wepham Down	112
28	Cocking	116

29	Chanctonbury	119
30	Harting Downs	124
31	Alfriston	128
32	Firle Beacon	131
33	Ditchling Beacon	134
34	The South Downs Way: Queen Elizabeth Country Park to Steyning	136
35	The South Downs Way: Steyning to Eastbourne	141
	YORKSHIRE DALES	
36	Gayles	146
37	Malham	149
38	Grassington	152
39	Marske	155
40	Nidderdale	158
41	North of Reeth	160
42	South of Reeth	163
43	Kexwith and Barningham Moor	166
44	Gunnerside	170
45	Kisdon Force	173
46	Scar House Reservoir	176
	THE LAKE DISTRICT	
47	Grizedale	180
48	Ullswater	183
49	Loadpot Hill	185
50	Helvellyn	188
	Useful Addresses	192

Introduction

Here are fifty offroad mountain bike or all-terrain bike rides which I have researched and ridden, and for the most part greatly enjoyed! Some are better than others and some are classics, but I'm not telling you which, because I don't want my favourite trails packed solid with riders!

So far as I am aware none of the rides go on footpaths which are absolutely illegal to all riders whether on bike or horse, and if they do go on a footpath, you walk. For the most part they stick to bridleways which are legal rights of way for walkers, horseriders, and now cyclists who have never really been able to enjoy them until the advent of the offroad bike. If you want to know more about rights of way, the Countryside Commission publish a useful booklet called *Out in the Country*, available from Countryside Commission Publications, 19/23 Albert Road, Manchester M19 2EQ (tel: 061 224 6287).

Bridleways must be shared with walkers and horse-riders. As walkers were there first and have first right to the trails, treat them with respect. My impression is that so far walkers cast a kind eye on offroad bikes, but this could quickly change if you go barging past, whooping as they

Stick to legal trails! Lester Noble begins the long descent on the Helvellyn ride.

scatter to avoid you. Walkers don't always expect bikes, so as you come up behind them be polite and ask them in the nicest possible way if you might squeeze past. If they're coming towards you don't assume that they should stand aside and let you by; they often do, so why not stop for a change and do the same for them. Remember that walkers and the Ramblers' Association form a powerful lobby group and if they develop a dislike for offroad bikes it is quite possible that bikes could be banned from some bridleways, as has happened on many trails in the USA. Act sensibly and be courteous and this won't happen in England.

Horses have also been around far longer than bikes, though I must say that if they were invented now they would almost certainly be banned because of the way in which they churn up and massacre the tracks – any horsy bridleway is worth avoiding in wet weather! When you meet horses and their riders be as polite and careful as you are with walkers, and remember that occasionally horses can be fairly dangerous with their riders only in semi-control. You will have to take things as you find them, remembering once again that horseriders are a fairly powerful lobby.

What about bikes and the environment? Ridden carefully, a bike is without doubt much kinder to tracks and trails than any horse; perhaps even kinder than a pair of walking boots. Apart from a whirr and a clickety-click we don't make much noise, but we do go faster!

The Rides

The fifty rides in this book are divided into seven principal areas in England which have a lot to offer the offroad biker. All, except the two rides along the length of the South Downs Way, are circular, ranging in length from just under 10 to well over 20 miles (16–32 km). I have assumed that you will either ride to the start point, or take your bike by car or train. Putting your bike on a train is a free service on most routes, but there are restrictions on some and charges at certain times, so it is wise to check. British Rail publish a guide called *Biking by Train*. Bikes travel in the guard's van, and BR recommend that your bike should be labelled, with all valuables and loose items removed, and that you arrive in plenty of time to get it on the train. If five or more of you are travelling with your bikes you should telephone and make prior arrangements since the guard's van may not have enough room to hold them all. Finally, don't ride on the platform!

Details given for each ride include the relevant OS map and the grid reference of the start point, the nearest BR station, and the approximate length in miles. Each ride is graded 'easy', 'moderate' or 'hard', though how *you* find it will to some extent depend on your own riding ability, inclination, and the weather – a track that is 'easy' in dry weather can soon become 'hard' when it's wet. I have also indicated where there are climbs, and most of these rides demand some uphill riding, for what goes up must come down and that's the best part of it! *Difficulties* you may encounter include mud, poor signposting, your way blocked or ploughed up, or too many walkers. *High Points* gives some idea what the ride is about and why you should go for it. Finally, under *R & R* are listed pubs, cafés, and other amenities, which will be much needed during or after a long, hard ride!

Finding the Way

Navigation is easy where there is good signposting; and can be very difficult where it is poor. The best signposting I know is in West Sussex where wooden or metal bridleway signs clearly point where every bridleway goes. In other

A bridleway sign shows where you can go, but in some areas signposting is non-existent.

areas of England you will find blue arrows (yellow for footpaths) painted on posts to give a rough idea of direction; or blue blobs daubed on trees or posts, telling you that it is a bridleway, but giving no indication of direction. Many of these blue blobs become hopelessly faded with time, which give little more help than the many tracks that are completely unmarked and signposted.

Looking after the bridleways and their signposting is the duty of the local highway authority and if you feel incensed by the lack of signposting or a bridleway that's blocked, you should complain to the relevant district council's Rights of Way Officer as soon as possible.

Taking the correct OS map – and being able to read it – is recommended for enjoying these rides. A compass is a must – there are times when working out which is north and which is south isn't easy, and knowing makes all the difference between finding the way and getting irretrievably lost.

Time Taken

Offroad riding is surprisingly slow. On these rides my average speeds ranged from just below 4 mph (6.4 kmph) to somewhere over 8 mph (12.8 kmph) depending on the type of terrain encountered. A mere 4 mph (6.4 kmph) may seem slow, but if you consider the times you stop to consult the map it becomes a realistic speed. If you don't know the terrain it makes sense to take it easy on the downhills, and by the time you have stopped at a pub and put in a few other diversions, many of these rides make good, full day outings which can also usually be extended with the aid of an OS map.

Preparation

I would always recommend carrying some drink (non alcoholic), and if the weather is hot you will need a lot of it to avoid the dehydration which comes on insidiously. Food stops are equally important, and you should carry snacks unless you can be certain of finding places to stop and buy something on the way.

Your bike should of course be in good working order – fully lubricated, and with the brakes providing failsafe

Dehydration sets in quickly, so carry plenty of liquid.

stopping. Carry a pump, a spare tube, tyre levers, and a puncture repair kit at all times. Punctures are an inevitable part of offroading, though not as frequent as you might expect – I had about ten in total during these fifty rides. The only other tool I needed was a chain link extractor, having broken the same chain three times running, but I suspect it was a rogue chain. Apart from a bag to carry your tools and a good pump, other extras you may go for are toe straps – a matter of personal preference for those who like to be locked to the pedals – and a milometer which is handy for recording progress and can also be a help with your navigation.

Clothing

Specialist cycle clothing isn't vital, but it's certainly the most comfortable thing to wear. Starting from the bottom I wear a good pair of offroad lightweight riding/hiking boots by AXO with medium thick socks; proper cycling shorts with good reinforcement, or long tights depending on the weather; a stretchy cycling shirt with a zip neck and big back pockets to carry an OS map; and a cyclist's thermal overshirt with the same neck zip and back pockets.

When the going gets cold a pair of waterproof mittens are recommended, being warmer than gloves. When the going gets wet there is no easy answer, but in my experience the type of lightweight anoraks that fold into a tiny bundle to be carried on a waistband are effective enough to keep you moderately dry, even though they sweat and may not last long.

What about safety protection? Whether you wear a helmet or not is up to you. Of course it's safer if you do – going over the handlebars can easily happen, and you may connect your head with a rock, tree, or something else hard, in which case head protection could be a lifesaver. Some experienced riders won't be without a helmet, while others only wear one if they have to during an organised race. Either way you should aim to ride carefully enough not to come off. You may like to wear gloves to protect your hands while riding through thorns and brambles, but in my experience this is unnecessary.

You may want to carry some kind of first aid kit, though it's likely you won't be able to include everything you could need. With careful riding the chances of an accident are small. The only time I came off at speed during the fifty rides in this book was when I chose to look backwards, trying to read a bridleway signpost while going forwards at about 30 mph. The front wheel hit a rut which I could have controlled if I was concentrating on forward motion, but instead I wiped out immediately. My forearm took the brunt of the crash, with a deep rip resulting in a scar which I bear today, but being close to civilisation I was able to get myself fixed up at a surgery fairly quickly. The moral of the story is *look where you're going, concentrate, and don't overcook it!*

The Right Bike

I almost believe that all mountain bikes are exactly the same – just painted different colours! If you go for models in the middle price bracket and upwards their specifications will be almost identical. Salesmen may hail such things as minute differences in seat angle as 'revolutionary', but in reality these are of little account when compared to the power of your legs and lungs, and the will to keep on riding. A good bike takes some getting used to, and it is only with experience that you will gain the necessary skill to make a really fast descent or negotiate a difficult track.

Not all mountain bikes are the same; this one is circa 1988.

Care and Repair

After the ride is over, you must care for and repair your bike. Hose and wash off any mud, which if left on will rust and do terrible things to the gears. Keep the chain well oiled, and every now and then give the brake and gear cables a complete lube to keep them moving freely. Change brake blocks as soon as they're worn, and leave more weighty matters of maintenance to other bike books or your local bike shop.

Dartmoor

Dartmoor is the biggest wilderness in south-west England. It's a wilderness by name and by nature, with an unforgiving terrain that demands careful preparation when setting out on a ride in inclement weather. Many of the 'bridleways' marked on the maps are lost in moorland and riding off the tracks can be frustrating, with rocks and bogs ready to trap the unwary.

The upside is that Dartmoor is a very beautiful area. Little villages nestle in green valleys, and after a good ride there are cream teas, pubs and West Country cider ready and waiting for you!

Ride 1 CASTLE DROGO

Area: Drewsteignton, north Dartmoor.
Start: OS Outdoor Leisure 28 grid ref 736908; limited parking by church at Drewsteignton.
Nearest BR station: Yeoford.
Approx length: 8.5 miles (13.6 km).
Ride: Easy.
Climbs: Three climbs, all of which are moderate.
Conditions: Hard tracks; some mud possible.
Difficulties: Track round Castle Drogo may become congested by walkers.
High Points: Good woodland riding; magnificent views over the Teign Valley; Castle Drogo well worth a visit.
R & R: Pub in Drewsteignton; National Trust café at Castle Drogo and Fingle Bridge.

This is a short ride but really enjoyable – especially if you like visiting National Trust houses, since it revolves around a visit to Castle Drogo (open daily from Good Friday to the end of October).

Park by the church in Drewsteignton in front of the post office; the pub is next door, and a village shop and a restaurant are close by. If there is no room to park at Drewsteignton, try the large car park at Fingle Bridge down the hill and adjust the ride to start from there.

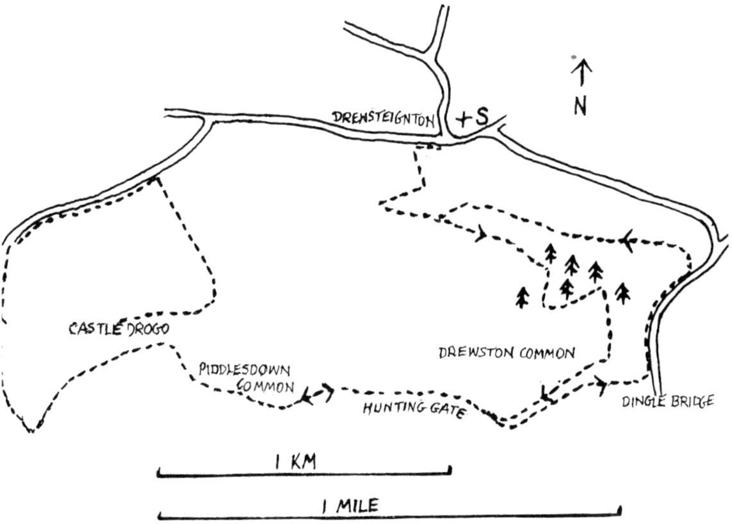

From the church ride south down the hill, then turn right towards Drogo and Sandy Park. Just past the school the bridleway is clearly indicated on the left; head downhill on a good track into a valley bearing left. At the bottom turn left on the bridleway, ignoring the footpath sign to the right. After a short distance the track splits left and right with a signpost to Fingle Bridge and Hunter's Path.

Take the Hunter's Path route which winds its way through the woodland on a very good track – amazingly good for Dartmoor! It's an up and down ride (though mainly up!) and the way is clearly marked as you gradually gain height through the woods before breaking into the open at the top of Drewston Common. After this long, steady climb, which is easily ridable all the way, the view that awaits you down the heavily wooded valley of the River Teign with moorland beyond on the far side is superb.

From here there's a really good hard track that runs level along the hillside, past Hunting Gate and Piddledown Common. It's good for fast riding with the same incredible views all the way, but watch out for pedestrians! When I did this ride on a weekday in May there were quite a few out and about, and on a weekend in high summer this track could well be too crowded to be enjoyable.

Castle Drogo comes into view round one of the bends looking for all the world like a vastly overgrown pillbox.

The track passes below and round the side of it, before heading down and joining a tarmac track which leads up to the road. From here there's a stiff pedal uphill and the road can be busy with all the car-borne visitors who flock to the castle and Fingle Bridge.

At the top of the hill turn right up the long driveway to Castle Drogo, forking right into the car park where there's a kiosk which sells pasties and great ice-cream, and in the castle itself there's a very good café serving lunches and teas. The castle was designed by Lutyens and built for Julius Drewe between 1910 and 1930, and is both hideous and magnificent with its gloomy baronial rooms and memorably funereal chapel. Mr Drewe had made his fortune and retired by the age of 33, so it's mind boggling that he could afford to build this vast place. The gardens are also splendid, and in particular there's a beautiful circular croquet lawn for which you can hire mallets from the shop.

The quickest way back to your start point is along the road, but it's more fun to head back via Fingle Bridge. Retrace your tracks around Hunter's Tor on the Hunter's Track. Past Hunting Gate and just by a bench, the track splits as indicated by the signposts. The left-hand track going down into trees is the way you came up; the right-hander going down more steeply leads straight down through the woods to Fingle Bridge on a good fast surface – but there's no room for manoeuvre, so watch out for pedestrians.

At the bottom you come out on the road just above Fingle Bridge which is a nice spot with riverside walks and another good National Trust shop and café. After taking a look, head back up the road for about 500 yards (440 m) until you come to a track heading off to the left. This leads along the edge of the woods, running alongside a stream on an easy gradient – however it is likely to be muddy in wet weather. Eventually you rejoin your outward track at the western end of the woods, from where you turn right, back up to Drewsteignton.

Allow two hours for the riding, two for Drogo, and an hour or two for Fingle Bridge and Drewsteignton and you should have a great day out!

Ride 2 BURRATOR

Area: Burrator Reservoir near Princetown, south Dartmoor.
Start: OS Outdoor Leisure 28 grid ref 557707; small car park on south side of road near Princetown.
Nearest BR station: Gunnislake.
Approx length: 13.25 miles (21.2 km).
Ride: Moderate.
Climbs: A few steady climbs.
Conditions: Mainly hard, rough tracks.
Difficulties: Usual safety precautions on open moorland should apply.
High Points: A fine ride round Burrator Reservoir with plenty of variety.
R & R: Pub, café and shop in Princetown.

This is easy/moderate riding which should pose minimal navigation problems in good weather. If you want to include a R & R stop, you could head straight for the pub in Princetown on the track that runs NNW from Nun's Cross Farm adding around 5 miles (8 km) there and back. Princetown is a somewhat grim and gloomy place with the famous prison dominating it – and you want to take care not to extend your stay . . .

The most convenient car park for this ride is three miles south-west from Princetown on the B3212. It's easy to spot,

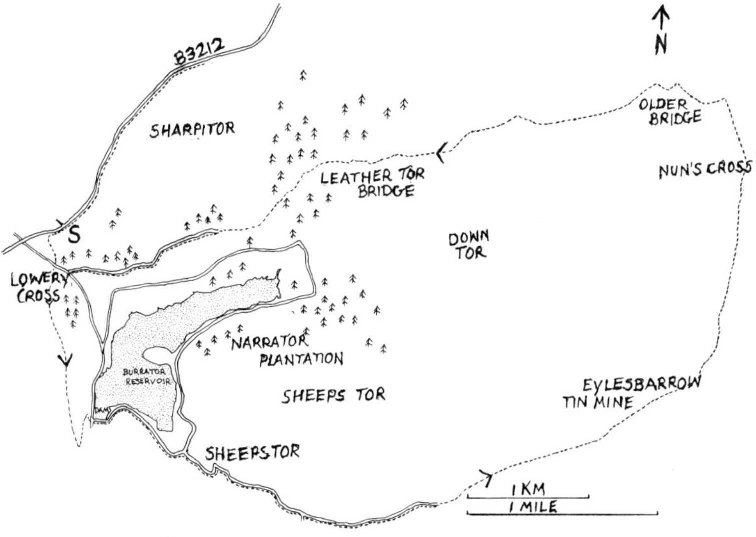

being at the top of a hill with a small pond alongside and Sharpitor's bleak peak behind. Alternatively, there are a couple of parking spots further down the road towards the cattle grid, but they are only big enough for a very few cars.

Ride down the road in a south-west direction, going over the cattle grid with woods on your left. A little further on you'll see the raised embankment of an old railway line, which could itself have made a fine cycleway! About 100 yards (88 m) further on, the bridleway is clearly indicated to the left. Go through the gate and up across a grassy field, bearing diagonally across it. When you come to a road, cross over it and ride out on to the right-hand side of the woods at Lowery Cross. Follow the perimeter of the woods which are bounded by an old stone wall – the going is good and fast on firm grass, and the area is well used by horses.

Burrator Reservoir soon comes into view on your left. Keep your height as you leave the woods behind, heading across the grassland and then a little down to the left through gorse. Eventually you will come to an old stone wall, and beyond it you join a hard crossing track which zig-zags its way down to the dam at the south-west end of the reservoir. Find your way down to the dam, taking the 'bike severe' direct route if you feel up to it, though the usual warnings about going head-over-heels on hard rocks apply.

Follow the road over the dam and keep on this quiet lane for the hamlet of Sheepstor, ignoring a turning to the left. You pass the entrance to a country house hotel, and then the very pretty church with its old cross before it. Keep straight on along the side of a waterway on this really nice lane which then starts to climb out of Sheepstor. Ignore a road turning to the right, and bear left with the magnificent mass of Sheeps Tor (the hill not the village) looking particularly fine across the valley.

The road soon peters out by a small parking spot with an MOD sign informing you that no vehicles should pass this point. Ignore the track that goes uphill to the right, and keep on ahead on a rough track which crosses a ford and then goes gradually uphill past a clump of trees sheltering a scout hut. The track is easy to follow, and though some of the going is hard and rocky you can ride on the grassland alongside it.

Keep on across the wild moor, steadily gaining height until you come to the Eylesbarrow Tin Mine which is recognisable by its old walls and workings. Where the track divides, bear left through the workings, and when it divides again take either track – the right track goes round the outside of the mine and is the easy route, while the left track goes right through the workings and is harder to ride, but gives fascinating glimpses of sunken pits and other strange devices. This must indeed have been a terrible place to work in!

Beyond the mine the track bears left to the north, when the large radio mast above Princetown comes into view. Keep on downhill, with Nun's Cross Farm, a truly isolated settlement, to your right. The track gets worse, but is still rideable, and you soon come down to the conspicuous Nun's Cross next to a wall about 300 yards (265 m) from the farmhouse. Push on along the track which becomes less distinct, passing two sets of roadside stones. Eventually you come to a clearly defined crossing track. Turn left here, and follow it round to the right heading towards another crossing track with the strange canal system of the tin mines running off to the left.

Turn left at the crossing track and cross the canal at Older Bridge. You then push on down the track with Burrator Reservoir once again ahead of you. It's a long, gradual downhill, but the going is so rocky that you can't go fast in any safety. Where the track reaches the corner of the woods you go through a gate, and it then runs down the side of the woods with a fine view to Down Tor on the left. After about 300 yards (265 m) take the unmarked right turning into the trees, then bear immediately left on a downhill track that leads to Leather Tor Bridge.

At the bridge the track divides, going either side of the river. If you wish to extend the ride you could bear left along the very pleasant track down to the Norsworthy Bridge car park, joining the bridleway at Narrator Plantation and finding your way back round the south side of the reservoir. To get back more directly, cross Leather Tor Bridge and then head uphill on the track that gradually takes you to the road, revealing another fine view of the reservoir and Sheeps Tor, a great place for a picnic.

Bear right along the road for a short distance, and then bear right again uphill on another more minor road which soon levels out towards Lower Lowery and makes for delightful riding with more of those strange waterways following alongside the road. Pedal up a final uphill, and then rejoin the outward bridleway at Lowery Cross and head back to your start point.

Ride 3 HOLNE and SCORRITON

Area: Holne and Scorriton to the north-west of Buckfastleigh, south Dartmoor.
Start: OS Outdoor Leisure 28 grid ref 706696; free car park just beyond pub opposite café at Holne.
Nearest BR station: Totnes.
Approx length: 12.5 miles (20 km).
Ride: Moderate.
Climbs: Steady climbs up from Holne and Scorriton; severe climb back to Holne on Two Moors Way.
Conditions: Mixed terrain and mainly easy going.
Difficulties: None.
High Points: Fine views, lots of variety, convenient half-way stop.
R & R: Pub and café at Holne; pub at Scorriton.

Holne is a little place out on the south-east edge of the moor which can be reached via narrow roads from Buckfastleigh, Ashburton or Two Bridges. The car park is just past the ancient pub, conveniently opposite a café/restaurant which you will probably welcome after this very pleasant double circuit.

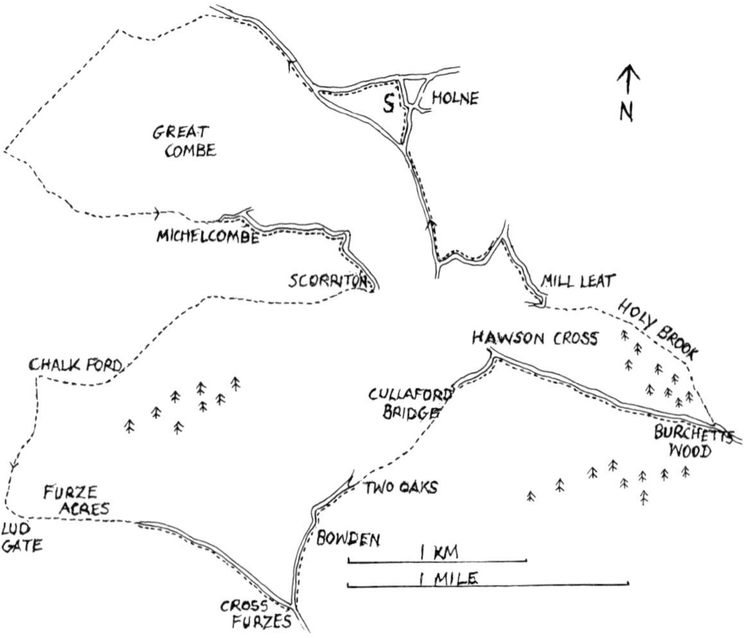

Turn right out of the car park, and at the pub bear left up the hill and then left again at the T-junction. Continue plugging up this long uphill which takes you out to open moorland. Just past the cattle grid a clear, unmarked track bears off to the left about a mile from Holne. This takes you on to the moor with a gradual climb on quite a good track with a hill called Great Combe to your left. Keep along this track until it begins to drop downhill to some stoneworks, with a clear view of Venford Reservoir down to the right.

Here the track bends left uphill on broken ground in a south-west direction, passing through old tin mine workings indicated by strange lumps, bumps and clefts in the ground. Carry on straight up the hill heading for the summit where there's a lonely tor and a single wind-blasted tree. Here you join the old Sandy Way track which leads out to more tin mine workings to the west. Bear left along the grassy track (despite its name!) with fine views of moorland all around. The track soon heads on a long downhill into the valley, crossing a stream and eventually coming to a bridleway gate.

Go through this gate, and carry on down a long track which is very rubbly and rocky. This takes you down to a bridleway sign pointing left to Holne via Great Combe. Ignore this and keep straight ahead on through another gate to join the road. From here, follow the signs on a very pretty lane to Scorriton. When you come to an unmarked T-junction by an ivy-clad farmhouse bear right downhill, and then uphill to the welcoming Tradesman's Arms. This is a finely situated pub with views over the valley, plenty of outside seating, a children's room, good food, and Ruddles and Ushers on draught. After 5 miles, it's as pleasant a place to stop as any.

To continue on the second circuit carry on past the pub for about 50 yards (44 m), turning right up a track with a dead-end sign. This track has a good surface and it leads gradually up between Michelcombe and Higher Coombe. After passing a driveway to the right it bends left and continues downhill, with fine views across to Scae Wood to the south. At the top of the hill there's a driveway going right to Scorriton Down Farm, and a gate ahead. Go through the gate, passing a footpath sign to the right. Then follow the bridleway down the side of the hill to Chalk Ford on a very pleasant track, and at Chalk Ford cross the bridge and follow the bridleway sign for Lud Gate, heading left steeply uphill.

The direction you are travelling is south with a touch of west as you plug up this steep section on grass. Carry on with the woods on your left, picking your way up the indistinct track. After a good climb you should come to a crossing track coming down from the direction of Pupers Hill which is conspicuous on your right. The track runs down to Furze Acres, a green building set in the corner of the woods to your left. Go through the gate set in the wall by Furze Acres, and carry on along the track beyond.

This track brings you gradually downhill on a reasonable stony surface. Bear right past Lodge on to a minor road which takes you down to Cross Furzes; then turn left and ride along and downhill past the farm at Bowden on your right. A little further on at Two Oaks there's a distinctive track going to the right towards a gate with fields beyond. Just by this gate there's a bridleway sign sending you down to the left on to a dried-up river bed track. This is a good technical section in an enclosed gully which bumps you downhill on a rocky surface, and it's tricky to ride in places.

Eventually you come down to Cullaford Bridge with the kind of cottage that an estate agent would describe as 'idyllic' on the left. Ride uphill on the road here to Hawson Cross, which indeed has a cross and a bus shelter opposite (from here you could cut short the ride by following the road signs to Holne). Turn right past the shelter along the road, and after an uphill and a long downhill past Hawson Court, put on the brakes when you reach the end of the woods on your left where there's a small cottage. Here turn hard left on to a signposted bridleway track, and go through a gate into Burchetts Wood which has a National Trust sign.

Keep along the track through the very pretty woods. The going is mainly good, though there are likely to be some muddy parts and the surface becomes rubbly when it runs alongside Holy Brook. At the end you reach a bridge to cross the brook; it's better to ride through and risk wet feet!

Turn right on to a quiet road which almost immediately bends left and starts a steep uphill past farm buildings. Plug on up, and at the top you have the choice of either taking the direct road route as signposted to Holne, or bearing left downhill for a final offroad section along the Two Moors Way. We chose the latter, knowing full well that what goes down also has to go up! Ride down the hill past a cottage on the right, and a little further on where the

James Ellis crosses the ford near the end of the Holne and Scorriton ride, and stays dry.

road bends hard left there's a track going steeply up to the right. This is a hard climb on a rough surface – a real test for those bikers who consider that they are super-macho! Grind on up, and as the track improves and levels out it becomes tarmac and then joins the road.

Bear right here, and then right again when you see the village sign for Holne at the top of the hill. Ride downhill past a few houses, and you will soon return to your start point in time for afternoon tea in the lee of the church, or maybe an early evening drink at the pub.

Ride 4 CHALLACOMBE DOWN

Area: Bennett's Cross north-east of Postbridge, north Dartmoor.
Start: OS Outdoor Leisure 28 grid ref 681817; limited parking on south side of road at Bennett's Cross.
Nearest BR station: Totnes.
Approx length: 7 miles (11.2 km).
Ride: Moderate.
Climbs: Moderately hard climb up to Grimpspound.
Conditions: Mainly good tracks.
Difficulties: None.
High Points: Fine views and lots of variety packed into a short circuit; Grimpspound worth seeing.
R & R: Warren House Inn near Bennett's Cross.

This is a short circuit but it's a good ride with lots of variety both in riding and scenery, with no real problems. Start at the parking space on the south side of the B3212 at Bennett's Cross, just by the well-worn cross itself. About 300 yards (265 m) further along the road is the Warren House Inn by another parking spot which could make an alternative start point.

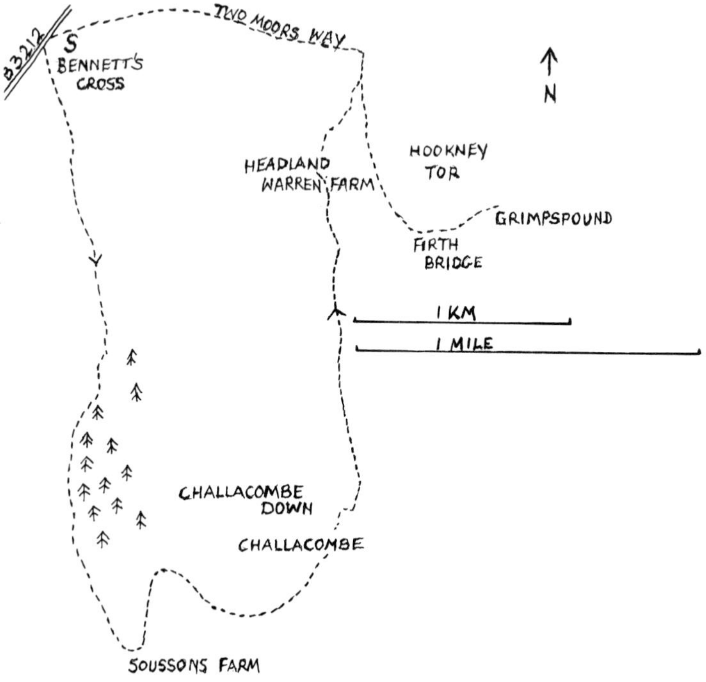

Looking out over the moor you will see the forest of Soussons ahead of you, with a gap over towards the left side where you are heading. Head downhill on a grassy track in a southerly direction. The track soon deteriorates, but it is easy enough to pick your way, passing through old mine workings. After a time you join a good track which rapidly takes you to the woods. Go through a gate and a short way further on turn right into the woods as indicated by a bridleway sign which also points straight ahead.

Follow the signs through the woods – the going is mainly good, but in some parts it may be muddy and the going heavy. When you come to a gate with woods on the right and open ground to the left, go straight on along the grassy track which brings you to Soussons Farm. Here you go through the gate, and immediately turn left through another gate into the farmyard of this lovely old farmstead. Go out through the gate on the other side and turn left through another gate, heading up across a grassy field back towards the eastern edge of the woods. Ignore the next gate and go through the one beyond where there's a tin shack ahead of you on the edge of the woods.

Here the track clearly bends round to the right and downhill along the valley, crossing a stream, and then heading up to a gate on the other side. Go through this gate and follow the track up over a grassy field with views over another valley and a road opening out to your right. Follow this very pleasant hillside track past Challacombe and Challacombe Cottages, opening and closing gates as you go. Headland Warren Farm comes into view in a commanding position on the right-hand side of the valley ahead, with the mass of rocks which is Hookney Tor conspicuous to the right above it.

Carry on towards Headland Warren Farm, bearing up towards it. Just before you get to the house there's a footpath which will take you up to the road if you want to walk up what becomes quite a steep uphill; alternatively the bridleway continues round the front of the house to a gate complete with blue blobs, and then joins a rough track going up to the right which is ridable if you're an experienced cyclist.

When you hit the road turn right downhill, passing above Headland Warren Farm with quite superb views looking down the immense valley in front of you. Before the road bends right and you cross a stream at Firth Bridge (well before the driveway to Headland Warren Farm), you'll see a grassy track bearing uphill to the left, with a post set in the open grassy space. This track is rideable with difficulty and leads up to Grimpspound, an enormous, mysterious circle of stones which was an enclosed prehistoric settlement set between Hameldown Tor and Hookney Tor.

From here I had planned to ride east across the moor to Heathercombe, returning in a great circuit via Coombe Down which would effectively more than double the length of this ride, but the lack of any rideable track in the vicinity put me off the idea of crossing 1½ miles (2.4 km) of open moorland! However, you may like to give it a go . . .

From Grimpspound head back down to the road, and then go uphill passing the outward bridleway coming up from Headland Warren Farm. Further up the Two Moors Way crosses the road just before the brow of the hill. It's a distinctive narrow track, coming down by walls to the right and heading uphill to the left. Turn left westwards along it and you'll find that the riding is OK, though some of the track is too sunken for pedal clearance so you'll need to ride through the heather on either side. As you come up the hill you'll see the B3212 and fine views to the north. Head on and the track soon brings you back down to Bennett's Cross.

Ride 5 POSTBRIDGE

Area: Postbridge, north Dartmoor.
Start: OS Outdoor Leisure 28 grid ref 647789; large car park with Dartmoor Information Centre.
Nearest BR station: Gunnislake.
Approx length: 10.5 miles (16.8 km).
Ride: Moderate.
Climbs: A few, though none are too strenuous.
Conditions: Moorland, grass, hard tracks, and possibly mud.
Difficulties: Hard riding on open moorland.
High Points: A lot of variety; pleasant riverside riding.
R & R: Pub, shop and hotel in Postbridge; tea at Brimpts Farm.

This ride combines open moorland, forestry, and a delightful river section. Riding across the moorland is interesting, but treat it with caution for the going is hard and the

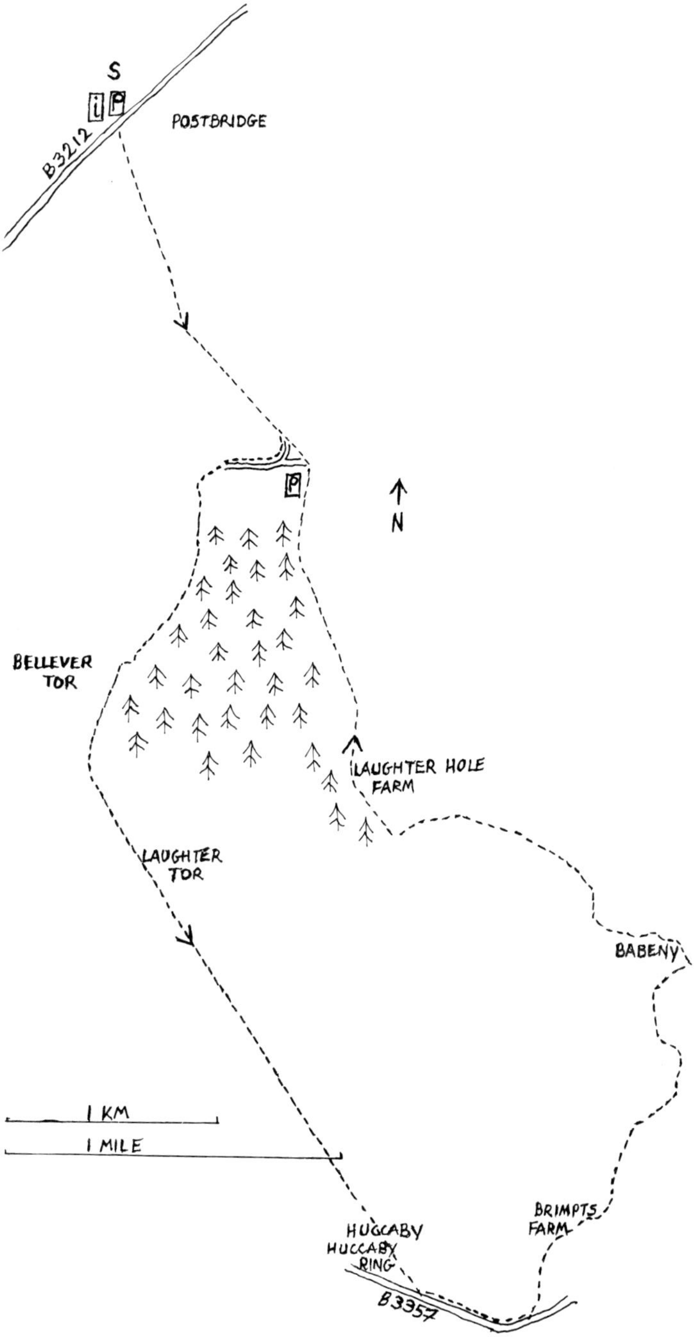
S
i
P
POSTBRIDGE
B3212
P
N
BELLEVER
TOR
LAUGHTER HOLE
FARM
LAUGHTER
TOR
BABENY
1 KM
1 MILE
BRIMPTS
FARM
HUCCABY
HUCCABY
RING
B3357

territory is wild. Even in dry, clear weather you're well advised to tackle it in company – if you rode alone and had a knockout prang it could be a long time before someone found you!

Start at the car park about 100 yards (88 m) from the Postbridge bridge on the north side of the B3212. It has a staffed information centre selling maps and guides, and loos if you need them. Turn left out of the car park, and the bridleway starts through a gate on the right side of the road about 25 yards (22 m) before the bridge. Go through it and along the track which is good until you come to a second gate where there's a short and very sharp uphill!

This brings you up on to open moorland which is quite hard riding. Head SSE, bearing over towards the road that runs along the perimeter of the woods to your right. The bridleway runs alongside this road, but since there's no specific track, you can take any course across the moorland. Bellever comes into view as you start to go downhill, with a small number of rather modern houses and a conspicuous bridge over to the left. Aim for the right-hand side of the houses, joining the road just by a post-box and phone box. Follow this minor road round to the right, and where it bears left continue straight on along the track which goes past the YHA and Forestry Office.

Go through a gate and then up a severe hill – it's short, but quite steep with a broken rock surface. At the top where you meet the woods, the bridleway sign indicates left and right. Go left along a good forestry track with forest to your right and fine views over the top of the woods to your left. Keep on this track which bears right into the woods and then downhill. Where the track bears left out of the woods into a cleared area, leave it and follow the sign going steeply uphill towards Bellever Tor, a high pile of rock with a trig point on its summit.

The bridleway turns left along the edge of the forestry before heading off across open moorland with Laughter Tor to the left. From here on it's hard riding through the undergrowth, but there are few dangerous hidden rocks to throw you off. Keep on heading south-east, leaving Laughter Tor behind and passing a conspicuous standing stone. From there you go on through an old wall and across the bridleway crossing track that connects Laughter Hole with Dunnabridge. As you head on across the moor there are no very obvious trails, but aim for Outer Huccaby Ring, a large pile of rocks on a mound. You then start to head down towards the road, aiming for the bottom right-hand corner of the woods of Snider Park Plantation.

When you reach the road you'll find a gate about 50 yards from Huccaby Cottage. Go left along the road, past a right-hand turning down to the Forest Inn about a mile distant to which you might like to divert. A short way further on turn left on to a track with a Forestry Commission sign, and a sign for Brimpts Farm telling you that they would be pleased to sell you a cream tea or coffee. Go over the cattle grid and follow this good track down to the farmhouse. From there the bridleway goes round the back and straight on through a gate to the right of a small cottage. Go right downhill here to the next gate where you turn sharp left, and from here the next section is very well marked with signposts and blue blobs.

The track goes downhill along the side of the valley with fine views over the East Dart River to Yar Tor. It comes down to the river and follows a delightful riverside trail, although you will need to jump off and push when you come across the occasional rock. This narrow track curves round to the left with the river, eventually coming to a sign directing you across stepping stones to the other side –

Stepping stones across the river on the Postbridge ride. It's easy to carry your bike over.

riding across them would be the ultimate test of your technical ability! Carry straight ahead, riding along the left bank of a tributary which you cross by a stone bridge. The bridleway then goes on ahead across open grassland, bearing left across a stream via a very narrow bridge – ride it if you dare! – before coming to the road by a collection of stones.

Turn left along the road into the tiny homestead of Belbeny, going uphill and then turning right as indicated by the bridleway sign up a steep track with a rough surface. This well-marked track takes you up above Belbeny with fine views of the moor opening out to the left. Eventually it comes to open grassland, and the going becomes harder as you head downhill towards Laughter Hole House on the left-hand side of the forestry. After wet weather this section could be extremely muddy, and it's not that easy when dry!

Keep on towards Laughter Hole House on a difficult and very steep downhill. Go through a gate at the edge of the woods and use the stepping stones to cross the East Dart River once again. Head up the narrow gravel track past the house which has a wonderful view south up the valley, and then follow the bridleway sign up a difficult track through forestry. When the track breaks out into the open, the bridleway turns right through an old stone gateway, heading across forestry devastation towards Laughter Hole Farm on the side of the hill. Pass the farm, and then join a much better track coming up from the right and going through a forestry gate.

Keep on ahead along a very good, wide track which takes you through the woods, bringing you down to Bellever once again. Bear right through the gate to hit the road, and then follow the bridleway sign diagonally across the grass to cut off the corner before rejoining the road near the same phone box that you passed on the way out. From here you can retrace your wheel tracks across the moorland, or, if you prefer to take it easy, ride up the quiet road which gives you the option of riding some way on tarmac and some on grass, bringing you down to the B3212 a short way from the start car park.

(Note: The forestry track that runs due south to the west of the Bellever-Postbridge road looks like the perfect route to take on the way out. However it's labelled as a footpath with a sign which says 'No Riding', despite the fact that it would clearly be much better suited to bike riders than walkers. Such inconsistencies can be frustrating.)

Ride 6 LUSTLEIGH CLEAVE

Area: Manaton and Lustleigh, north Dartmoor.
Start: OS Outdoor Leisure 28 grid ref 749812; free car park by church at Manaton.
Nearest BR station: Newton Abbot.
Approx length: 8.5 miles (13.6 km).
Ride: Hard.
Climbs: Very hard climb from Lustleigh to Sharpitor; moderate climb back to Manaton.
Difficulties: A lot of hard technical riding through rock strewn terrain.
High Points: Visit to Lustleigh; mega views over Lustleigh Cleave.
R & R: Pub in Manaton; pub and tea/coffee house in Lustleigh.

The ride starts from Manaton to the north-west of Bovey Tracey on the edge of Dartmoor. Originally Manaton Magna and Manaton Parva ('large' and 'small') there is a charming village green by the 15th century church and some picturesque cottages which were once the local school, post office and public house. The Kestor Inn is now down at the lower end of the village where there is also a general store.

Ride out of the car park heading up the green, and cross over it to the other side joining the narrow lane going north out of Manaton. After a short while fork right where you see a bridleway sign, going through a gate and on a moderately

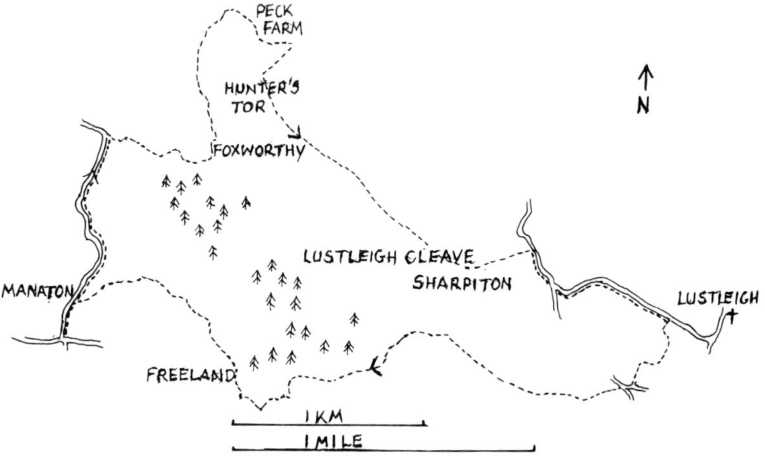

good track that brings you down to a T-junction with a footpath to the left and bridleway sign right.

Turn right here for Freeland along a track which is rocky in places. At Freeland a bridleway sign points left and right with a farmyard ahead of you, and since Freeland is not particularly worth investigating you might as well take the left fork and start the long downhill to the bottom of the valley. The track becomes difficult, though it can be ridden with skill. If in doubt it's safer to walk, since there are plenty of rocks to crack a bone on!

The track goes down through pretty woods with abundant ferns showing the damp nature of the surroundings. Keep on and cross the River Bovey on a bridge like a glorified treetrunk. On the other side go up on a track through silver birches and woodland – it's all very pretty but the riding is not easy, and you may have to do a fair amount of hopping off and pushing, depending on your ability.

After a short time you reach a bridleway sign pointing left, or straight on for Pethybridge. Continue to Pethybridge on the narrow track which follows the side of the valley, riding as much as you can. Eventually you come up to a gate where you join a wider track going down to the road. Turn right here, and then almost immediately left down a steep hill. Just before Pethybridge's phone and post-box bear right down a narrow road by the side of a thatched cottage, and carry on downhill past the affluent dwellings that dot the hillside above Lustleigh, turning right and left to bring you down to the village.

Lustleigh is very twee, and has a pub, tea/coffee shop, general store, and antique shop. To continue, retrace your tracks over the bridge and turn right up the hill. Continue straight up this hill which becomes seriously steep, wiggling its way between farm buildings and ducks and geese all over the place, before joining another minor road. Bear right here, and after about ¼ mile you'll see a bridleway sign pointing left near Grove House which has dual signs directing you to Hunter's Tor and back to Lustleigh.

Go up the narrow, difficult track, through a gate, and at the next set of bridleway signs bear right. There then follows a shattering hill which I found 100 per cent unridable, though some macho spirits will no doubt manage parts of it. Toil on up past strange rock formations – and wish you were on a horse! As with all great climbs the reward is the view, and this one brings you out high on top of the valley with fabulous views to the south-west past Freeland and the gaunt moors beyond. Weather permitting, this would be a great place for a picnic.

Pick your way along the track which runs along the top of the hillside. It's easy to follow, but owing to the liberal number of boulders scattered around it is difficult to ride without stopping. Eventually the going improves as you come down to the ancient fort which is now no more than earthworks, with the unusual rock formation of Hunter's Tor jutting out over the valley beyond. Go through a gate here, and follow the bridleway down to the right alongside a wall, and then left as indicated by the signs. The track is mostly rideable until you reach the gate going into the field next to Peck Farm. When I rode along it one would have imagined it had played host to a cows' disco on the previous evening, and though hard in its dry state I can't imagine what it would have been like after a certain amount of rain!

The gate out of this field is in the far right corner by the farm, where you join a good track carrying on downhill. Just after a stream the bridleway sign indicates left or right for the road. Go left through the gate here, and along a reasonable track which could however become very muddy with rain. This brings you down to Foxworthy where there are some twee converted farm buildings; bear right on a hard track over the bridge, ignoring the bridleway sign to the left which heads down through Lustleigh Cleave. The bridleway bears off to the left for a short section before rejoining the farm track about 75 yards (66 m) further on – you have now covered the last technical section of the ride!

When you hit the road turn left, and then there's a long plug uphill into Manaton. Overall this is a hard ride and very technical, and is probably best not attempted during or after heavy rain. The signposting is very good and there is no open moorland work, but at weekends some of the narrow tracks may get bunged up by horses – however on a weekday in May I saw nary a soul.

If you want to do some more investigating in the area, the Bowerman's Nose is worth a look and is reached by a narrow lane running south from the church at Manaton, and then a bridleway which branches right off it. The 'Nose' is said to be the remains of a hunter who was turned to stone by witches in revenge for him knocking over their cauldron while he was hurrying on his way – it should teach you to behave when you're out on your bike!

Ride 7 COSDON BEACON

Area: South Zeal, north Dartmoor.
Start: OS Outdoor Leisure 28 grid ref 652935; car park in South Zeal.
Nearest BR station: Yeoford.
Approx length: 7.5 miles (12 km).
Ride: Hard.
Climbs: Very hard climb up Cosdon Hill.
Conditions: Very hard going – rocky tracks, gorse, boulders and bogs!
Difficulties: Very poor tracks around the sides of the hill; some very hard riding.
High Points: You made it! Cosdon Beacon and Little Hound Tor are fine points from which to survey an untouched world.
R & R: Pub and hotel in South Zeal.

Cosdon Hill is one of the highest parts of the moor, dominating the surrounding area. This ride which takes you up it and then back down round its perimeter is extremely arduous, and can only be recommended to those who want a taxing physical and technical challenge. Otherwise it's considerably easier on foot or on horseback! Riding through the rock-strewn landscape should only be undertaken on a day when the weather is set fine; you should do it in company; and you should be equipped with map, compass, food, drink and also extra clothing, for this area of the moor can rapidly become very inhospitable. I would also recommend that you wear a helmet if you're going to ride rather than push, since any falls may well be hard landings. A 75 per cent riding ratio is possible, but you would need to be good to accomplish it.

Start from South Zeal on the A30. The village is downhill south of the road and has an old pub and old hotel, plus two general stores. The free car park is just past the post office pleasantly situated next to the recreation grounds with swings and slides for the kids, loos, and also a bubbling stream from the moor in which to wash your tired feet when it's over!

Ride uphill and fork right after about 200 yards (176m). This brings you out on to the main road by a garage. Cross straight over and follow the bridleway sign up a track. It starts OK, but soon develops into a severe climb! Follow it up, bearing right and then following the signs up on to the

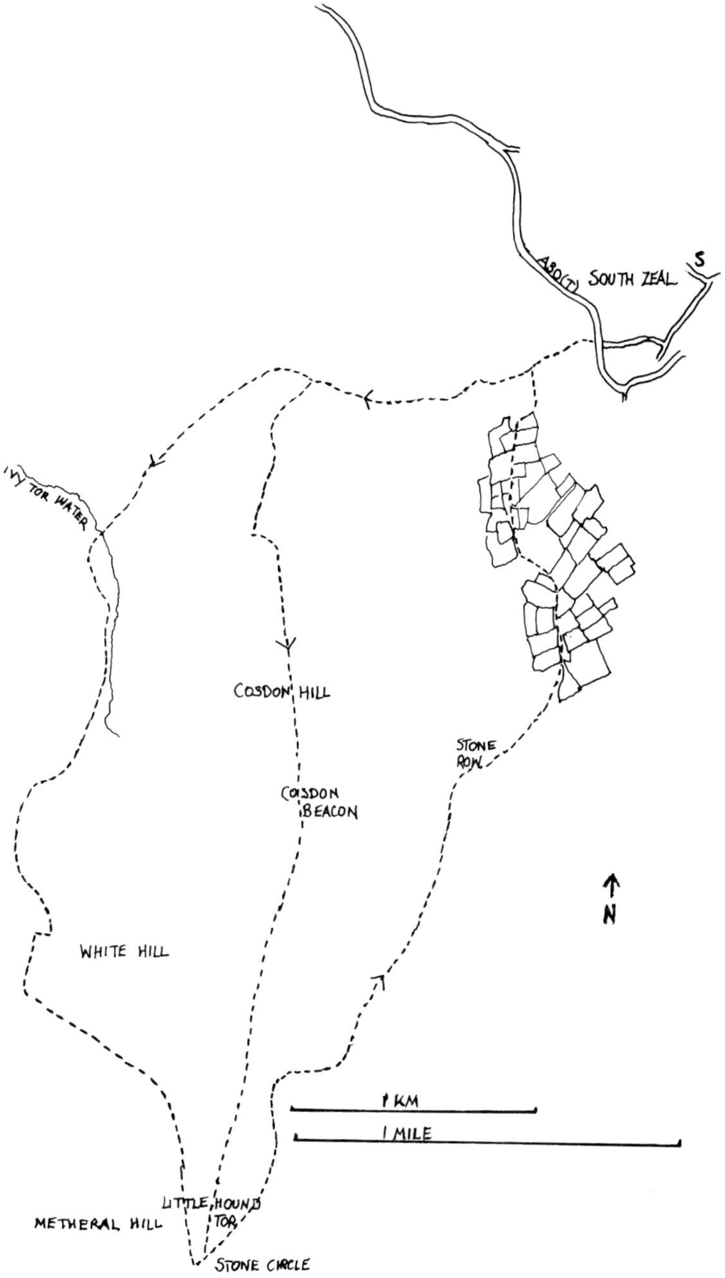
A30(T)
SOUTH ZEAL
S
IVY TOR WATER
COSDON HILL
COSDON BEACON
STONE ROW
N
WHITE HILL
1 KM
1 MILE
LITTLE HOUND TOR
METHERAL HILL
STONE CIRCLE

moor as the track gradually deteriorates with a lot of loose stones and rock.

Keep on into open moorland, heading west all the time. When the track appears to peter out into grassland you should be able to pick out a distinct track to the south heading straight up the hill. This track soon disappears and the going again becomes very tough as you navigate through the boulders hidden in the heathery undergrowth. The top of this vast hill seems to be a long time coming, but the track does reappear and improve near the top, leading to the trig point of Cosdon Beacon with a conspicuous cairn in the form of a pointed pile of rocks. The views all around are of course very fine – they ought to be after such a climb!

The track continues from Cosdon Beacon going due south downhill to Little Hound Tor, and although totally unmarked on the OS map I would strongly recommend this short and easy option. I took the other option, following the bridleway route back down the hill and then round its western flank. Here good tracks are even more non-existent than on the way up, and I would only recommend it to those who enjoy a very hard slog.

At first the grassy track is fine, following a disused 'leat' like a ditch in the grass, but as you swing south with Belstone on your right the going becomes much worse. The trick is to keep well up the hillside away from the boggy ground down by Ivy Tor Water. Ahead of you Metheral Hill has a distinctive top, with Higher Tor and Oke Tor over to the right – both great lumps of granite against the skyline in an area which is much favoured by hang-gliders. Bearing south-east towards Little Hound Tor which is the hump south of Cosdon Hill, you rejoin the track running down from Cosdon Beacon.

This track is the only easy part of the ride, a gentle downhill with superb views. Little Hound Tor is marked by a small cairn of piled rocks, and just beyond you come to one of Dartmoor's strange stone circles – very megalithic and druidical with a conspicuous single standing rock some 200 yards (176 m) beyond. Here the track once again disappears, though you could try your luck and push on for Hound Tor and beyond, allowing plenty of time to get back.

I resolved to head back via the OS map bridleway route running along the east side of Cosdon Hill. This section was also anything but easy! Once again you need to keep well up the hillside. If you get down into the marshy area towards Raybarrow Pool and Blackaton Brook you can

The bleak circle of standing stones at Cosdon Beacon with wild, open moorland all around.

almost sink in to your waist, so stick to the high contours and stay dry as you pick your way towards the north. The going improves as tracks develop further up the east side where you will probably meet some cattle, and you then come to a very conspicuous twin row of ancient stones which is marked on the map.

Pass straight through the stones, keeping north and resisting the temptation to ease off downhill towards the walled fields on your right, for any height lost will need to be regained. The going demands very good technical ability as you follow horse tracks going round the hillside towards South Zeal, and you eventually reach the end of the walled fields. Here you can rejoin your outward rubble-strewn track which is not much easier to ride downhill than it was uphill! Then it's a short way back to the car park after a memorably hard ride.

Exmoor

Exmoor has some fine biking terrain and is well laced with bridleways. Many of the tracks are good, and the views both inland and to the north over the sea to Wales are famous, with the going much more forgiving than in rocky Dartmoor. These three rides offer just a taster of the many biking options available in one of the prettiest corners of the English landscape.

Ride 8 DOONE COUNTRY

Area: North Exmoor, on the Somerset/Devon border.
Start: OS Landranger 180 grid ref 793486 (OS Landranger 181 also required); free car park at County Gate on the A39 coast road.
Nearest BR station: Minehead.
Approx length: 8.5 miles (13.6 km).
Ride: Moderate.
Climbs: Moderate climb up to South Common; hard climb back up to County Gate.
Conditions: Good tracks along Badgworthy Water; exposed but generally good going on South Common.
Difficulties: The bridleway route up over South Common to Oare is not at all clear.
High Points: Fine views and good riding with a lot of variety packed into a short length.
R & R: Information Centre at County Gate sells some food; Cloud Farm sells soft drinks, ploughman's lunches, and cream teas. Both open Easter to late October.

This is an excellent introduction to Exmoor. Although comparatively short, it takes in all kinds of terrain and is rideable most of the way. It can also be easily extended, for example west over Brendon Common or north on to the bridleway section of the long-distance coast path. In summer watch out for walkers who frequently go along the Badgworthy Water section of this ride.

Start from the free car park at County Gate in a magnificent position on the coast road between Lynton and Porlock.

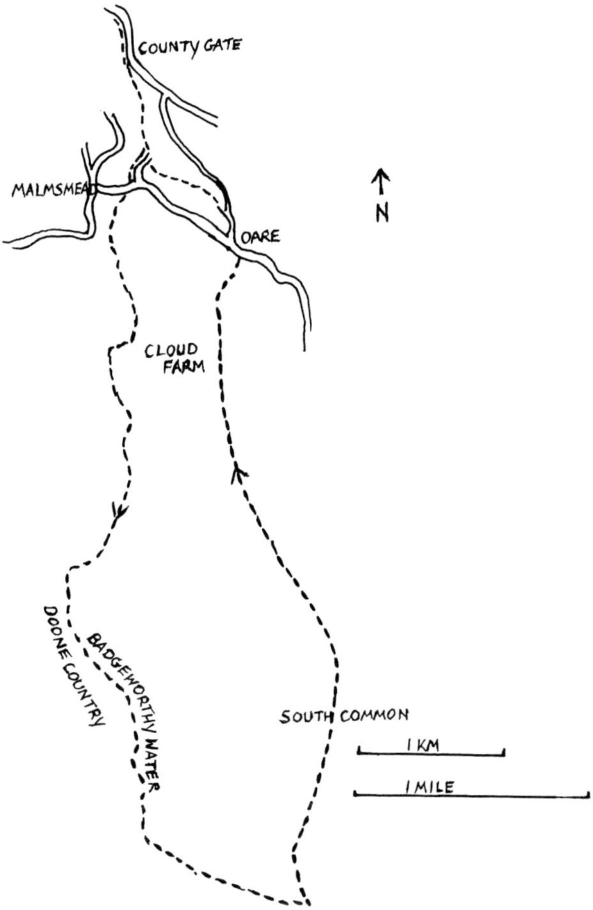

From here you can get an unbeatable view out over the moor. There's an Information Centre (Easter to October, 10 a.m. – 5 p.m.) which sells local OS maps as well as other publications dealing with Exmoor, in particular the Lorna Doone connection for which this part of the moor is famous.

From the car park head back towards the road, as if turning right for Porlock. Just before the road, go right through a gate and follow the bridleway sign to Malmsmead in the valley, heading along the side of a wire fence. This leads you down a steep downhill which gets steeper; plunge down with brakes on and a great view laid out ahead. Going down is fine, but you do have to go back up to finish this ride, and you may ask why not start and finish at Malmsmead where there is also a car park? You can, but hill climbing is a part of offroad biking, and I would recommend the County Gate start for the fine views which condition you for the ride, for its useful info centre, and because it's much easier to get to from the main road.

At the bottom, bear right before a stile to cross the East Lyn River, heading straight ahead and then bearing left up by the side of a farmhouse which brings you to a minor road. Here you turn right past a large house, taking the first left over a cattle grid signposted to Cloud Farm. The track up to the farm is mostly tarmac, and is fast riding on a fairly level surface. At the farm you can stop for something to eat or drink (unlicensed) in the pleasant garden, or bear right down to the river – Badgworthy Water – which you cross and then turn left on a good track which runs along the other side.

Keep along this track, passing a large stone which is the R. D. Blackmore Memorial (author of Lorna Doone) on the right. The track follows the side of Badgworthy Water, going through a gate and into oak woods just by the infamous 'water slide' (uphill to the right) from Lorna Doone. On the far side of the woods carry on past a track going off up to the right, cross over a narrow bridge and head along a much narrower track between rhododendrons. This leads past a short unridably rocky section to more open country, heading into wild moorland as the track follows the right side of the valley.

Ahead you will see a clump of trees down to the left. Where the track bears right up Hoccombe Combe, turn left down to the three-way sign by these trees and follow the direction for Exford, crossing a narrow bridge over a stream which feeds Badgworthy Water. Bear round to the right to continue alongside the river in the same southerly direction, riding along the track until it once again bears right, this time turning west along Hoccombe Water. Here you go left through a gate to go over the fairly large bridge which crosses Badgworthy water.

On the other side go up a short, steep hill following the signposted direction to Exbridge. When you reach the top and start to head down, look out for an unmarked grass track going off up to the left at an acute angle, well before you reach the next dip where the track heads on uphill into even wilder country, approaching a long stone wall. This acute turning takes you back up towards the north; from here on the track goes across South Common and down to Oare and is unmarked and not that obvious to follow.

A short way on, fork right where the uphill track forks right and left, and follow the moorland track as it appears and disappears through the heather towards the top of the ridge, heading more or less ENE most of the way. At the top it becomes much better defined, bearing to the left which is more to the north. The corner of a huge green field cut into the moor comes into view, and the track carries on down to a gate leading into it. Head across this field, bearing left to follow its boundary wall on the moorland side – from here you should be able to see your start point at County Gate in the distance way ahead of you.

Where the field heads down into a rough gulley, turn left through a single gate in the wall, bearing right downhill to pick up a track that runs through the heather in much the same direction. This narrow track continues on up the other side of the gulley to cross an expanse of heather, before coming to a gate set in a wall. Go through and ride along the right side of the field ahead which will probably be full of sheep, steadily losing height as you approach the gate to the next field. Here you continue in the same direction along the right-hand side boundary, going more steeply downhill to work up a good fast cruising pace.

When you come to a gate on the right, turn into the next field and head downhill towards the hamlet of Oare, which until now has been hidden from view. Look for a clump of trees in a gulley heading down the hillside towards a large house on the other side of the valley, and ride over to it where you will find a signpost pointing down to Oare Church, taking you downhill across a couple of fields and coming out at a minor road just alongside it. This turning to head down to Oare is quite easy to miss. If you overshoot while riding along the ridge, the clump of trees and the house will come into view to the right. You then go through the left-hand of two gates at the end of the field ahead, and turn right downhill along a track that doubles back down to the trees.

Oare Church is worth a look inside if you are interested in small old churches; and you can see where Lorna Doone was shot while standing at the altar! From here turn right downhill on the road, crossing the bridge over Gare Water and bearing left up the other side. After about 75 yards (66m) turn left through a double green painted gate, following the sign (a footpath sign but marked on the OS map as a bridleway) to Malmsmead with a fine riverside ride. This takes you past the back of a large farm, and then on to the stile at the foot of the hill which leads back up to your start point at County Gate. This is a long, hard climb which will defeat all but a handful of riders.

Ride 9 EXFORD TO SIMONSBATH

Area: Exford, on the B3224 west of Wheddon Cross.
Start: OS Landranger 181 grid ref 854383 (OS Landranger 180 also required); free car park on south-east side of Exford.
Nearest BR station: Minehead.
Approx length: 16 miles (25.6 km).
Ride: Moderate to energetic.
Climbs: Stiff climb from Court Farm up Road Hill; long climb out of Withypool.
Conditions: Mainly good going, though first leg south from Exford could be muddy.
Difficulties: None, unless you take in the Great Bradley circuit.
High Points: Fine views on the high level ride along the Two Moors Way towards Simonsbath.
R & R: Pubs, cafés, etc in Exford; pub in Withypool; two hotels in Simonsbath.

Exford lies in the middle of Exmoor, down in a valley to the south of the Lorna Doone trail. It's in an area which is well laced with bridleways, and this route could be the basis for all sorts of diversions with the aid of a trusty OS map. Most of the bridleways are marked with red blobs; so when you see them follow the dabs of red paint all the way. It's also prime hunting country, so if you see a stag hunt (local speciality) in progress you can either cheer or jeer them on their way.

From the free car park turn left through Exford, heading over the bridge and then immediately taking the left turning on a side road signposted to Withypool. Head steeply uphill, and, where the road bends sharp right, turn left downhill to Court Farm. Ride through the farm following the red bridleway sign, bearing right and left between the buildings and then going through a gate and on up a rough track. From here head along the side of a field, bearing round to the right and following numerous red blobs to the next gate where you bear left steeply downhill.

At the bottom the track bears left again, going up a narrow track which soon becomes formidably steep and unrid-

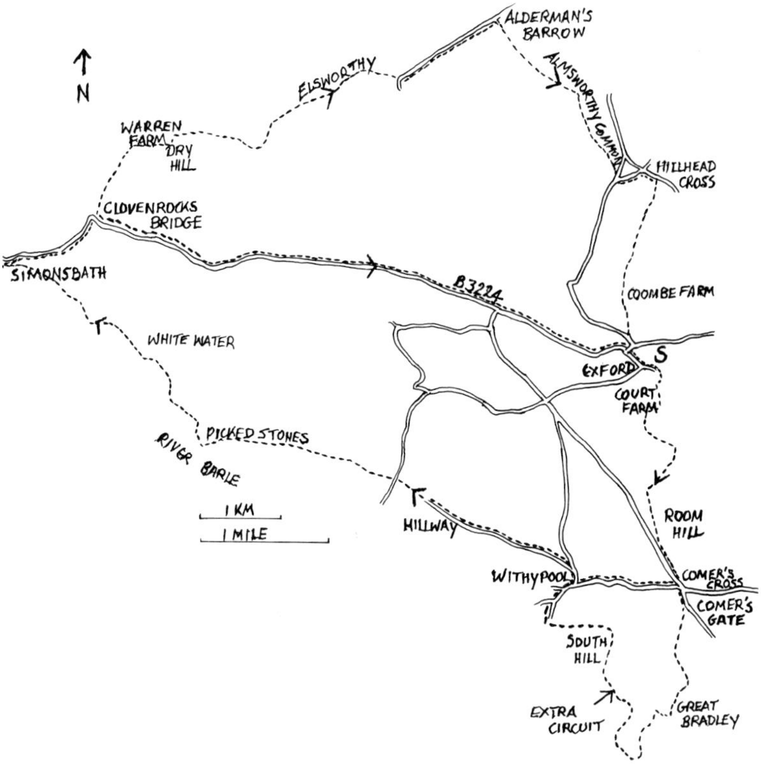

able. At the top go through a gate and straight across the field ahead, following the grass track which runs parallel with the valley below. Turn right at the next gate, heading up towards an impressive avenue of trees which runs along the hilltop to the left. Go through another gate here and on past the second line of trees, forking right on to a rough track signposted to Withypool and leaving the better track which goes on to Winsford. With deep ruts this is not easy riding, but it soon leads you out to the road below Room Hill. From here turn left down to the crossroads at Comer's Cross, where you turn right for a long downhill into Withypool.

At this point I went off in a different direction, putting in an extra circuit which didn't really prove satisfactory – maybe I was off form, or maybe it was the weather, which was pretty poor. At Comer's Cross I headed straight on, turning right towards the entrance to Great Bardley. A long track leads to the entrance where it's unmarked bridleway from the cattle grid on a steep downhill. Past the farmhouse the track goes down to a stream in the valley, becoming rough and difficult riding. Over the stream you bear left on the track which leads steeply up the other side of the valley, hitting open ground at the top and then going into a belt of woods where the track bears left downhill to the River Barle down in the next valley. This route is not that easy to find, but once on the riverside track it's a pleasant ride towards Withypool. Not far short of the village the track becomes a permissive right of way which appears to be a footpath – a sign tells you about this. To the left you'll see a line of stepping stones which is the way the bridleway crosses the river; unfortunately the stones are in poor condition; in anything but a drought you'll get wet feet, while in winter it may well be uncrossable. Presuming that you do get across, you head up a steep hill through a farmyard, and then out on to the road where you turn right down to Withypool.

Withypool is a small place on the river with a single pub. To get on to the Two Moors Way take the turning uphill just east of the church, and after a hundred yards or so bear left on to a minor lane signposted 'Hotel'. Ride on a steady uphill which passes a few houses – you are now on part of the Two Moors Way which connects Dartmoor to Exmoor. At a gate above Hillway the lane continues as a track across the moor, coming to a minor road where you cross straight over, riding on along the good track ahead. Where this forks, follow it off to the right, signposted to Picked Stones, which takes you on across the moor and then across a field to a farm track where you turn left down to the farmhouse at Picked Stones.

Bear right through the farm buildings and out through a gate the other side. From here you keep to the right side of the field which plunges down into the valley of the River Barle with a large clump of trees down to the left. Keep ahead, and you soon join an up and down track with great views down this wild valley towards Simonsbath. The track heads right downhill to cross the stream called White Water, turning left through a gate and up the other side where you head up a grassy slope and then bear left over to a line of trees on the hilltop, heading for a faded red blob marking the way on a disused gatepost.

Follow these trees along the hilltop heading north-west towards Simonsbath, and keep in the same direction until you start to head downhill towards Winstitchen Farm alongside which there's a straight track leading to the road.

Before reaching the farmhouse you bear left around the edge of the field, and then turn right through a gate by stables, keeping right and heading on towards the woods above Simonsbath where a track takes you down to this small hamlet which boasts two hotels.

From Simonsbath turn right onroad towards Exford, starting with a long uphill. After about 1 mile (1.6km) a bridleway goes off to the left on the sharp right-hand bend at Clovenrocks Bridge, signposted to Alderman's Barrow which is 4.5 miles (7.2km) distant. This was the way I had intended to go, but on what was the 50th and last ride of this book (despite being labelled as number 9!) the weather intervened in a serious way, with torrential rain joining the gale force winds I had suffered all day. This forced me to cut short my planned route for the first and last time, and I had to ride directly onroad to Exford some 4 miles (6.4 km) distant.

The offroad route would be about 7.5 miles (12 km), heading via Warren Farm and Dry Hill along the high ground at Elsworthy and on to Alderman's Barrow. Here I intended heading down Almsworthy Common to Hillhead Cross, and from there continuing offroad to Exford on the bridleway that goes via Coombe Farm. With the aid of an OS map I'll leave it to you to discover if this route is good, bad, or indifferent – I am sure it won't be the latter!

Ride 10 DUNKERY BEACON

Area: Dunkery Hill to Winsford, west of Wheddon Cross on the A396.
Start: OS Landranger 181 grid ref 924388; free car park by the crossroads at Wheddon Cross.
Nearest BR Station: Minehead.
Approx Length: 16.25 miles (26 km).
Ride: Moderate to Hard.
Climbs: Three climbs, all quite hard.
Conditions: Mainly good, but some of the tracks near Wheddon Cross are hard going.
Difficulties: Mud in woods near Wheddon Cross; hard climb up Mansley Combe.
High Points: The climb up Dunkery Beacon, highest point on Exmoor!
R & R: Pubs at Wheddon Cross and Winsford; seasonal café at Winsford.

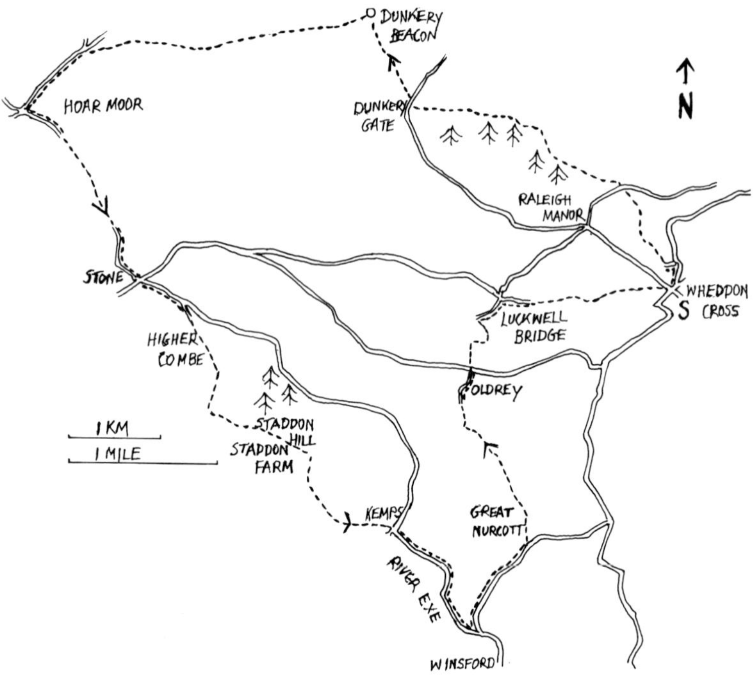

This is an excellent ride, but energetic! Be warned that it starts hard and ends hard on some difficult tracks around Wheddon Cross.

From the car park turn left on to the A396 towards Dunster and Minehead, heading down the hill. Where the road bends left a bridleway track is indicated turning sharp left by a large barn; go down here, and then bear right on the track signposted to Raleigh Manor.

Continue over a cattle grid and along a tarmac lane towards the manor, and just before you reach it turn off to the right as indicated by a bridleway sign. This leads you down a rough track to a gate, beyond which you go steeply downhill. Most of the way down here proved very muddy and badly chewed up by horse hooves, and it could be appalling in wet weather. Eventually you come down to a crossing lane. Go straight over here and bear left through a gate as indicated by a bridleway sign. Head down the hill on a good track, crossing a stream at the bottom and going through a gate into the woods ahead.

Carry on along the track which follows the right side of the woods. Ignore a track forking off to the left, and a little further on ignore a track going uphill to the right, although both are bridleways. Keep on ahead, crossing a few streams while the track gets muddier, slower and more difficult to ride. Eventually you come out of the woods and begin a long, hard uphill on a good track running up the side of Mansley Combe. Near the top – the view is worth it! – carry on over grass towards a gate where you ride on up across the next field, making for the right-hand side of the trees ahead. The going is hard, and it doesn't get any easier for some time!

Just before the trees you reach a rough, deeply rutted crossing track. Turn left along this, following it along the side of the trees. After a while it starts to bear right and the going gets better – ride towards a gate in the wall ahead, and from there on to the car park by the roadside at Dunkery Gate which is clearly marked by a National Trust sign. Turn right along the road here, and then after about 50 yards go left on to the track which heads up to the summit of Dunkery Beacon (519 m). This is a long steady ascent, and not at all bad. When you reach the top there's a magnificent view looking out over Exmoor to the west, Wales to the north, and the Quantocks to the east. It's worth the effort!

From Dunkery Beacon take the left hand track heading due west downhill. After a fast descent this levels out on a good surface, reaching a quiet road by a junction above Exmoor Common about 2 miles (3.2 km) from the beacon. Turn left on the road here, which soon takes you on a fast downhill. At the first right turning, turn left on to a track with a bridleway sign, and bomb down towards a gate, ignoring the bridleway turning to the right. Carry on over open moorland below Hoar Moor, following the track through a number of gates until you head down a rock staircase which makes a long, bumpy, and somewhat unusual descent.

This leads you to a tarmac track, passing a pond on the right and emerging through two fine entrance pillars to hit the road at Stone. Go left and immediately right here, and then some way on take the first turning to the right along a narrow tarmac lane. Go past the right turning to Higher Combe and head on uphill, going through a gate and out into open country, but still on a made-up track which follows the side of the valley. Bear right and then left up Staddon Hill, with magnificent views over to Dunkery Beacon in the north.

At the next gate, go ahead on to a grass track as indicated by a bridleway sign, leaving the made-up track which turns right down to Staddon Farm. Continue ahead, and then turn right with the track at the start of a long downhill which takes you towards the River Exe at the bottom of the valley, with varying steepnesses and varying surfaces on the way down, passing the farm buildings at Kemps and eventually hitting the road on a sharp left-hand bend.

Go straight ahead here and follow the road up and down into Winsford which is about 1 mile (1.6 km) distant. When you come into the village turn right by the garage, and the excellent Royal Oak pub is about 100 yards along on the left; there is also a seasonal café just by the green. Allow about two hours for this first part of the ride.

To head back to Wheddon Cross, start to retrace your tracks out of Winsford. A short way out, take the first narrow road going off uphill to the right. This is another long, long uphill which will be heavy going if you've over-indulged in the Royal Oak! When it levels out, a track goes off to the left beside a barn, about 75 yards (66 m) before a right-hand bend in the road. Head uphill on this track past the farm buildings at Great Nurcott, keeping straight on to the top, where you start to head downhill on the track which is now much narrower. Eventually you come out into the open, joining a track coming from the left, where you bear right through the farm buildings at Oldrey and then come down to a minor road.

Go straight over here, following the track ahead which soon narrows and bears right and left, bringing you quickly downhill to a lane leading into Luckwell Bridge. Just past the old chapel, turn right along the side of the River Quarme as indicated by a bridleway sign – note that from here on the route follows yellow footpath signs, although the tracks are bridleways as shown on the OS map. Follow the track through a gate and down past the right side of a cottage, keeping on ahead along the right side of the river before eventually coming down a field past a solitary white boulder to a bridge where you cross over the river. Bear up the right side of the field ahead, and go through the gate beside a stile. From here the track runs straight ahead uphill to Wheddon Cross, but much of it is strangely and impossibly rutted. As a result, the last half mile or so is a hard uphill push, and you can only ride easily near the end where a flat grass field runs alongside. This soon leads to the Wheddon Cross sports pavilion, and from here it's a short ride back to your start point.

Dorset and the Purbecks

The Purbeck Hills which run along the south Dorset coastline offer some magical offroading, with fine views and good tracks that run within sight of the sea west and east of Weymouth. However, when riding in this area you are never far from civilisation, and near the coast in summer traffic jams can be a problem getting to and from the rides. Inland, the area round the county capital of Dorchester offers some good riding, while the easy hills round Blandford to the east are a favourite with offroaders from Poole.

Ride 11 Blandford

Area: Blandford Forum, Dorset.
Start: OS Landranger 194 grid ref 884062; Pay & Display car park fours hours max or free car park at end of main street.
Nearest BR Station: Poole.
Approx Length: 15.5 miles (24.8 km).
Ride: Easy.
Climbs: A few minor climbs; steady climb up from Durweston.
Conditions: Mainly very good tracks, though some sections can be muddy.
Difficulties: None, though it's possible to choose the wrong tracks through Blandford Forest.
High Points: A lot of good woodland riding on mainly good tracks with minimal ups and downs.
R & R: Pub at Okeford Fitzpaine; pubs, cafés, etc in Blandford Forum.

The Blandford area is well endowed with bridleways and is highly rated by offroaders in the area. This route is based on one provided by Jerry Cooper of the Inside Park (tel: 0258 53719), a caravan and camping site in Blandford which would be delighted to play host to more bikers. The riding is easy because essentially the tracks are good and

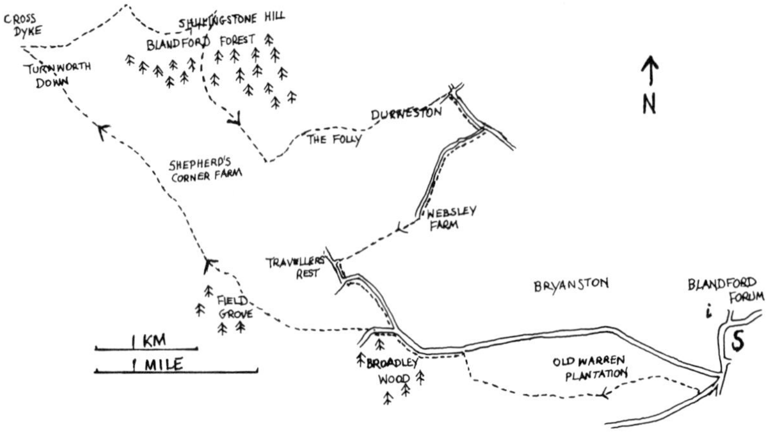

well signposted by blue bridleway blobs, with not much up and down and a lot of riding through pleasant woodlands.

If you've come by car the easiest starting point is the large car park by the information centre next to Safeway, just by the River Stour. However, waiting is limited to four hours and at least three should be allowed for the ride, so if you plan diversions, stops at pubs, and so on, it's better to leave your car at the end of the main street on the other side of the town.

From the information centre turn left and ride over the River Stour, passing the entrance to Bryanston School. A little further on you pass a right-hand turning signposted 'Bryanston ¼ mile'; go past this and take the right-hand fork signposted to Winterborne Strickland. Ride up an easy hill with farm buildings on the right, and just past the last building turn right down the main driveway to the farm by a bridleway sign which incorrectly points straight across the field. Follow the drive past a line-up of beautifully painted old ploughs and round to the left past the front of the immaculate farm house.

The drive becomes a farm track, passing through a gate and heading towards trees at Old Warren Plantation with fields on either side. Just before the trees you go through a gate and then follow the narrow track round the left side of the plantation, heading down to another gate. Go through and head straight across grass towards more trees ahead, with a farmhouse and a large, old barn down in the valley to the right. Go into the trees through a gate, and follow the woodland track ahead, ignoring crossing tracks. You eventually come out of the trees at another gate, and head across open grassland to the next gate with houses at 'Kennels' ahead.

Go through a gate by the fairly modern house, joining a track and bearing right over a cattle grid past a large farmstead to the right. Take the next 90 degree right turning down a tarmac lane which soon brings you past a few houses to the road. Turn left here, and follow this fairly quiet country road past Broadley Wood on your left. Ignore a right-hand fork, and a little further on where the road bends left with open fields and a gate ahead, look for the bridleway sign which is on the right-hand side pointing along the edge of the field.

Ride along this narrow track which bears left round the edge of the woods, and does not go straight across the field as shown on the OS map – an obvious case of a compromise which is better for both farmer and biker/horserider/walker. The track heads into the woods on a good surface, coming down to a left and right fork marked by bridleway blobs. Take the right fork here, and continue to follow your nose straight ahead through the woods at Field Grove, ignoring all side turnings.

You eventually come out of the woods, passing through a gate and riding along the edge of a field with Blandford Forest ahead. Go ahead over a crossing track which is the bridleway leading down to the road from Shepherd's Corner Farm, and on along a much rougher track which is slow going and could make for heavy riding in wet weather. Follow this track into the woods, keeping left on a better surface which runs along the woods' perimeter, coming into the open at Turnworth Down. Keep on ahead across the right-hand side of the field here, following the track past the next woods until you come to a T-junction crossing track at Cross Dyke within earshot of the road.

Turn right, passing the Forestry Commission sign for Wareham Forest. (If you want to head for the pub at Okeford Fitzpaine, turn left along the edge of the woods and take the second bridleway turning which bears left over to the road and then heads up towards Okeford Fitzpaine.)

Go into the woods on a fast forestry track which soon bears left with open ground on your right. After a while the track splits, with the right-hand fork passing a trig. point which is easily spotted. Keep to the main left-hand track here and follow it on a gradual descent through the woods along Shillingstone Hill – watch out for the deer which have a habit of darting across the track. Keep to the main track until you come to a right hairpin bend turning which is the way you go. This is easily spotted – the track sweeps round to the right uphill, almost doubling back on itself, while straight ahead there is the start of a steep downhill with trees on either side. The latter track leads down to the road below Hod Hill where there are no connecting bridleways.

Follow the track round to the right and into the open with fields on either side. Pass a bridleway sign to the right, following the sign straight on and going once more into the woods ahead on a slight downhill. Here you take the right-hand fork along the good, wide track through the woods which bears left around Bensley Common passing a couple of huts on the left. Go through a gate and follow the track across open ground towards more woods, going through a gate and riding along the left side of the trees until you reach the minor road ahead.

Turn left here past a few houses, the last of which is called 'The Folly'. A little further downhill past a large barn, turn right through a five-bar metal gate with a bridleway sign. Head straight on down towards the trees ahead on a fast grass descent, looking for the gate at the bottom of the hill which soon comes into view. Once through the gate keep to the right hand track along the edge of trees, following it on a narrow woodland trail, and then through a narrow gate with a large field up to the left. This soon brings you down to a gate by a small equestrian centre. Ride straight through past the stables, and join the road in the petite village of Durweston.

Turn right along the road; right again; then immediately left passing the church. Keep on along this road past the houses, until you see a footpath sign showing the way ahead to Bryanston ('1 mile') along a long avenue of trees. Just to the right a bridleway sign points straight up the hill, a route which does not quite agree with the OS map. Head up here, and go through a gate at the top of the field with Knighton House School on your right. Turn right along a faint track above the school, and go through a gate and on to a rough crossing track.

Turn left uphill here, gradually heading up to Websley Farm, bearing left and right between the farmhouse and stables. From here on follow the track straight ahead and down to the road opposite the farm at Travellers' Rest where there are a few choice buildings. Turn left along the road, bearing left uphill and following it past Broadley Wood. From here you can keep along this road which will take you down past Bryanston to Blandford; though I returned offroad by retracing the outward route. Where the road goes straight after Broadley Wood, look for the unmarked right turning by a cottage on the opposite corner. The offroad way back is mainly on a gentle downhill and consequently more fun than on the way out, and you're soon back in Blandford after two to three hours in the saddle.

Ride 12 Chaldon Down

Area: Chaldon Down near Weymouth, Dorset.
Start: OS Landranger 194 grid ref 760824; good parking in National Trust car park west of Chaldon Down.
Nearest BR station: Broadwey.
Approx length: 11.5 miles (18.4 km).
Ride: Easy.
Climbs: A few minor hills.
Conditions: Can be slippery after rain; muddy around Holworth.
Difficulties: Very exposed to wind and rain.
High Points: Fine views; easy navigation; little onroading.
R & R: Pub at Chaldon Herring.

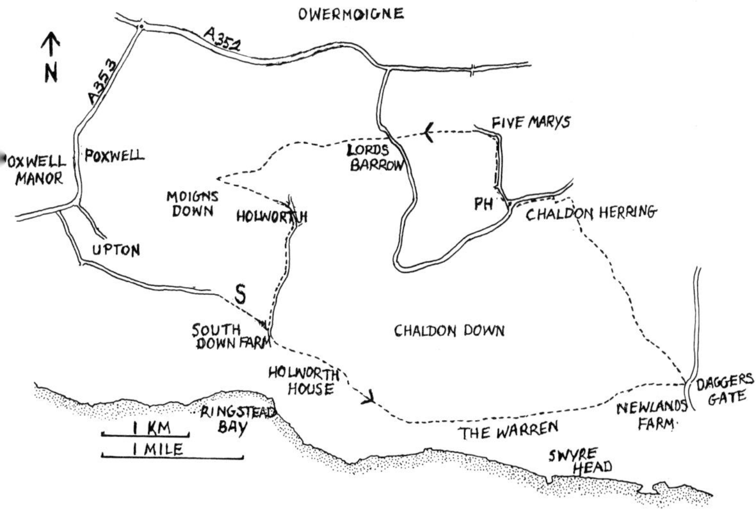

This is a relatively easy ride, even though it has a few climbs. However, it's not recommended on a wet or windy day as most of the route is very exposed with little shelter, and you'd probably get blown off the top of Chaldon Down!

To get to the start point head along the A353 south towards Weymouth. At Poxwell you will easily identify Poxwell Manor which is a fine building on the right, sometimes with a helicopter parked there in place of a car. Shortly after this the road bends round to the right, and then there's a turning downhill to the left signposted to Ringstead which is easy to miss, so go slowly.

Follow the narrow road through Upton, keeping left and ignoring the turning to Ringstead. Head up the long hill and over the cattle grid which brings you to a large National Trust car park with a fine view over Ringstead Bay. On my visit in winter this was deserted, but on a fine summer day it no doubt becomes quite crowded. Before you leave take a look at the National Trust information panel which tells you about the area – its geology, sea life, the White Nothe nature reserve, the zig-zag path which featured in the book *Moonfleet*, and the Trust's Southdown Farm which is worked in a traditional, conservationist way.

Follow the track through the car park, heading south-east and then east towards Daggers Gate. The route is well marked by bridleway signs and the going is mostly good, though it can be slippery and after wet weather I came off a couple of times. There are gentle ups and downs, but nothing that requires much exertion.

Go past Sea Barn Farm with its old-fashioned thatched barn on the right of the track, on past a ruin, and then across grassy fields with great views of Swyre Head to the south and rolling hills all around you. This is a really fine ride for a still, sunny day. After passing through numerous gates a fast downhill takes you towards the road at Daggers Gate with a large modern barn on the left. About 10 yards (8.8 m) before you reach the road, follow the sign for East Chaldon which takes you up the hill to the left. Head on up a good track, then down to a couple of old barns where you bear right following blue bridleway signs, and head on down into a deep and tranquil valley.

Ride through the valley, keeping straight ahead and following the blue blobs which clearly mark the way. Close all gates behind you for there will probably be plenty of sheep around! Eventually the bridleway goes on to a hard track which comes in from the left, bringing you out at the

This lonely barn at Sea Barn Farm is on the Chaldon Down ride, after the downhill from the car park.

village with two names – East Chaldon or Chaldon Herring. Turn left along the road through this quiet place, bearing right past the Sailor's Return, a pub which appeared busy on a Sunday lunchtime.

Keep on uphill on the road, and where the road bends left you'll see a bridleway coming in from the right. Keep on up to the top of the hill where at Five Marys you turn left and due west through a gate with a bridleway blob. Keep west along the top of the down through fields with fine views to north and south and on a clear day you'll see Dorchester.

Cross straight over the road at Lord's Barrow and at the next road. Here the track bends to the left before resuming its westerly direction. When you reach a gate with a stile on the right, you've arrived just below Moigns Down. You will be able to see farm buildings down a track in the valley ahead, and you'll find the bridleway and footpath blobs are all indicated on the bottom gate, downhill from the stile. (If you want to extend the ride into Ride 18, carry on north-west for Poxwell here.)

Turn hard left and head ESE directly ahead and downhill from the gate – keep left and don't bear all the way down the hill to the right where there's a good track and an inviting gate. The bridleway follows a much inferior path along the side of the hill, through a gate, and across a field, which on my visit was unridable due to the presence of many heavy-hooved cows who really wanted to check out the specification of my bike!

Head for the left-hand side of the Holworth farm buildings, crossing the stile and turning right along the track past the duckpond. Here you follow the bridleway sign for Ringstead Bay, bearing right uphill. The track is good and fast, and soon brings you back to your outward track just above Sea Barn Farm where you turn right to get back to the car park.

Ride 13 MAIDEN CASTLE and HARDY'S MONUMENT

Area: Dorchester, Dorset.
Start: OS Landranger 194 grid ref 669889; good parking in free car park below Maiden Castle near Dorchester.
Nearest BR station: Dorchester.
Approx length: 15 miles (24 km).
Ride: Easy/Moderate.
Climbs: A few minor climbs.
Conditions: Good tracks.
Difficulties: None.
High Points: A well-signposted ride through fine country with some good views.
R & R: Pub in Martinstown; pubs, cafés, tea shops, etc in Dorchester.

This is a great ride. The tracks are really good and they should be OK in wet weather. You pass through some fine country and the bridleways are clearly marked or signposted most of the way.

Take the signposted turning for Maiden Castle off the A354 Dorchester–Weymouth road on the town side of the bypass. Drive or ride until you reach the car park at the foot of the Maiden Castle earthworks. This is a splendid iron-age fort composed of massive concentric ditches. There's an information panel in the car park which makes interesting reading, and it's worth a walk round the fortifications to see what their builders achieved, and what any attackers were up against.

Go through the gate by the car park and ride up the hill to the right-hand side of Maiden Castle. When you reach the padlocked main gate and kissing gate entrance to the fortifications with an English Heritage sign, bear right and pick up the bridle track which continues round to the left with a blue blob showing you the way. Follow this track

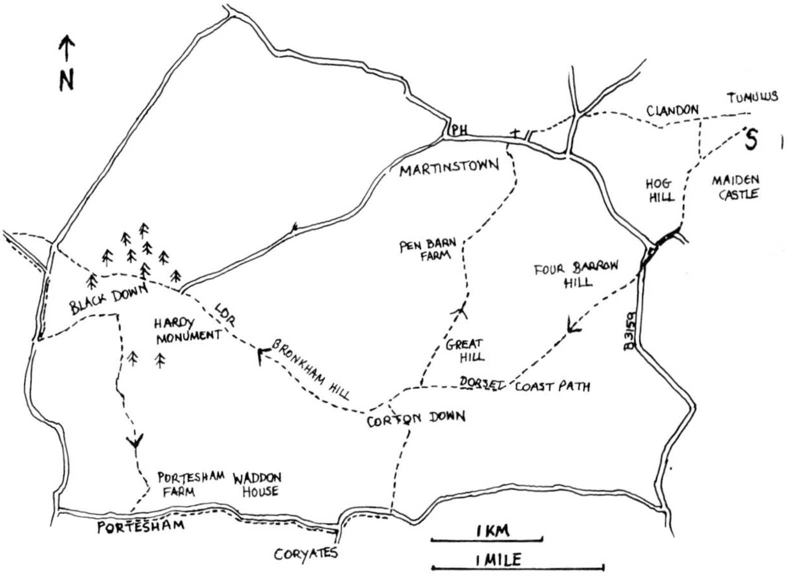

round the north-west side of the fortifications with Hog Hill on your right, and then go through a gate and ride down a valley with Ashton Farm ahead of you.

Here you join a minor road for no more than a couple of minutes' onroading. Bear round to the right, and then keep straight on until you reach a more major road coming from the right a short way on. Bear left here, and almost immediately cross the road and head down to the right on the bridleway track which passes some houses and heads through another farm.

The bridleway is well signposted, heading out on a hard chalk track and then bearing left and right into a field – just follow the blue blobs. Keep along the right-hand side of the grassy field with the valley on your left, bearing left around the top until you see the bridleway blob on the second gate. This leads to a field which was planted with fully grown corn when I rode through, but a narrow track had been left intact, slicing diagonally in a south-west direction. Head across this field, passing through a grassy section with tumuli to the right, then head across more of the field until you reach a gate in the corner.

Go through and bear left along a clear track which runs along the side of the next field, soon bringing you down to a crossing track bounded by a wall which is the Dorset Coast Path. Ahead there is a fine view south over Dorset countryside as it slopes down towards Portland. Turn right along the Dorset Coast Path, and keep to it towards the Thomas Hardy Monument. This is a tall, narrow tower which you will soon see ahead in the distance. The Dorset Coast Path is a really good track with fine views on both sides, and there's no way you can get lost! The only vague section is where the track disappears along the edge of a field with Pen Barn Farm – a large, modern farmstead – over to the right. You rejoin the track on the other side of the field, steadily gaining height towards the monument.

Just before you reach the monument, the track goes downhill towards a road. I met an old local on the Dorset Coast Path who had plotted a 40-mile (64 km), mainly offroad, route for the day – he knew the local tracks like the back of his hand, and he was riding an old tourer! He recommended crossing straight over at the road, and trying the bridle track that runs through Black Down woods, and he was dead right.

Go straight through the woods, following the bridleway signs on this narrow track and bearing left as shown. It's a great up and down woodland ride, which after a time breaks into the open as you ride along the head of a valley with the woods still on your left. Keep on and cross the next road, then follow the track which bears round to the left before joining a very minor road. Turn left here and you come back to the same road that you crossed a short time before. Ahead is a track which would take you back towards the monument, but is unfortunately not shown as a right of way, so turn right and then first left along the road until the monument once again comes into view.

Just before the monument there is a track going down to the right along the edge of a strip of woods. Go down this, and keep on down into the woods on a really good, fast descent. Carry on downhill and if in doubt bear right, until you come to a clearing in the valley with a bridleway sign over to the left showing another track heading back up to the monument. Ignore this and go straight ahead through a gate, heading up the steep hill on the other side of the valley and leaving behind a few ruined barns.

At the top of the hill the track goes through Portesham Farm, and then bears right downhill and turns to tarmac. Here the ground formations become really unusual with all sorts of hills and hillocks to the right which would make an interesting technical section. You also get a real grandstand view of Chesil Beach, the enormous strip of pebbles running up the coast from Portland. The track soon comes down to a very minor road. Turn left and ramble along, meeting scarcely a car. You pass by Waddon House, a most imposing building, and a little further on bear left uphill when you join a road coming up from Coryates.

Ignore the first bridleway track which goes off to the left at the next right-hand bend. Carry on uphill and join the bridleway a short way on, which goes left alongside the first house you come to with power-lines ahead. Keep on up this made-up track past the farmstead on the left, crossing under the power-lines once, and then again when the track bends left. Riding over Corton Down you eventually rejoin the Dorset Coast Path on the crossing track that goes on up to Pen Barn Farm.

Turn right back along the Dorset Coast Path here, and ride through the next field and go through the gate. A little further on there's a three-way bridleway sign. Take the left turn to Martinstown, following the track across a field and then on a long steep descent down Great Hill. The bridleway becomes a proper farm track, and then you reach another three-way bridleway sign in the valley showing ahead to Martinstown, back the way you came to Great Hill, and acute left to Bronkham Hill.

Carry straight on for Martinstown following the track round to the right. However, don't go up the hill which starts about 50 yards (44 m) past the sign. The bridleway goes along the left-hand side of the long valley to your right, a turn which is not clearly indicated. Follow this direction, going through a gate and then gaining height up the side of the valley. At the top turn left through a narrow bridleway gate, and head across the field ahead which brings you back to the farm track. Turn right, and this soon takes you down into Martinstown just opposite the church.

Here you can go left to inspect the pub. To push on, turn right for a short way along the road, and then turn left at the first turning by a house called Fishers' Barn. Ride up the hill for about 75 yards (66 m), and then just past the last house turn right through a bridleway gate. From here ride across a small field, go through a gate, and then along an avenue of trees until you join a minor road. Turn right, cross over the next road which you come to immediately, and go straight offroad on to the track which bears off to the left. Follow this track up to the farm buildings at Clandon –

go straight through them and out the other side, passing a small modern house on the left. Maiden Castle and the car park soon come into view. Just keep on downhill, and then turn back to the right for the car park.

Ride 14 BLOXWORTH

Area: Wareham Forest and Bere Regis, Dorset.
Start: OS Outdoor Leisure 15 grid ref 906893; Forestry Commission car park near Wareham.
Approx length: 19.5 miles (31.2 km).
Ride: Easy/Moderate.
Climbs: Two minor climbs.
Conditions: Some tricky forestry sections; generally good going.
Difficulties: None.
High Points: An easy cruise which can be as demanding on your technical ability as you make it; some good views; plenty of variety.
R & R: Silent Woman pub near the start point; pubs, cafés and shops in Bere Regis or Wareham.

Although quite long this is an easy ride which would make a good day out. There is no hard climbing, but some of the

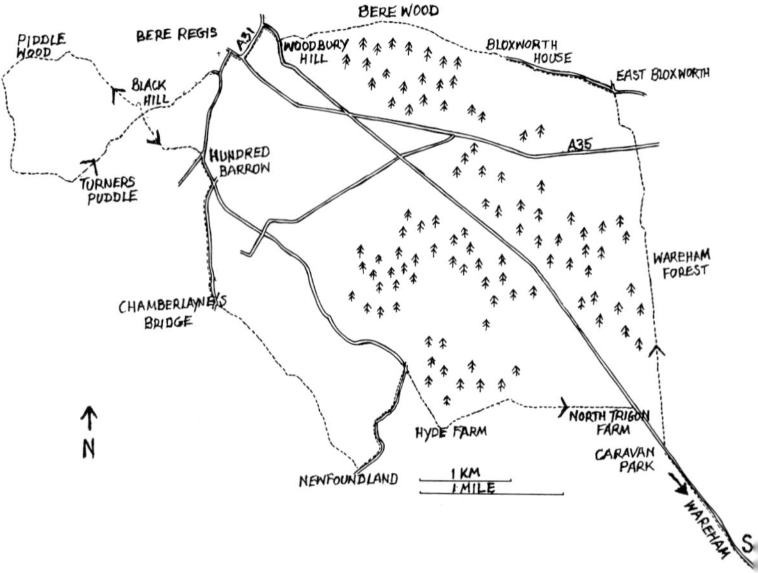

going through forestry is tricky – count the number of times you put a foot down, and then add your score up at the end!

Head north-west out of Wareham on the Bere Regis road. When you come into forest, the Forestry Commission car park is on the right about a mile out of town. From here carry on along the road for just under another mile. For the first hundred yards or so you can ride offroad along the right side of the road; then join the road and head on past the Silent Woman and a caravan park on the left. A little further on, the bridleway joins the road from the right. Cross the road and the bridleway goes through a gate in some new fencing.

Head up this bridleway, keeping due north all the way to Bloxworth. At first it goes down a narrow track hemmed in by a wire fence with open ground on the right. This section is surprisingly tricky due to the narrowness of the track and the bumps and lumps of tree roots under your wheels – watch out also for the stream which suddenly cuts a great trench across your path.

Head on into Wareham Forest where the track gets much better. Keep straight ahead through forest and open land, past Woolbarrow Fort on your left. Wherever the track deviates there are clear blue bridleway blobs to guide you on your way, and eventually you ride through a stream and come out on to the A35.

Go straight across here and keep ahead on a track which bends left past some houses, and then right taking you out on to the Bloxworth Road at East Bloxworth. Turn left for about ¾ mile (1.2 km) of quiet onroading past the few sleepy houses of Bloxworth with fine views of the Dorset countryside away to your right. Keep on ahead at the dead-end road sign, past a building with a brewery sign (which may or may not be a pub) sited next to the church. Pass a few modern 'executive style' bungalows, and then go through the gate ahead with a bridleway sign pointing straight across the field. To your right is Bloxworth House, a magnificent Jacobean pile hidden by trees.

The next gate is set in the perimeter of the woods on the far side of the field. At first sight these fields are welcoming with plenty of bluebells in the spring, and there's a rusty sign which tells you that a 'Boundary Oak' has been planted here to replace the one believed to have been there since the Domesday Book – although the modern replacement didn't seem to be in evidence.

From here the track degenerates due to being badly

chewed up by tractors. After wet weather much of this short section is barely ridable; I also punctured a tyre on a thorn, so beware! You soon cross a track where the bridleway greatly improves, becoming grassy and hard under your wheels with trees and rhododendrons on either side. Where the track forks, go left uphill as indicated by the blue bridleway blob; this is the first uphill of the ride and is short and easy.

You then continue west along a fine open section with good views to the north and to the south where you may see the vague outlines of the Atomic Energy Establishment at Winfrith – just hope that the wind is not blowing in your direction! The track enters trees and then goes through a gate by farm buildings, over a track, and through another gate. Head on down the track which bears right and left, coming to a twin bar gate which takes you across a field that goes steeply downhill with views of Bere Regis beyond. Head diagonally across this field following the horse tracks, and there's a good 'bike extreme' downhill in the bottom left corner leading down to a gate by a house from where a short track leads down to the road.

Turn right down this road past the farm and join the busy A31. Turn left for a short distance along it, turning right into Bere Regis at the roundabout. Follow the road round to the left, stopping if you like to check out the church which is advertised as 'medieval with an interesting carved roof'. The road crosses the river, and immediately after you take the turning to the right for Southbrook, following it round to the left past a footpath sign until you see the cemetery ahead of you. The bridleway track goes up the right-hand side of the cemetery on a good surface, heading into trees where there's an up-and-down 'Technical Sections Area' used by local BMX riders – you might like to pause there a while to show off your skills.

Bridleway blobs indicate left and straight ahead. Go straight ahead up a short, steep hill and off to the right and on to open heath heading south-west. After a while you come to a crossing track where you turn right, heading north-west across the heath. Ignore a track doubling back to the left (marked 'Tumuli' on the OS map) and keep straight on until you reach a gate with bridleways indicated downhill to the left and straight ahead towards some modern farm buildings. Keep on towards the farm buildings, and when you reach them turn left through a gate following a bridleway blob. The track which goes straight

Out of the woods and ready to head for the road with the end of the Bloxworth ride in sight.

ahead looks fast and inviting, but it goes the wrong way! Instead, bear right across the field (south-west) and into trees where you'll find a bridleway gate.

Head on down a good fast track through Piddle Wood. When you pass an old shack on the left the track dips down to a crossroads where you turn left, heading on downhill in a southerly direction, and eventually breaking into open country. After a good, fast descent turn left when you reach the crossing track and head east for Turner's Puddle, a small hamlet with a few houses, an attractive church, and a farm. Just past the last barn the bridleway goes up to the left, heading up Damer Hill to Black Hill. This is the hardest uphill of the ride, but would only be rated moderate at worst. After going up through trees the track breaks into open ground where you come to a crossroads with a large unusual rock which presumably is a boundary stone. Carry on to the next crossroads at the top of Black Hill – where you turned right on the way out – and this time turn right in the other direction, along past the quarry, before bearing left on a good downhill via Hundred Barrow past a caravan park.

Here you join the road. Cross over and turn right for Wool, ignoring the turning to Bere Heath. After about a mile you cross the River Piddle at Chamberlayne's Bridge, and then bear left on to a track with a faded bridleway blob before you reach the pylons. Head along this track past farm and other buildings, crossing a stream and going into rhododendron woods. These woods are very pretty despite a few mini dumps of building materials, and the route of the bridleway is clearly marked. Eventually you emerge on the right-hand side of a square clearing. Keep straight ahead, and then go through a lumber yard and out on to the road via a gate opposite Newfoundland.

Turn left along this minor road which snakes its way across the Piddle and its offshoots, past a house named Woodlands on the left, before bending left, running straight, and then bending left again when the forest comes into view with pylons beyond. Bere Lodge is a small, white building on the right side of this bend with the bridleway running beside it – the first time it can be easily missed. Turn down the bridleway heading SSE on a good track with woods to your left and open ground to the right. When you come to a crossroads turn left as indicated by a very faded bridleway blob. The track continues on a hard gravel surface with rhododendrons on either side which must be magnificent when in flower.

After about ½ mile (0.8 km) turn right off this track and into woods, as indicated by two bridleway blobs. On my visit the woods here had been decimated by the foresters, but the area may have been properly cleared by the time you get to it. The bridleway was indicated by a mass of blobs through the remains of the woods, as far as open heathland where there's a conspicuous rock with faded footpath and bridleway blobs. Follow the bridleway direction, straight ahead and due east, taking you out on to the road just above North Trigon Farm. Here you turn right and ride back just over 1 mile (1.6 km) to your start point, perhaps pausing at the Silent Woman on the way.

Ride 15 NINE BARROW DOWN

Area: Studland, Dorset.
Start: OS Outdoor Leisure 15 grid ref 038825; National Trust car park by Bankes Arms in Studland, plus other car parks in the village (pay in season).
Nearest BR station: Branksome.
Approx length: 16 miles (25.6 km)
Ride: Moderate.
Climbs: Two hard climbs, one moderate.
Conditions: Mainly hard chalk and grass; some mud and sand.

Difficulties: Studland has a traffic problem in high summer; unmarked bridleways.
High Points: Fine views from Nine Barrow Down; Corfe Castle interesting.
R & R: Pubs, hotels and cafés at Studland and Corfe.

This is a really fine Isle of Purbeck ride with little time spent onroad. However, beware that Studland can get hemmed in by cars during summer, and in particular the chain ferry that connects Studland to the Sandbanks peninsula develops very long car queues going to Studland in the mornings, and back in the late afternoon.

Start at the car park alongside the Bankes Arms pub and hotel. If this is full there is another large car park by the beach a short way to the north – to find a space it is necessary to get there early to beat beach-users if it's a hot summer day.

From the pub head down the hill, round the bend to the right, and up to the farmyard. Here, turn left up a rough road which heads straight up the hill to the Glebe Estate. Carry straight on up, passing the houses on your right, until you come to the last one which is a large, red brick, two-storey affair. Bear right here and then left up through a gate and on to a track past the National Trust sign

Go on up past a bomb crater where an enemy bomber jettisoned its load in the Second World War. Eventually you'll come to a stone seat marked 'Rest And Be Thankful', with a fine view behind you over Poole Harbour and Bournemouth Bay as far as the Isle of Wight, and ahead

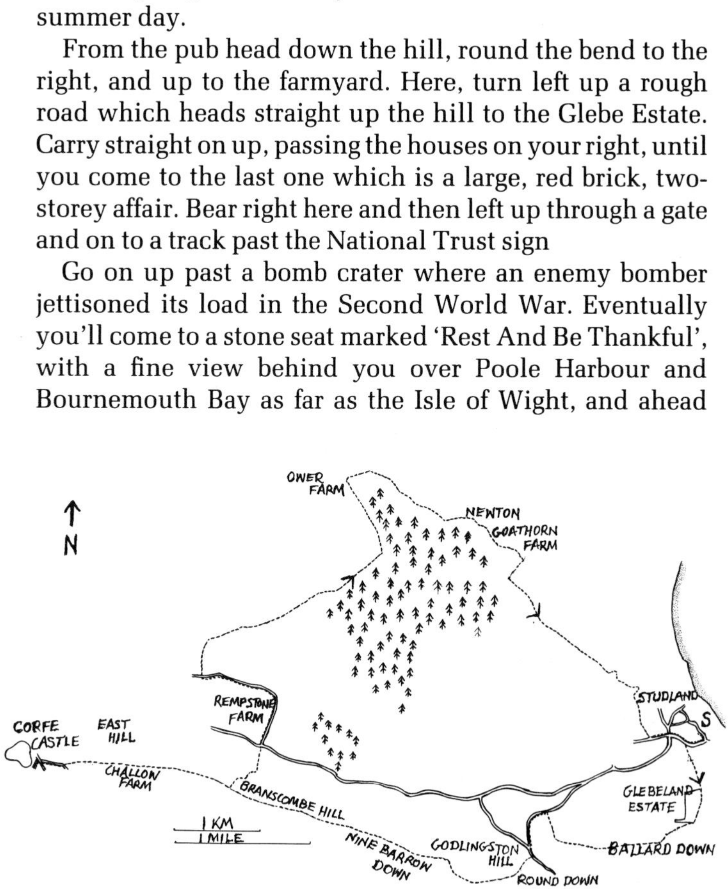

over Swanage. Turn right through a gate here, and ride along Ballard Down in a westerly direction. After about ¾ mile (1.2 km) you'll come to a large obelisk; bear off to the right past it, and head downhill until you come to the road.

Turn left along the road (which can be busy with holiday traffic) for about ⅕ mile (0.32 km). After you pass a road forking up to the right, the road bends left and on the opposite side there's a gate with a National Trust sign for Godlingston Hill which you can see wending its way up the hill. Plug up this track which is a long, hard haul, but the going *is* good as it's on solid ground.

At the top, bear left by the old gun emplacements, following the footpath sign and keeping west along the top of Nine Barrow Down. The going is mainly on grass, and you soon pass over Ailwood Down, marked by National Trust signs, and then on along the increasingly fast track past Branscombe Hill. When you come to the large radio mast at the top of Ronnington Hill (unmarked on the OS map), bear left and ahead down a track which will take you past Challow Farm. Alternatively, if you are looking for a technical section and are sure it won't hassle anyone, head from the radio mast along the left-hand edge of the field ahead of you, and when you reach the wire fence turn left at 90 degrees for a 'bike extreme' downhill that joins the track to Challow Farm.

From Challow Farm the road leads down under a bridge to the base of Corfe Castle, where you turn left and up into the village square. There are all sorts of shops and cafés, and predictably the place can become very crowded in summer. The ruined National Trust castle is worth a look if you like antiquities, but unfortunately you can't ride its 'bike extreme' hillside!

After watering yourself and your bike in Corfe, head back up to the top of Ronnington Hill via Challow Farm – it's an easy plug back up on the mainly hard chalk track. Retrace your tracks from the radio mast, looking for a bridleway turning to the left (north) after about ¾ mile (1.2 km). This turning is easy to miss as it is completely unmarked. You will come across a grassy plateau with a fenced field to the left ahead of you with a rather decrepit gate, and a gravel track going down to the south to the right. The bridleway is a narrow grass track going into gorse on your left, but if you overshoot it don't worry – you'll come to a gate with the National Trust sign for Ailwood Down, and about 25 yards (22 m) beyond it is an unmarked gate on the left which joins a track going left downhill to join up with the one you missed. Both are steep downhills, eventually leading to the Corfe–Studland road.

At the road go straight over and on down a minor road past Rempstone Farm, following the road left and ignoring narrow roads ahead and to the right. You pass Rempstone Old Farm on the bend, and then some way on you come to a house both on the right and on the left where you turn right down an unmarked track. If you overshoot you will come to a phone box and a few more houses – in all it's about a mile onroad.

Head down this track, and when you come to a smallholding on the left, there is a bridleway sign showing you the way to go to the right through a gate and across a field. Turn right at the next sign, and then ride along what was once a narrow gauge railway line and is now a very pretty track lined with old pine trees and blazing gorse in the spring. Some of the going is muddy but it's mostly easy; just keep straight on in an ENE direction and eventually you'll come to a tarmacadam crossroads with an industrial unit on your right.

Head straight over here, and on to a rough road with a sign saying 'BP Vehicles 20 mph Only'. Keep on along this forestry road, and you'll come to a bridleway crossroads indicated by daubs of blue paint (blue for a bridleway; yellow for a footpath). Turn left through thicker trees, and when you break into the open, follow the bridleway sign straight ahead, through a gate, and across a field. Cross to the far side, then turn right along its perimeter, keeping to the left down a track which can become very muddy. Ower Farm is to your left, and you may also see a couple of the 'nodding donkeys' which work the well-disguised oil wells in this region.

Keep on along this track which winds round Newton Bay, a very pretty spot which would be fine for a stop. Ahead you'll see a large old farmhouse which is Newton, marked on the OS map; head for the right-hand corner of the building where the bridleway gate is, and then out on to a track where you bear left, keeping left and following the bridleway signs past Goathorn Farm. Here ignore the bridleway blue daub pointing straight on across a muddy field, and bear right with the track past a couple of buildings marked as Greenland.

You soon come to a bridleway T-junction with the track bearing left and due east towards the road which you can probably hear. Instead turn right through the narrow National Trust gate which has the word 'Bridleway' written on it. Head straight on through several similar gates and past a barn (occupied by horses when we passed by), turning left where bridleway blue daubs indicate the options of left and straight ahead. Here you head diagonally across the field, through a couple more National Trust bridleway gates. (If you follow the direction implied by the daub – straight up to the left side of the field – you will eventually come out through a gate with a sign saying that you have just left an 'Alsatian Guard Dog Training Ground'! This is your local friendly landowner at play. We didn't get a sniff of so much as a poodle!)

Head on across the heath which is wild territory. There is a fair amount of boggy ground, and as you cross over towards Studland village it becomes increasingly sandy, which is bad news for both your brakes and gears. On your right you'll see the unusual looking Agglestone Rock – said to have been thrown there by the devil when he tripped over Old Harry – and then you head down into trees, bearing right across a stream over a narrow bridge.

The track leads up round the back of the Knoll House Hotel, past some buildings, and then comes to a crossing track with a gate complete with blue daubs on the left. Turn up the gravel bridleway track to the right, and almost immediately left again. The section which follows could be the muddiest of the ride and is usually badly chewed up by horses, but is thankfully short. It leads out on to Agglestone Road where you turn left until you hit the main road, turning left and then forking right back to your start point at the Bankes Arms.

Ride 16 WINTERBORNE KINGSTON

Area: Winterborne Kingston, south-west of Blandford Forum, Dorset.
Start: OS Landranger 194 grid ref 861977; parking on road.
Nearest BR station: Poole.
Approx length: 19 miles (30.4 km).
Ride: Moderate.
Climbs: Nothing to worry about.
Conditions: A number of sections along the sides of fields may be difficult if the weather is wet and/or the fields are ploughed; some bridleways are also very overgrown.

Difficulties: Riding difficulties will depend on the conditions; signposting is very poor, making navigation tricky.
High Points: A bracing circuit with some good views from high ground.
R & R: Pubs and village shop in Winterborne Kingston and Milborne St Andrew.

This ride can be started at Winterborne Kingston or at Milborne St Andrew, whichever is more convenient. From Winterborne Kingston, ride round the back of the church to East Street where you head east. Beyond the houses the lane becomes a track which comes to farm buildings on the left. Here the main track goes through a gate and curves round to the left, but you keep to the right and head straight along the side of the field ahead. Follow this good track on to the next field where you meet a track coming up from a farm to the right. This goes ahead for a short distance and then turns 90 degrees to the left, at which point you go straight ahead on a narrow track running along the left-hand side of a hedge. Keep on in the same direction, following the track across the open field beyond and coming to a gate where you drop down on to a gravelled crossing track.

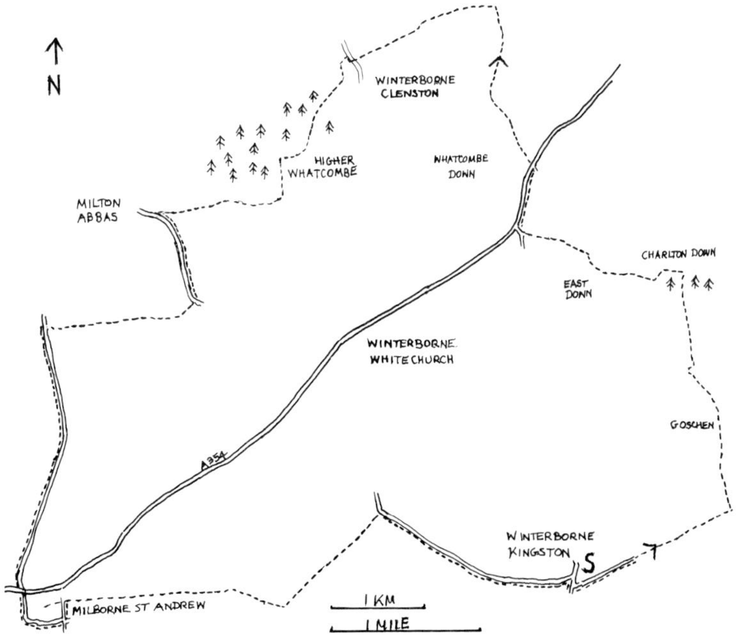

Turn left here, and follow the track which passes farm buildings on the left at Goschen, bears right and left, and then after about a mile becomes a grass track heading straight into the woods. Go into these woods which are on the top of Charlton Down, and turn left on the first crossing track which takes you out to the west side. Here you turn left on a narrow track running along the side of the wire boundary fence, soon coming to a gate where you leave the woods. Ignore the turning to the left and head across to a narrow track going straight ahead into the bushes. This was fairly overgrown but ridable when I tackled it, heading downhill. After a time you will meet a wide track coming from the left; turn left along it, keeping left until you see a couple of posts with a blue bridleway mark ahead. Go through here, and ride on downhill by the side of a battery egg farm, joining the tarmac driveway and eventually coming out at the road past a yellow road barrier by a sign for East Down House – a bridleway sign pointing back the way you came confirms that this is the right way!

Turn right along the road which leads to the busy A354 after 50 yards (44 m). Turn right, and ride along past a driveway going down to the farmstead at Whatcombe Down on the left. A few hundred yards further on a footpath sign on the left points up a track going uphill to the right, with the left-hand sign apparently broken off. You turn left here, heading across the field on what was a good clear track when I rode it. At the far side of the field you go through a gate and join a narrow track between a hedge and wire fence running up the side of the field ahead. When I rode it this was so overgrown as to be almost impossible – I leave it up to you to find the best way through! Keep on going until you come to a gate at the end of this awful track, and there bear left into a field which goes down and uphill ahead of you. There is no clear indication of where you should ride, but since the bridleway gate is in the far right-hand corner it seems sensible to keep to the right side of the field.

Go through the gate and continue to ride along the side of the field, coming out by the side of an electricity pylon where you cross underneath the power-lines by riding down the left side of the field ahead. When you start to head uphill, look for a narrow track through the thick hedge on the left. This takes you to a gate, where you head straight across the left side of the field ahead with a pylon on your right. You soon join a rough track which bears left and right, taking you down past the large farmstead at Winterborne Clenston, and then steeply downhill to the road by an impressive old barn.

Turn right along the road here, passing the front of the manor house. Well before the phone box a bridleway track going up to the left is indicated, passing through a locked green gate – it appears that horses are expected to squeeze round the side. Follow the tarmac track uphill as it bears round to the left and into thick woods. It goes past an incongruously placed garage on level ground, and from there straight on through another locked gate to a narrow, overgrown track through Oatclose Wood. This leads to an old gate where you turn on to a better track that bears left through the woods, eventually bringing you into the open by another gate. Turn right inside the fence here, and head steeply downhill by the side of the woods with the clearing of Higher Whatcombe to your left. At the bottom go through a gate and turn left on a crossing track, riding to the south-west corner of the clearing where you turn right on to a wide Forestry Track by the Wareham Forest sign.

Follow this track until it bears right and the bridleway leaves it to go straight ahead through the trees. This turn-off is easily missed, in which case the forestry track goes on and on, heading north and then bearing west past a solitary cottage after which it emerges on the road just outside Milton Abbas. The correct bridleway track takes you through the woods to the edge of a large field heading up to Hoggen Down. Turn left up the edge of the field, joining a good track which runs along the top, bringing you to the road by a house with a large farmstead down to the right.

Turn left on the road, and after about ½ mile (0.8 km) where the road bends left, look for a track off to the right. This is the bridleway, following the right-hand side of the field and then turning left along the bottom where it comes to a gate. Turn right through this gate, and go straight ahead along the right side of the next field until you come to a gate in the far right corner. Here you turn right and left along the perimeter of another field, joining a track which passes a modern barn on the left and soon brings you down to the road by Hewish Farm next to a field with geese.

Turn left along the road here, and ride on for 1½ miles (2.4 km) into Milborne St Andrew. At the main road – the pub is a short way to the right – turn left and then first right, following a quiet lane straight on and round to the left, where it goes uphill past houses. At the crossroads turn left, and then look for a gate on the right with a faded blue bridleway arrow. Turn right here, heading along the left side of the hedge across farmland. Go through the next gate, and in the field beyond go through the gate on the right so that you follow the hedge on your left, keeping in the same direction. The bridleway passes a cottage on the right, heading downhill and then uphill, following the line of hedges on the left. Eventually it comes to the road where you turn right to ride for just over 1 mile (1.6 km) into Winterborne Kingston.

Ride 17 ST ALBAN'S HEAD

Area: Corfe Castle, Dorset.
Start: OS Outdoor Leisure 15 grid ref 958818 at Corfe Castle; car park 50p in season.
Nearest BR station: Wareham.
Approx length: 17.5 miles (28 km).
Ride: Moderate.
Climbs: Two moderate climbs, but nothing severe.
Conditions: Variable with mud; some sections slippery.
Difficulties: Tricky ride down to Hill Bottom, and along final section to Challow Farm after rain.
High Points: Great views of Corfe Castle; fine 800-year-old chapel at St Alban's head; pretty coastline.
R & R: Pubs, hotels and cafés in Corfe; pub and shop at Worth Matravers; shop at Harman's Cross.

This is not a ride for a wild, wet and windy day! The section out to St Alban's Head is very exposed, as is much of the Priest's Way, so reserve it for a day when the weather is reasonably settled. It is a good ride with some fine views, and it's worth allowing extra time to check out such pretty spots as Chapman's Pool and Dancing Ledge.

The ride starts from the car park off West Street in Corfe, which is right past the church from the square. Turn right out of the car park (which has loos) and follow the road to its end where the footpath ahead is indicated, but there's no sign for the bridleway which runs south-east. Head left across Corfe Common, crossing the B3069 at a gate, and then heading straight on through a gate across the other side of the common. Aim towards Peaked Close House on the corner which brings you out on to the road.

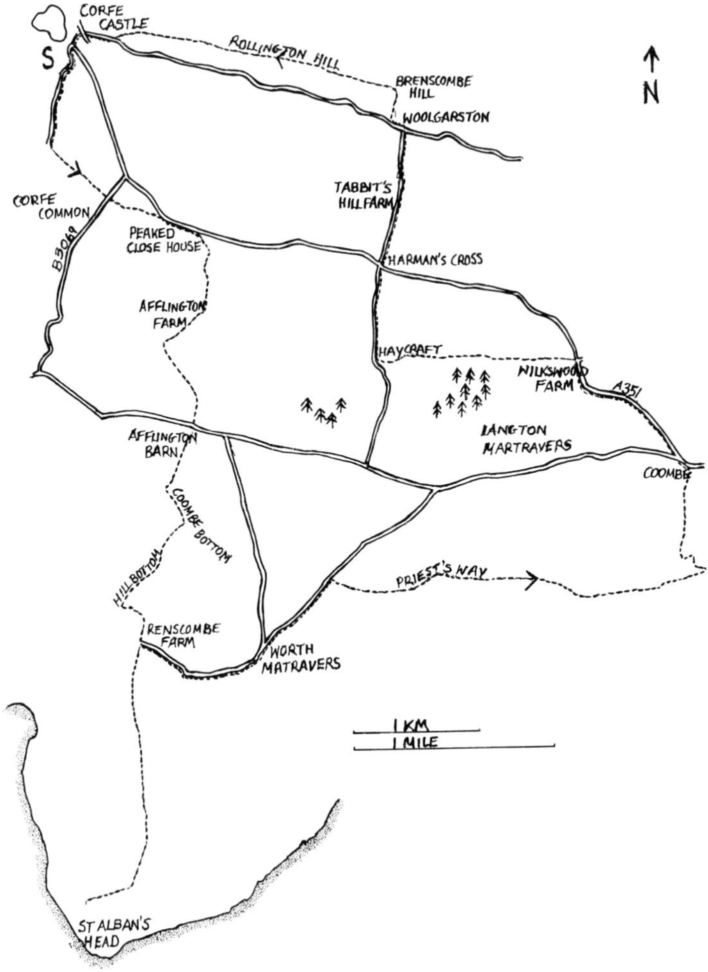

Turn right here for a couple of hundred yards. Just past a copse a track bears right to Afflington Farm. Follow it, keeping on for the farm and ignoring the footpath sign which follows the old railway. When you come to the farm bear right round the back of the buildings and south-west up the hill. The track soon becomes muddy and has been ripped up by tractors, but the view behind of Corfe and the Purbecks compensates. You soon come to a poorly marked bridleway crossroads where you head off to the left across a field – again on a poor track – keeping south-east and then bearing straight up the hill on a hard track towards Afflington Barn. This section is not at all clearly marked and is tricky to follow until you hit the track to the barn which is easily identified.

Cross the road here. The bridleway carries on between the house and the barn, going down what can be a muddy track. Keep straight ahead with Swanworth Quarry coming into view on the left ahead, and follow the track as it dips down a short 'bike extreme' hill with a gate at the bottom. There follows a tricky section through Combe Bottom and Hill Bottom in the small valley beneath the quarry. After wet weather the going can be exceptionally slippery and parts are rocky, so a helmet is recommended if you want to ride it at any kind of speed – otherwise pushing is easier and safer!

After a time you come to a footpath sign pointing left to Worth, and straight on towards Chapman's Pool which is the way you go. On your right you'll see a waterworks manhole cover set in the ground, and then to your left there's a made-up track going up the valley which you can't miss. Head up here and through Renscombe Farm where one of the cottages sells milk/cream to thirsty/greedy bikers. Follow the bridleway sign which takes you on a hard track out to St Alban's or 'St Alhelm's' Head, with a coastguard station and the tiny, 800-year-old Norman chapel – a place with a great sense of tranquillity once you're within its massive walls. From Corfe to here is around 5½ miles (8.8 km).

Head back towards Renscombe Farm, or take time out to investigate Chapman's Pool (for a swim?) via the track that goes down from Hill Bottom. From Renscombe head along the minor road through Worth Matravers, a pretty village with an interesting old pub on its outskirts named the Square & Compass, which can become very crowded. Head on in the direction of Langton Matravers, passing a footpath sign to the right. Not far after that you'll see a bridleway sign on the right opposite a modern barn – it's marked 'The Priest's Way' and tells you it's 3 miles (4.8 km) to Swanage.

The Priest's Way starts as a good, fast track through open country with fine views over the sea to your right. There are plenty of places worth investigating if you're looking for diversions, though there are no bridleways to the south. Dancing Ledge is particularly splendid. Keep on The Priest's Way for a couple of miles. The track goes through a gate with a modern barn to the left, and then bends left and heads downhill (north) just before you reach some houses.

The signposting by the National Trust as you approach St Alban's Head is admirably clear.

Keep on down for Gully where you turn left on to the busy A351 road, almost immediately bearing right for Corfe. After about ¾ mile (1.2 km) a road comes in from the left by a footpath sign; and a little further on there's a crossroads where you turn left towards Wilkswood Farm.

Bear right on to the bridleway past the National Trust sign. There follows a very pretty section through woods and on grass, eventually coming down to a rather ramshackle farm. On the map the bridleway goes straight ahead between the farm buildings; in reality it seems easier to go left through the gate with a yellow footpath blob, and then follow your nose west through a field and into a copse which brings you out into the Haycraft Caravan Park and onto the road where the bridleway is indicated on the map.

Turn right here along the quiet road, over the railway, and then straight over at the Harman's Cross crossroads. From here you head on up a minor road passing through Tabbit's Hill Farm where there's a bridleway indicated off to the left. In practice this bridleway proved difficult to follow, and a more satisfactory route is to push on up the road to the T-junction at Woolgarston where you turn left for about 50 yards (44 m), turning right up a bridleway track at a bend on a dip in the road with a house on either side. This road section is just over 1 mile (1.6 km).

Head up the track, bearing left (WNW) beneath Brenscombe Hill, ignoring the track which forks up to the right to the top of Brenscombe and Rollington Hills. Keep straight

Corfe Castle, a splendid landmark on both the Nine Barrow Down and St Alban's Head rides.

on in the direction of Challow Farm, with occasional glimpses of Corfe Castle showing that you do not have far to go. The track is more or less level but can be very slippery in places, with tricky narrow sections on the hillside and through woods before you eventually drop down to Challow Farm and rejoin the road, going under the bridge and turning left for your start point in Corfe where you can probably demolish a nice tea!

Ride 18 POXWELL and WHITE HORSE HILL

Area: Poxwell north-east from Weymouth, Dorset.
Start: OS Landranger 194 grid ref 760824; good parking in National Trust car park west of Chaldon Down.
Nearest BR station: Broadwey.
Approx length: 19 miles (30.4 km).
Ride: Moderate.
Climbs: A few medium climbs.
Conditions: Generally good going, but can be muddy after rain.
Difficulties: Very poor waymarking on first section demands careful navigation.
High Points: Fine return ride via the Dorset Coast Path.
R & R: Pub at West Knighton.

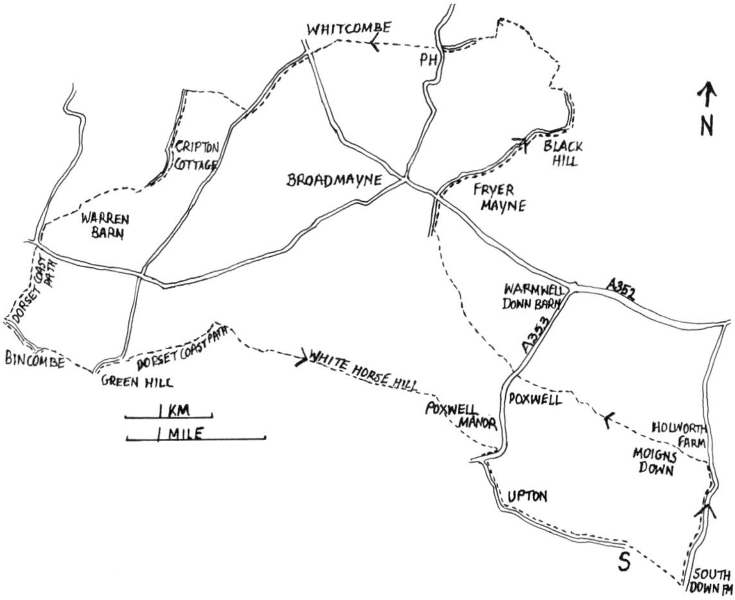

This ride starts from the same spot as No 12; in fact the two can easily be linked to make a taxing 30-mile (48 km) circuit – a very full day out on the hills above Weymouth!

Start eastwards along the car park as for ride No 12. Go downhill through two gates, and at the second turn left on to the unmarked bridleway which finishes the No 12 circuit. This is a clear track well before the bottom of the hill, and before the third gate leading to Sea Barn Farm.

This track takes you up and down on a good surface to Holworth Farm. Turn left over the stile just past the duckpond, and continue retracing the final section of No 12 in reverse order. Head across the field keeping the line of trees to your left; go through the metal gate; and head along the side of the hill until you join the wide track going up the hill ahead. The difference in riding this section one way on a damp day in May and the other way on a blazing day in June was noticeable! On the first occasion it was mainly a pushing job with thick mud much of the way, while on the second it was dry and could be ridden all the way, though it was certainly bone jarring!

Go up the hill until you reach the fence at the western-most point of No 12. The left-hand gate has a barrage of bridleway and footpath blobs – turn right here and join the track going straight down the valley from the next gate up.

This leads you downhill on a hard track to old farm buildings. Turn left through a gate just past the main barn where there is a very faded bridleway blob. A very steep hill confronts you, but don't go up it! Instead, ride round to the right and through an old metal gate by a completely ruined and overgrown house with its chimney poking up through the trees.

Go straight ahead up the hill until you reach a modern barn on the top. You join a track here which runs round its side, and then goes on down the side of a field past a conspicuous small tumulus which is fenced around. Just beyond it you leave the track (which bends left) and turn right through a gate into the next field, and then go left straight down the hill. This brings you down to the A353 above Poxwell.

Go straight over the road and through a gate with a bridleway blob. Go uphill across the field and through another gate where you ride up the side of the next field, keeping north-west. At the top bear right through a gate, and then head across a level grassy field aiming near the left-hand end of the strip of trees ahead. Go through the gates here, and then straight across the next field to another gate. Here you come to yet another field with Warmwell Down Barn away to the right. Bear right downhill across this field, and then go uphill until you hit the crossing track coming from the buildings.

Navigation on this stretch is not easy, but once you have reached the crossing track you'll find a proper bridleway sign pointing you in the direction of Broadmayne. Follow it uphill and along the left-hand side of a field which brings you to a gate in a belt of trees. Go through and then down the next field, heading for the farm buildings ahead. Beware of electric fences – I touched one here in a very sweaty state and got a nasty live wire shock!

The bridleway gate is over to the right by a small house. Go through, and then ride round to the left through the farm buildings, before bearing right on the tarmac track which takes you due north to the A352 road. Go straight over here, joining another tarmac track which gives you a very pleasant leafy-lane style of ride. Go past the old stables of Fryer Mayne, and a little further on the track bears left past farm buildings and roughens up. Just past here there is a bridleway track down to the left, but you go straight on through the woods, into the open, and turn left at the next bridleway crossroads.

Here go down a slight hill, crossing over watercress beds and the stream that feeds them. Go through the watercress farm buildings and then bear left uphill with a small house on your right. Keep left on a good track and you eventually come to a bridleway T-junction with a sand quarry ahead. Bear left on the track which goes round the edge of the quarry on a track of variable quality. It crosses under the overhead power-lines where it bears left, going past woods and through a gate downhill. A couple of hundred yards later – very bumpy in dry weather, but very muddy in wet – you come to a pretty thatched barn looking like an orphan in the sand and gravel pit wasteland. Bear left around the back of it, joining the main quarry track, and then almost immediately bear right on a long downhill which takes you to the road.

Here you could turn left and ride the 200 yards (176 m) or so to the New Inn pub, a pleasant looking place to stop. To continue, head back past the track you hit the road at, and about 20 yards (18 m) further on there's a track to the left running up the near side of some modern industrial units. This soon leads out into open countryside, running between fields on either side – when I rode past they were populated by the most alarming scarecrows, idly flapping their arms and looking for all the world like the Ku Klux Klan! Keep straight ahead on this track ignoring the bridleway going off to the right. After a time you'll hit a crossing track, with a grassy track going straight ahead towards a large farmstead called Whitcombe. Bear left here, and ride out on to the A352.

Cross straight over and continue along a minor road past an incredible-looking modern equestrian unit that did not appear on my up-to-date OS map. Carry on past this massive building to a dip in the road where there's a bridleway crossing track. Turn right here up the side of another field which brings you out on to a crossing track with a copse of trees to the right.

Turn left here on a good track past trees and then on down past Cripton Cottage, a pretty building on your left. The track bends left and right here past farm buildings, straightening out and coming to a gate with woods on both sides. Go on for about 50 yards (44 m), and then bear right through a gate with the customary faded bridleway blobs. On my ride there was a clear track through the next field bearing round to the left and going into another field, before coming to a modern barn at the end of a track.

Just before the barn, cross the track and go uphill into the adjoining field, and then bear left along the side of the field heading towards the right-hand side of the clump of trees ahead. Here you hit the road opposite a golf course which is advertised as a dangerous place for trespassers! Turn left along the road, and when you come to a T-junction after a couple of hundred yards, carry on straight over and follow the bridleway sign along a track heading due south – you're now on the inland section of the Dorset Coast Path.

Carry on down this good track which soon turns to tarmac with views over Weymouth opening out ahead. Ignore the first turning to the left and bear right downhill past a farmhouse until you hit the road at Bincombe. Turn left downhill through this quiet, charming place, and where the road bends right bear left on a rough track which takes you up past the church. Keep on climbing up this loose gravel track, gaining height until you reach the electricity pylons which disfigure an otherwise fine landscape. From here the bridleway is clearly indicated, going steeply downhill towards the road. When you reach the footpath sign for Osmington bear left down the grassy hill, heading towards Green Hill Barn which is conspicuous on the bend of the road.

Just beyond the cattle trough there's a gate. Turn left along the road here, and then take the first right past the barn signposted to Sutton Poyntz and Preston. About 20 yards (18 m) up the hill the bridleway is clearly indicated going off on a track to the left. Follow this uphill past a mass of tumuli, with a magnificent strip-farmed 'bowl' dropping away to your right. The track comes up to some ruined walls where you bear left through a gate, joining a crossing track with more overhead power-lines beyond.

Turn right along this track which will take you all the way to Poxwell. Ride through a succession of fields following the signs for Poxwell and Osmington, and then Poxwell alone. You will pass a trig. point at the top of White Horse Hill, and then gradually lose height on the way down to Poxwell. When you come down to a somewhat dilapidated barn on your right, cross over the track which leads down to Poxwell Manor, a splendiferous pile in the distance. Go up the short hill ahead and across the grassy field, bearing to the right and then down to the left where you join a track which becomes increasingly rough and steep on its approach to the road.

At the road you then have two main options. Unfortunately the track dead ahead, which is the most direct route, is labelled as a footpath so it can't be ridden. If you want to offroad it all the way back, turn left along the road for about 50 yards (44 m) and then right uphill at the first bridleway signpost. This takes you back via Moigns Down, rejoining your outward route through Holworth. Alternatively, the much quicker option is to turn right along the road and then left down and uphill to road it all the way back to the car park – it's a long, steady climb which is easy enough on tarmac.

The Isle of Wight

The Isle of Wight almost certainly has more bridleways per square mile than any other part of the UK. The south of the island is criss-crossed by a confusing maze of bridleways, with some fine long-distance tracks that culminate in the Tennyson Trail which forms the backbone of what is certainly one of the best rides in this book – a classic in good weather.

Don't assume that riding offroad on the Isle of Wight with its retirement home image is easy. There are a lot of ups and downs with stiff climbing and narrow tracks that demand both good technique and a good level of fitness. That said, the Isle of Wight is the perfect place for a heavy session of offroading over a weekend, with unlimited tracks to choose from.

Ride 19 THE SHEPHERDS TRAIL

Area: Mid-south of Isle of Wight.
Start: OS Outdoor Leisure 29 grid ref 484876; car park by Carisbrooke Castle.
Approx length: 15 or 17 miles (24 or 27.2 km).
Ride: Moderate.
Climbs: A few minor climbs; gets steep to Hoy's Monument.
Conditions: Variable tracks, some of which are tricky riding.
Difficulties: Some sections quite technical; could be very muddy in wet weather; overgrown on approach to Hoy's Monument.
High Points: A guided tour of the mass and maze of bridleways that this part of the Isle of Wight abounds in.
R & R: Pub at crossroads south of Rookley.

This is not the easiest Isle of Wight route, but it shows off the confusion of bridleways in the mid-south of the island. Some make for tricky riding and navigation is not always that easy, but they do give endless offroad options.

Carisbrooke Castle is to the south-west of Newport and is

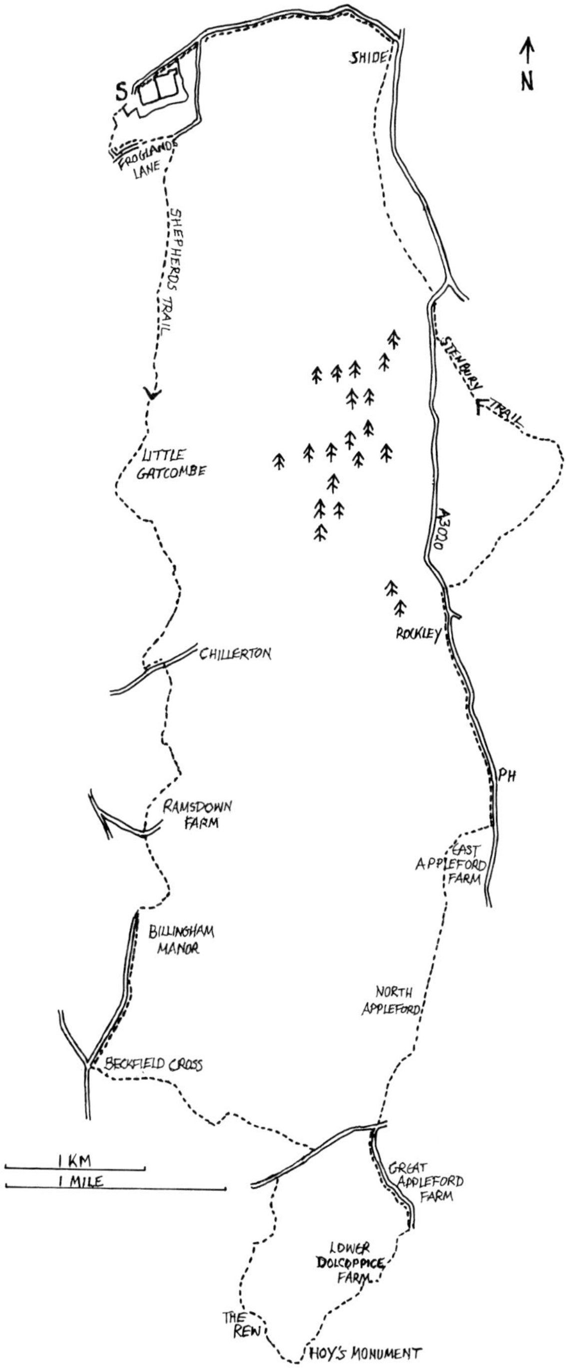
N
S
SHIDE
FROGLANDS LANE
SHEPHERDS TRAIL
STENBURY TRAIL
F
LITTLE GATCOMBE
A3020
ROCKLEY
CHILLERTON
PH
RAMSDOWN FARM
EAST APPLEFORD FARM
BILLINGHAM MANOR
NORTH APPLEFORD
BECKFIELD CROSS
1 KM
1 MILE
GREAT APPLEFORD FARM
LOWER DOLCOPPICE FARM
THE REW
HOY'S MONUMENT

well worth a look over; its south-facing ramparts also make a good place for a picnic on a fine day. The quickest way from the car park to the Shepherds Trail bridleway is to take your bike down a footpath which is over to the right as you go into the car park. Note that this is a *footpath* so don't ride. It's only about 75 yards (66 m) down to the lane where you can mount your bike, and it's considerably quicker than finding your way round by Millers' Lane.

Turn left along the lane at the bottom, crossing a ford and going slightly uphill before taking the next left turn into Froglands Lane. Head along it, steadily gaining height as you pass a sign for the woefully overgrown, direct footpath route to the castle which is over to your left. When you come to a road on a bend, take the bridleway sign up a track to the right which is the start of the Shepherds Trail.

At first this runs along the side of a field, before grinding up a narrow, subterranean passage which could become very wet and muddy in winter – and it's not easy riding in dry weather. Once back in the open, the Shepherds Trail continues along the top of fields, and you keep due south as you pass the red-brick tower of Whitecroft Hospital down in the valley to your left. A little further on the Shepherds Trail crosses a bridle track that goes down to Hill Farm at Gatcombe, and then it heads down into trees, dropping downhill between the farm buildings at Little Gatcombe with large hunting dog kennels on the left.

Ride down to the tarmac lane here where you turn right and then left up another lane, following the bridleway sign for Chillerton. At the next bridleway sign turn left for Chillerton up a rough track along the side of a field, heading up towards trees. Ignore the first track turning into them, and on the far side of the next field follow the bridleway sign round to the right. Ride down the side of this field, following its perimeter up to a gate where you continue along the side of a grassy field, through a gate, and then on down to the road at Chillerton just opposite Kervil Dairy.

Turn left here, and after about 100 yards (88 m) riding through the village turn right by a bridleway sign up Hollow Lane, heading towards Ramsdown Farm. The track narrows and keeps on going uphill, eventually coming up to a field where the bridleway goes left and right round its perimeter. At the bridleway T-junction ahead turn right for Ramsdown, heading downhill and bearing left through the farm buildings and out on to a country lane.

Turn right, bearing round to the left uphill. You soon

come to a bridleway sign pointing left where you turn down a steep, narrow track. After a short ride through trees the bridleway runs along the side of a field, and then goes through a gate set in the right-hand hedge, marked by a blue bridleway arrow. Bear left down through a five-bar gate here, heading down a rough track with Billingham Manor and West Billingham Farm ahead.

The track joins the road by Billingham Farm where I opted to push on due south and leave the Shepherds Trail which heads south-west before leading into a footpath. Turn left along the road, and after just over ½ mile (0.8 km) follow the bridleway sign left again at the crossroads at Beckfield Cross. This track leads through low-lying fields, eventually coming down to a sewage works. Just past this, turn 90 degrees left through a big metal gate, following the crossing track and then turning right at a bridleway sign after 100 yards (88 m) or so. Ride along this grassy track on a slight uphill, and then follow the edge of a field out on to the road.

From here I had intended to extend this ride south via Hoy's Monument as far as St Catherine's Hill, but had underestimated just how slow the Shepherds Trail would be. If you would like to find your way up to Hoy's Monument and read about the possibility of a big south-east circuit you should consult 'To Hoy's Monument' (below), while those who would prefer to head for home should move on.

To Hoy's Monument

The way up to Hoy's Monument and the top of St Catherine's is not an easy ride. Turn right along the road, and follow the first bridleway sign to the left along a lane past Upper Appleford Farm. Further on it becomes a rough track heading steadily uphill. Follow it, ignoring a right-hand fork down to a field, and it soon goes into a grass track on level ground. It then turns right through a narrow bridleway gate, and immediately left along the edge of a field which was badly overgrown when I rode it and made heavy going. The bridleway heads up through the trees of The Rew on a clearer track as it bears left uphill, coming out of the far side of The Rew at a gate. Here you turn right up the side of a field, heading up towards trees on the hillside with glimpses of Hoy's Monument above them.

This last climb was very overgrown, with a hard push uphill and a temperature of around 85C and an enthusiastic band of flies following my progress. At the base of the trees which surround the monument, the way for St Catherine's is to bear right straight up the hill. However I had run out of time on this ride, and decided to leave Hoy's Monument and St Catherine's Hill for another ride – No 22! Instead, I bore left on a much more obvious track which goes through a narrow gate and then on a good downhill across grass, with Hermitage Dairy over to the left. At the bottom of the field join the tarmac lane and follow it downhill to the left. After a swift descent, bear left by the entrance to Lower Dolcoppice Farm and ride on down to a road where you turn left past Great Appleford Farm. At the T-junction beyond carry straight over on to the bridleway track ahead and push on north for Carisbrooke.

Missing Out Hoy's Monument

After arriving at the road on the bridleway from Beckfield Cross turn left, and after a few hundred yards turn left again on to the bridleway track opposite the turning down to Great Appleford Farm.

This bridleway takes you north between fields towards Rookley. After a while the main track bears left up to North Appleford where you leave it and follow the side of the fields. Unlike most Isle of Wight riding the bridleway route is not that clear, and it is important to keep along the left side of the hedge which runs between the fields. Keep straight ahead at a footpath crossing track, and a little further on ride along the edge of a grassy field as you pass a copse of trees over to the left. Here the bridleway bears right on a track towards East Appleford Farm where it rejoins the road.

Turn left on the road, passing a pub at the next crossroads, where you may care to stop. Ride on through Rookley, bearing left on to the A3020. After a footpath sign on the left you turn off at a bridleway sign on the right a little further on. This track runs round the right-hand perimeter of a couple of fields, bearing left on a bumpy surface with trees on the right. Eventually it brings you out at a hard crossing track which is the Stenbury Trail. Turn left along this tarmac bridleway lane, passing Buckmore Farm and soon coming back out on the A3020.

Turn right on the road for a short distance, taking the first turning left where the road bends right past a garage. Just past the first house go through a narrow entrance, crossing a small bridge which takes you out on to the canalside cycleway – note that the entrance has no sign and can be easily missed. This is a delightful route on which to finish this ride, following a canal and stream with trees on both sides. After just over a mile of peaceful riding it brings you out at Shide on the busy outskirts of Newport. Here you turn left along the road, keeping straight ahead and following the signs (or lack of them) for Carisbrooke Castle which is a little over a mile away – if in doubt, just keep on ahead!

Ride 20 THE HAMSTEAD TRAIL

Area: Western end of the Isle of Wight.
Start: OS Outdoor Leisure 29 grid ref 347858; Pay & Display car park in Freshwater.
Approx length: 12 miles (19.2 km).
Ride: Moderate.
Climbs: Three climbs.
Conditions: Almost all good tracks.
Difficulties: None.
High Points: Pretty ride along the estuary to Yarmouth; good ride up to the top of Brook Down with fine views; fast final descent.
R & R: Pubs, cafés, tea shops, etc in Freshwater and Yarmouth.

This is a good circuit which in a comparatively short distance offers Isle of Wight downland views, an estuary ride, and a chance to visit Yarmouth. There's an uphill plug to the top of the downs plus a couple of shorter climbs, which will class this ride as either 'easy' or 'moderate', depending on your uphill enthusiasm.

Start from Freshwater as for ride No 21. Ride up the hill going east along the coast out of the village, taking the second turning to the left along a rough lane signposted to the golf club. Turn right into the golf club and ride up past the clubhouse; about 75 yards (66 m) further on a bridleway sign directs you downhill to the left on the Freshwater Way.

Follow this track north between fields until it opens out on to chalk and joins a tarmac lane. Turn right here, and then left on to the B3399 Newport road. Here you effectively cross straight over by almost immediately turning along a lane known as The Causeway. Ignore the first bridleway sign some way on, and look out for the second which indicates

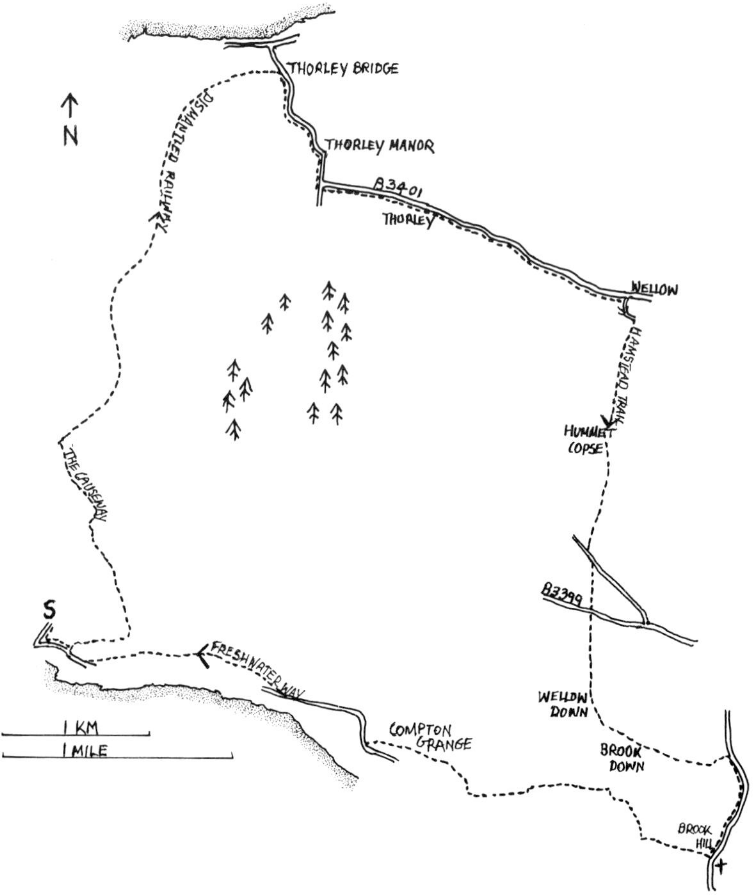

The Causeway crossing track by a bridge with a church across the estuary ahead of you. Turn right along this disused railway line which is a tranquil route alongside the Yarmouth estuary on an easy riding surface. It passes a short way south of Yarmouth, bending right by an old railway station before joining the road at Thorley Bridge after just over 3 miles (4.8 km).

Yarmouth is worth a detour, so if you want to investigate turn left here and head back into town. To push on, turn right along the road, and then take the first left past Thorley Manor signposted to Thorley village. Ride along the quiet road through Thorley past the church, and on into Wellow where you pass footpath signs right and left on the outskirts. A little further on, after just over 2 miles (3.2 km) onroad, take the first right on a lane passing the post office. Follow this lane round to the left by the village hall, and head down towards a small ford where a bridleway sign points right along what is the Hamstead Trail.

The track gradually gains height between fields, passing the trees of Hummet Copse over to the right. You go through a gate, keeping straight on south through a grassy gully, before joining a hard track that brings you to the road. Turn left and almost immediately right here, following the bridleway sign along a good track which crosses straight over the B3399 and then starts to head uphill. Keep on up, with woods ahead to the left. After going through a gate the bridleway climbs quite steeply up Wellow Down on a narrow track along the side of these woods, with a great crater in the hillside to the right which is probably something to do with old pit workings.

After a steep but ridable climb, the track goes through a gate and bears left along the side of the woods in a south-east direction. Here it starts to level off and becomes much easier pedalling. Go through double gates ahead, and the track then bears away from the woods and up towards the top of Brook Down which is not far ahead. Here the Hamstead Trail merges with the Tennyson Trail on a clear track heading east. Follow it round to the right side of the tumuli, and then enjoy the fine views after your climb. Anywhere along here would make a grandstand place for a picnic if the weather allows.

From here head downhill on the chalk track which is too heavily rutted to allow high speeds. Go through the gate at the bottom where you turn right along the road, heading down below Brook Hill. After about ½ mile (0.8 km) onroad you come to a church on the left. Turn right immediately opposite on to a private lane/bridleway signposted to Dunsbury Farm, and keep along this lane until you come to a bridle crossroads with the farm buildings in sight some way ahead of you. Turn right here, plugging up on the rough track until it reaches a crossing track where you turn left beneath Brook Down.

Head straight along, ignoring a fork downhill to the right and going through a gate and across a field where the track effectively disappears. Go through the next gate, and ride alongside the fence at the top of a field which slopes down to the right, with Compton Farm in the valley ahead and a fine view over Brook Bay to the south. After passing a foot-path stile the bridleway continues alongside the fence, before going through a gate at the far end. Here it bears right downhill on a sunken track which then bears left down to the farm. Go through the gate by the farmyard, and follow the farm track left towards the busy coastal road.

Turn right along this road, plugging uphill round the long left-hand bend. From here you can onroad it all the way back to Freshwater, but if you've got some energy turn off right on a steep uphill at the first bridleway sign which comes up after just under ½ mile (0.8 km). This is in fact an extremely steep track, which may make you wonder what you're doing offroad! However, after this short if savage climb you soon hit a clear chalk crossing track on the golf course which is the Tennyson Trail. Turn left here, and head down on a great high speed descent that makes the climb worthwhile, following the same finishing section as the longer Tennyson Trail ride, albeit further down the hill. All too soon you hit the road just outside Freshwater, from where it's a short downhill to your start point.

Ride 21 THE TENNYSON TRAIL

Area: South-west of the Isle of Wight.
Start: OS Outdoor Leisure 29 grid ref 347858; Pay & Display car park in Freshwater.
Approx length: 21.5 miles (34.4 km).
Ride: Moderate.
Climbs: Quite a few.
Conditions: Mainly good tracks.
Difficulties: None.
High Points: A classic circuit – virtually all offroad; some great views; long, fast final descent towards the Needles.
R & R: Pub, tea shops, etc in Freshwater.

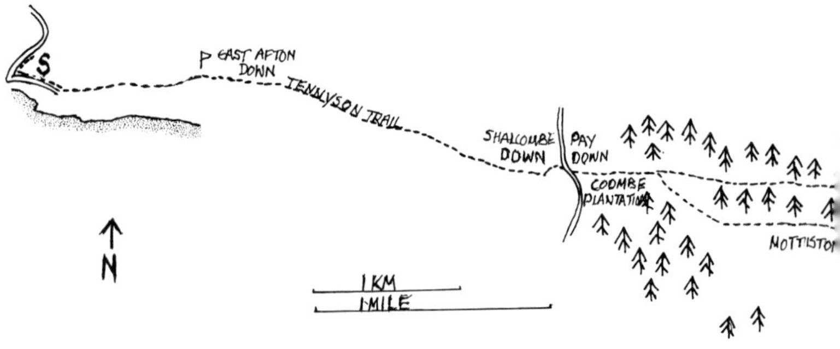

This is a very fine ride with superb views and fine tracks which appear very little used and are probably mainly quite ridable in wet weather. It's only a very short distance onroad, and yet you can average quite high speeds on the trails despite a fair amount of up and downing.

Start from the car park near the middle of Freshwater, just at the bottom of the hill that goes east out of the village. Ride up the hill, and a short way out of Freshwater take the first bridleway sign bearing off to the left. This takes you on a good chalk track uphill through the golf course. Plug on up this easily followed track as you gradually gain height, leaving the golf course at a gate. The track then heads straight on ahead, with fine views opening up. After a time you pass woods on the left as you ride along Shalcombe Down, and then you come to an area where a narrow track goes straight ahead and up and over cone-shaped tumuli.

It's worth riding over these tumuli past the Trig Point at Five Barrows for the mega views, followed by a steep descent ahead, bearing over to the right to rejoin the main track and taking care to avoid the disused pit with its sheer drop ahead – don't ride over the precipice! The track brings you down to a gate, and then to the road where you go straight over on to another track which heads up Pay Down towards woods. Go through a gate and into Coombe Plantation, keeping straight on up the wide track towards another gate. Follow the track ahead along Mottistone Down with

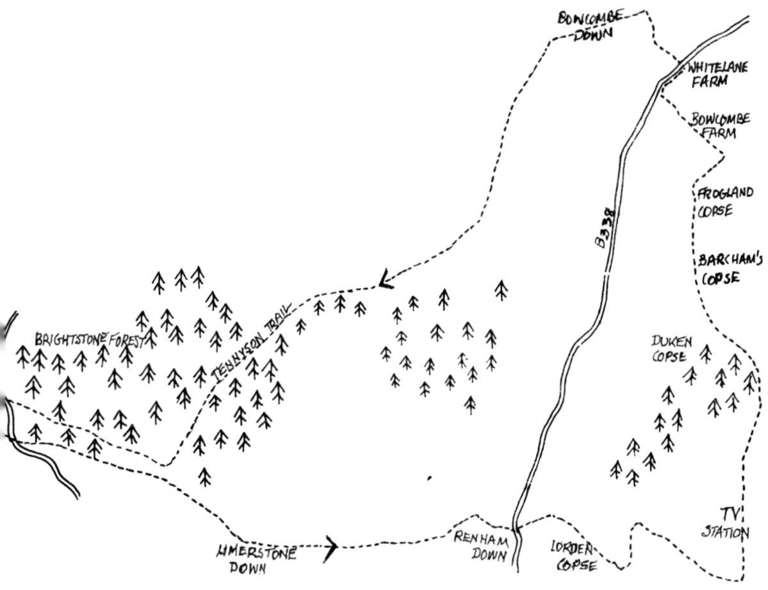

open ground to the south, heading on a good, long downhill towards the small car park and road at the bottom.

At the road turn right and immediately left on to an unmarked track (which is a bridleway), heading up along the side of woods on a loose gravel surface. After a time the track levels out and the surface improves. Ignore the left-hand bridleway turning for the Tennyson Trail, keeping on ahead and also ignoring two right turnings for Limerstone. The track passes the viewpoint on the top of Limerstone Down where there's a sort of miniature tower over to the right, and then heads downhill past a modern barn. The massive TV station mast which is the turning point of this ride is conspicuous on the hills ahead.

The track soon passes a strange place on the right which looks like some kind of radar station, joining a tarmac lane where you bear left, heading down Renham Down all the way to the road. Here you go straight over on to a rough track which goes steeply on a short uphill (change down in plenty of time), before levelling out and bearing right around the edge of Lorden Copse beside a field. After a steady uphill the track levels out completely, and then heads downhill to the left above New Barn Farm which is down in the valley. Bear left uphill through a gate here, keeping on uphill on the rough track which leads to a concrete crossing track leading up to the TV mast.

Turn right, following the track all the way to the TV station where the bridleway is indicated bearing off to the left through a gate, following a track to the west of the mast. Keep due north along this track which passes by a barn, going through a couple of gates on level, high ground and on into the pine woods at Duken Copse. There follows a good fast ride through the copse, keeping straight on past the right turning bridleway to Gatcombe. The track goes out through a gate and along the right side of two fields, heading downhill with Barcham's Copse on the right. This brings you to a steep, narrow downhill track which winds a short way down to a gate on the edge of Frogland Copse. Bear left and then right round the perimeter of the field ahead, turning left on a crossing track on the far side of the field and heading past Bowcombe Farm where you bear right and keep on ahead for the road.

Turn right for a short way along the road, passing a footpath on the left and then taking the next bridleway sign left by Whitelane Farm. Bear right through a gate with the farmyard on your left, and then steadily plug uphill on a narrow but good track. After a while you come to level ground with a crossing track by a rusty four-way signpost. This is the Tennyson Trail, and you turn left to follow it, bearing left at the end of the field and ignoring the right turning bridleway that heads towards Calbourne. Keep straight along the track, ignoring all turnings both right and left and gradually passing some more TV station masts which are well over to the right.

Go through a gate and straight over at a signposted crossing track, keeping ahead along the edge of a field and following the track which bears right through a couple of bridle gates along the north edge of woods. The Tennyson Trail then goes into Brighstone Forest for some good woodland riding, before emerging into a cleared area with newly-planted trees. Some care is needed to find the right turning here. Ignore the first right-hand bridleway signposted to the Calbourne/Brighstone road, and keep on for another 100 yards (88 m) or so until you come to a four-way bridleway sign on the edge of woods with another bridleway sign about 75 yards (66 m) over to the left. The sign pointing to the right downhill says 'Brighstone/Calbourne Road 1 mile', and that is the way you go on a good, wide forestry track with a loose gravel surface, bombing down to hit the road in record time.

Here you go straight over at Calbourne Bottom, heading uphill through woods and then riding level along Westover Down. After passing a bridleway crossroads the track bears left, and you soon come to the crossroads where you entered the Coombe Plantation on the outward leg. Turn right through the gate here, and retrace your wheel tracks down Pay Down and then over the road, heading straight up the steep track ahead which takes you beneath Five Barrows along Brook Down.

From here it had been my intention to bear north round the edge of the woods on to the Hamstead Trail, returning to Freshwater via Yarmouth and the disused railway Causeway track which would have extended the ride to some 28 miles (44.8 km). However, I had run out of time and decided to leave this extra circuit for another ride, retracing my tracks on the direct route. This proved to be an excellent decision. It's amazing how different a track can be when ridden in the other downhill direction! The Tennyson Trail along Wellow and Tapnell Down makes for great fast cruising, and then you finish the ride with a long and very fast downhill on East Afton Down, bombing down through the golf course on a good hard grass and chalk track. With the sun setting over the Needles ahead of you this is a great end to the ride, bringing you back down to Freshwater in record time. But take care to be courteous to any strolling golfers you may meet!

Ride 22 NITON TO LUCCOMBE DOWN

Area: South-east of the Isle of Wight.
Start: OS Outdoor Leisure 29 grid ref 491767; free car park at viewpoint above Blackgang.
Approx length: 18 miles (28.8 km).
Ride: Hard.
Climbs: A lot of them, and some are hard!
Conditions: Mainly good going on various surfaces, but mud could be a problem after wet weather.
Difficulties: Mud if wet; track up to Hoy's Monument badly overgrown.
High points: Magnificent views when you're up, and a fine ridge ride around Luccombe Down; good if you're into energetic riding.
R & R: Pubs, etc at Blackgang, Niton, Whitwell, Wroxall and Chale; refreshments van at start point; excellent farm shop in Chale.

This ride takes in a good selection of the network of bridleways in the south-east of the island. The going is up and down which makes it energetic, and you'll need to pace yourself accordingly.

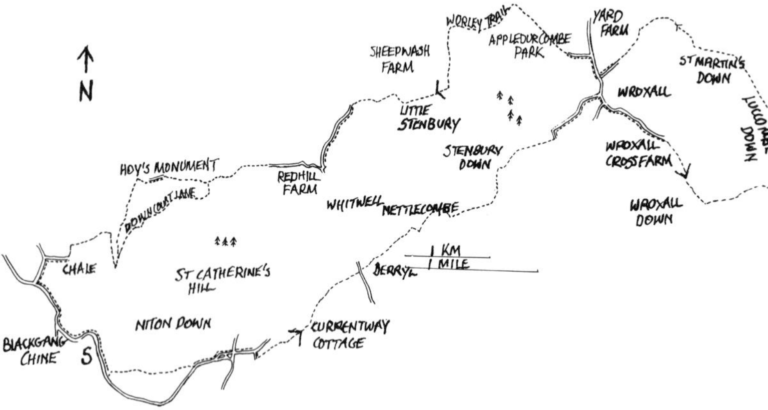

Start from the car park near the top of the hill above Blackgang Chine. From here turn right up the hill, and after a couple of hundred yards turn left on to a track heading up between fields. Turn right through the first gate following the bridleway sign along the left-hand side of a field, and follow the track as it narrows and goes downhill towards Niton where you rejoin the road.

Ride through Niton following the one-way system and carrying on straight ahead at the crossroads. Pass a footpath sign and the sign for Chatfield Road, and then take the next turning on the right where the road bends left. Follow this side road round to the left with modern houses on either side, and you'll eventually come to the bridle track going straight ahead. Follow it past a few houses on the right, and keep straight ahead where the main track bends right towards a friendly sign with a message to the effect of 'This is not a b-way so * * * * off!' Ahead a bridle gate goes into an impenetrably overgrown track leading up to the solitary Currentway Cottage; instead keep up the side of the field where there is a well-trodden track, joining a hard driveway just past the house.

This soon takes you down to the road by the YHA at Whitwell. Here you cross straight over on to a bridle track with a sign which is easily missed. Go downhill and through the gate, crossing a stream and then heading up towards the left-hand corner of the field. Here you go through a gate in the trees ahead, about 15 yards (13 m) to the right of the footpath stile. Follow the narrow track uphill and through another gate on to open grassland, riding up to the bridleway signs with a couple of houses at Berryl over to the right. The bridleway sign implies that you turn left along a clear track; in fact you head diagonally across the grass ahead, aiming for the right side of the farm buildings at Nettlecombe in the valley.

Go through the gate and pass the ponds on your left, going through another gate and turning right on to a marked bridle track running up between hedges. After 100 yards (88 m) turn left at the next bridleway sign, following the track up to an open field where you follow a bridleway sign and turn right along its perimeter. At the bottom of this field turn left, following the bridleway sign for Stenbury Down; an unmarked bridle track runs straight ahead here, with Week Farm downhill to the left. Ride along the side of a field and then up a track between hedges which were badly overgrown when I rode this route. Once on open ground ignore the right turning bridle track, and bear left up the hill, aiming for the next set of bridleway signs, through a gate and on to the Stenbury Trail on the hill top.

Turn left along the Stenbury Trail and ride towards the radio station, passing footpath and bridleway signs to the left. After a short blast take the next right-hand turn downhill on a made-up track which will take you down to a crossing road in record time. Turn left here, following this road round to the right and past houses until you hit the main B3327 road which runs through Wroxall. Turn right here, and then bear left off the main road uphill past the pub. Keep left and you soon leave the houses of Wroxall behind, riding along a country lane which passes the rather splendid Wroxall Cross Farm. Ride on and at the bridleway sign take the right-hand fork on a slight uphill, keeping straight on between the buildings and ignoring the next sign pointing up a track to the right.

Beyond the farm buildings the track goes into trees and then heads steadily uphill between fields, before going into the woods of Wroxall Copse. Here it becomes mega steep and quite unridable, and it's a hard plug to the top pushing your bike. As you break out of the trees, follow the track off to the left, ignoring the gates on the right with the rather ambiguous bridleway sign. The track soon brings you to the top of Wroxall Down by a radio station, with magnificent views out over the island.

Turn left along the tarmac lane here, following it round past the radar station and then going through a gate to join the bridle track which runs north along the top of Luccombe Down. This is great ridge riding with immense views on either side. Ignore the first bridleway turning downhill to the left, and continue until you come to the second bridleway turning signposted to Wroxall with a footpath going straight ahead. Ride downhill on a grassy track, going through a gate and then bearing right for a gap in the trees where you pick up the next bridleway sign for Wroxall. This takes you downhill on the right side of an enormous crater on St Martin's Down, through a gate and along a narrow track running through trees which is tricky to ride in places and could be very muddy in wet weather.

Follow the signs beyond the trees, bearing left up to a gate and then turning downhill. Here I must admit I lost the bridleway; having hit a hard track I assume it was the right way and zoomed off downhill, eventually emerging on the road by Yard Farm about ½ mile (0.8 km) from where I

Approaching the gatehouse in Appledurcombe Park leading to the Worsley Trail.

should have been! The correct route keeps close to the trees and goes down past the cemetery, before joining the road in the middle of Wroxall.

Turn right along the road here, and then take the left turning downhill signposted to Appledurcombe Park. Follow this road to the Appledurcombe car park, where you go through the gate on the left and on to a bridleway bearing right across fields. Follow it through a gate, and then over grass towards a magnificent old gatehouse, which is sadly in ruins. Go through the left-hand gate, and after 10 yards turn left on to the Worsley Trail.

The track heads up through woods, and then out on to open grassland where it follows round the left side of Gat Cliff with a fair amount of uphill riding. It goes through a gate into trees, and then there's a short, steep downhill into more trees where you follow the bridleway sign left round the side of Gat Cliff. From here there's a tricky ride along a very narrow track which has mega lumps, heading steeply up a short hill and then along the left side of a field when Gat Cliff is left behind. Riding along the top of this field you will see Sheepwash Farm and Little Stenbury downhill to the right. Go into trees at the end of the field, and where the track heads steeply uphill, turn right down an unmarked track with trees and bushes on both sides. This soon leads down past Little Stenbury on a good surface, and by following your nose you're soon back down on the road.

Turn left here, and then take the first lane to the right

heading towards Redhill Farm. When you reach the farm head straight over, and go up the bridle track which soon bears left past the farm buildings and logging shed at Moorhills. This takes you through a gate, and across a grassy field where you bear right uphill to the fence and then follow it round to the left on a track that heads downhill and leads to a clear crossing track.

Almost directly opposite is a narrow unmarked track heading up the hill. This is the bridleway that leads up to Hoy's Monument – a huge stone pillar with a ball on top – which had been luring me on. However the bridleway proved to be so overgrown as to be almost impassable and extremely unpleasant, rather putting the kybosh on what had been a very good ride. I would recommend, if it appears equally overgrown when you reach it, that you retreat back to the crossing track and follow it south to the next right turning track which is Downcourt Lane. This leads through Downcourt Farm to the top of St Catherine's Hill, and though I have not ridden it I suspect that it would be a relatively easy ascent.

If the track up to Hoy's Monument has been cleared you can follow it up to a small cottage on the edge of the woods where you then join a hard track. Follow this uphill past the left turning track to Downcourt Farm, and at the next bridleway sign bear left along the side of a wall beneath another cottage on the hillside. Go through a bridle gate by a National Trust sign, turning directly up the hill on a steepish track which soon bears left and levels out as it approaches the top of St Catherine's Down.

Once at the top you get more fine views and good riding on hard packed grass – this appears to be a popular place for gallops. Head south along the top away from Hoy's Monument towards the radar scanner on the hill ahead. Go through a gate by a National Trust sign, and then bear right towards another gate which takes you on to a rough track heading right down the hillside. With a bumpy, hard ride – no doubt very muddy when wet – this bears left downhill to Chale farm where you join a narrow lane and turn right out on to the road. Turn left and a little way further on there's a farm shop which sells ice-cold orange juice and a vast selection of home-made ice-cream – manna from heaven after such a ride on a hot day! From this little oasis ride on through Chale, joining the main coastal road and turning left for the longish plug uphill back to your start point above Blackgang.

Sussex and the South Downs

The South Downs run all the way across the breadth of Sussex, and are well laced with bridleways giving the most excellent offroad conditions in some wonderful countryside. The most famous bridleway of them all is the South Downs Way, a non-stop 75 miles (120 km) that runs from the Hampshire border to Eastbourne on an up-and-down route that demands major commitment. Many of the rides which follow use sections of the South Downs Way as part of the circuit, while others follow other parts of the downs in what is probably the best mountain bike territory in the south of England.

Ride 23 WEY SOUTH PATH

Area: Wisborough Green, West Sussex.
Start: OS Landranger 197 grid ref 047258; park by green.
Nearest BR station: Billingshurst.
Approx length: 12 miles (19.2 km).
Ride: Easy.
Climbs: A few minor climbs; otherwise flat.
Conditions: Some sections liable to be muddy and badly churned up by horses.
Difficulties: Mud in wet weather.
High Points: Easy ride with short offroad sections and quite a bit of variety.
R & R: Two pubs and village stores in Wisborough Green.

This is an easy ride some way to the north of the South Downs. Most of the going is flat and it's relatively short, but be warned that some sections are liable to be badly churned up by horses and much too muddy to ride in wet weather.

Start from the green at Wisborough Green where cricket is played in summer. Head along the A272 towards Billingshurst, and not far past the church look for a right-hand turning with a bridleway sign. Head down this track which is tarmac initially. It passes a few houses and then comes to

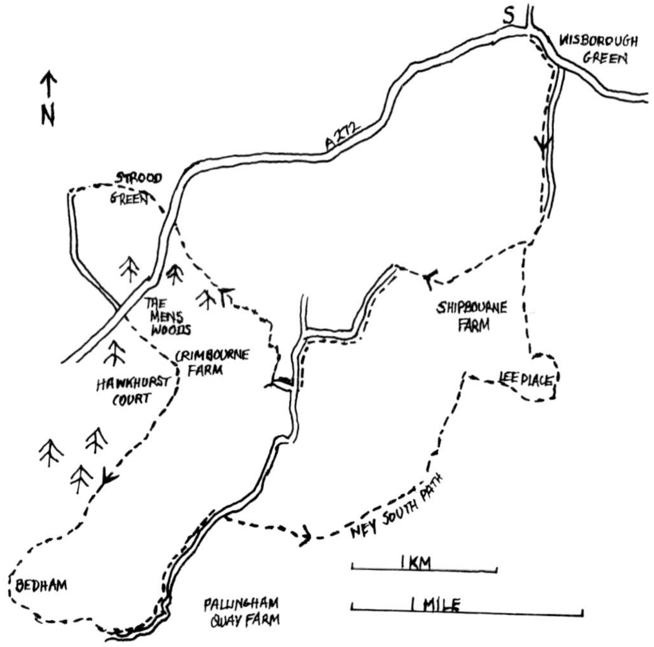

the farm beyond Harsfold Manor where it goes through a gate and into fields.

Keep on ahead on a good track. After a short time you come to a bridleway sign pointing straight on and right. Take the right turn, following a track which can be rough going in places as it comes down near to the river. Go through a gate and straight ahead across a grassy field, picking up the bridle track which continues through trees. From here it goes to another gate where there's a bridleway sign directing you right along the track and through another gate. This brings you into a field with Lowfold farmstead over to the right. Keep straight ahead here, heading for a gate in the corner of the field which takes you to a crossing track where you turn left.

The going here is good, and you soon come to a bridleway/ footpath T-junction just east of Shipbourne farm. Turn left here, and the track soon brings you out on to the road where you turn left and ride a couple of hundred yards to the first right turning signposted to Kirdford. Fifty yards (44 m) or so along where the road bends left, a bridleway sign points right down an overgrown track besides a wooden hut. The direction of this track is easy to follow and at first the going is good, but you soon run into problems with the ground badly churned up by horse hooves – this is prime horse-riding territory. Keep on through a tricky section which is good for improving your technical riding – impossible if muddy – and the going improves as the track eventually joins up to a hard driveway passing through houses in The Mens' woods.

This takes you to the A272 which you cross straight over, picking up the bridleway sign on the opposite side of the road. Go straight down the lane as indicated, and a short way further on you come to a house with a bridleway sign pointing right and a footpath sign left. This is somewhat confusing, for the bridleway in fact runs down a narrow track by the right side of the house, and continues through woods all the way to the road at Strood Green. Again, the direction of the track is easy to follow, but the going is even more difficult with horses once again the main culprits. This is as much a pushing section as a riding one, but is none the less enjoyable for those who like to take time out in the country.

The track bears left slightly uphill through grass to hit the road. Here you turn left and head back down to the A272 on a quiet lane. Go straight over the A272 and on to the lane on the other side, and after about ⅓ mile (0.5 km) you'll see Crimbourne Farm, an imposing building with outbuildings on the left, and on the right the lane up to Hawkhurst Court with a bridleway sign. Ride up to Hawkhurst Court where you take the right-hand driveway and then bear left round the buildings. This takes you on to an up-and-down tarmac lane through woods (watch for the sleeping policemen) until you see a bridleway sign on the right at a dip in the road.

Go offroad here and follow the track through the woods – the going is mainly good, though muddy in places. This will in time bring you down between two cottages on the edge of the woods where you hit a lane and follow the bridleway sign right. The lane passes the front door of a cottage, and a short way on you'll see another bridleway sign pointing straight ahead into the woods as the lane bends left.

This is the way that you go and it takes you up to a two-way bridleway sign where you turn left, heading uphill on a good track above a house beside a green field. You pass a small ruined chapel in a clearing which is something of an oddity, and then after another short uphill you come out on to a lane with a large barn opposite. Turn left here for just

The ruined chapel on the South Wey Path ride, with a sign showing the trail.

over a mile of onroading. The lane goes downhill past the well-to-do/well-hidden houses of Bedham, and you then follow the left-hand turning signposted to Wisborough Green. After more downhill the lane wiggles through an S-bend, passing the bridleway turning for Pallingham Quay Farm. Further on it levels out past some houses, coming to a farm on the right with a house and stables on the left.

Look out for the bridleway track on the right here with a sign that is quite well hidden. Head through a couple of gates along this good track which is the start of the Wey South Path. The going from here on is mainly good as you bear left round the top of an open green field, following its perimeter down to a gate where you cross a lane by a farm cottage. Follow the bridleway sign into the next grassy field, keeping to the right and then following the bridleway sign left when you come to it.

This leads through a pair of gates and on to a bridge which crosses the River Wey. From the bridge go straight up to a gate, where you follow the bridleway sign left and right round the edge of the field on a good track. At the far side of the field turn right on the bridleway by a left-turning footpath sign, riding along below Lee Place which is the imposing place on the hillside. You come to a lane where you turn left, coming to a three-way sign by the entrance to Lee Place. Follow the bridleway straight ahead here, going over the cattle grid and heading for some cottages. The bridle track bears round the left side of these cottages, picking up another sign behind them which directs you to the right and down towards the river.

Here you cross over the Wey once again on a venerable bridge and then follow the track straight ahead between fields. You soon pick up your outward wheel tracks, and from there it's a short ride back to Wisborough Green.

Ride 24 WATERGATE HANGER

Area: North of Funtington, near Emsworth on the Sussex/Hampshire border.
Start: OS Landranger 197 grid ref 801083; parking opposite pub in Funtington.
Nearest BR station: Southbourne.
Approx length: 12 miles (19.2 km).
Ride: Easy.
Climbs: A steady climb up towards Kingley Vale and up from Stoughton.
Conditions: Some sections could be very muddy in wet weather.
Difficulties: None, though horseriders may congest the way.
High Points: An easy introduction to South Downs riding, passing the splendid Stansted House and Racton Monument.
R & R: Pubs in Funtington and Stoughton; café at Stansted House when open.

This is an easy two-hour circuit, though it could be heavy going in wet weather. If you ride it in the summer you may like to leave time for a visit to Stansted House which is open to the public. If 12 miles (19.2 km) isn't long enough for you, the route can also be linked with the Kingley Vale ride (No 25) which follows.

Start from the car park opposite the pub in Funtington. Turn left out of it, and then immediately right on the road signposted to Petersfield. After less than ½ mile (0.8 km) take the first right past a grass island, following the sign to Asdean House. About 50 yards (44 m) up the driveway a bridleway sign points up a track to the right. You turn up here to go offroad.

The track takes you on a good surface steadily and easily uphill, mainly through woods. At a T-junction crossing track turn right, and continue to follow the track along the

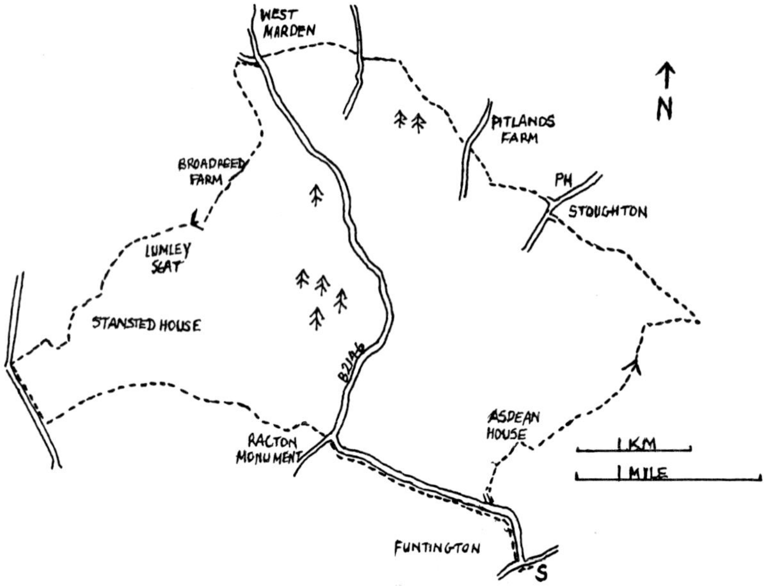

side of a field as it bears sharply left uphill with open ground on your left and woods on your right. Keep on ahead to the top of the hill passing the right turnings to the tumuli on top of Kingley Vale which would link this ride to No 25, which follows, if you wanted to make a grand circuit.

Keep on along the same track which starts to bear left downhill. This takes you on a long descent towards Stoughton, but it's a rough track and not easy to go fast on. At the bottom turn right along the road, and then left at the green. If you want to visit a pub at this stage, it's a bit further on down the road. At the back of the green a bridleway track is indicated bearing uphill to the left. Head up this and follow it along the side of trees, bearing right on a bumpy downhill which brings you down the side of a field to another road just south of Pitlands Farm.

Cross straight over here, heading steadily uphill. Ignore a bridleway turning to the left, keeping on up what is the steepest hill of the ride. It eventually levels out through woods, and then emerges with a big open field to the left. Here you glimpse a house ahead to the right, and at the three-way bridleway sign you take the left turning heading across the field and gradually downhill. When you reach a lane turn right, and then left on to another bridleway track which is signposted after about 25 yards (2.2 m).

This leads through more woods to a fast downhill between hedges which brings you to the B2146 road just south of West Marden. Go straight over here and head up the lane ahead, taking the first bridleway to the left after about 75 yards (66 m). From here you ride along a good flat track through the woods of Watergate Hanger, running parallel to the road. Keep on ahead, and it eventually bears uphill to the right bringing you out into the open by a solitary house. Head on along the gravel track past this house, and keep on the track past Broadreed Farm which is a smart-looking place on your right. From here the track turns to tarmac – though still a bridleway – quickly bringing you to a house on the corner of a sharp right-hand bend.

From here you have two options. We followed the track round to the right on what is to all intents and purposes a private road, passing a secluded, large house called Lumley Seat on the left and coming to one of the Stansted House lodges where a bridleway sign points left and right. However, going back to the sharp right-hand bend a bridleway is signposted going straight ahead down a track, which is not shown on the OS map. We did not ride this way, but it appears that after a few hundred yards this track turns sharp right by a copse of trees, bringing you to the same lodge by an offroad track.

From the lodge turn right on the private road which passes the entrance to Stansted House which is well worth a visit if open. Just past this entrance a bridleway sign points left along the side of a field – a turning which is easily missed. Ride along the side of the field with Stansted House revealed on the left, on a narrow track which could be hard going in wet weather. Keep on along the fence until you come to another driveway, and follow it to the right away from the house on a loose gravel surface. After about 100 yards (88 m) a bridleway sign points right across grass towards trees; follow the narrow track which bears left before coming to the road at the southern end of Stansted Forest.

Turn left down the road, and about ½ mile (0.8 km) further on look for a sharp left bridleway sign at the end of the woods pointing to another track which could be easily missed. Follow this track (the Sussex Border Path) as it bears around to the right, and keep on along it as it heads eastwards on a good surface through quiet countryside. Towards the end it passes a reservoir and then comes to the Racton Monument, an incredible ruined tower in a wonderful position which someone is apparently attempting to turn into a house. Keep on past the monument and head downhill, soon coming to the B2146 road. Turn left and then immediately right onroad, and after about a mile it will take you past the entrance to Asdean down to your start point at Funtington.

Ride 25 KINGLEY VALE

Area: Kingley Vale, near Chichester, West Sussex.
Start: OS Landranger 197 grid ref 815089; near West Stoke.
Nearest BR station: Bosham.
Approx length: 10–15 miles (16–24 km).
Ride: Moderate.
Climbs: Three climbs, one of which is severe.
Conditions: Some sections very muddy after wet weather, and they take a long time to dry out.
Difficulties: Some of the narrow bridleway sections can become congested by horseriders.
High Points: Magnificent views from 'tumuli'.
R & R: Pub en route with others nearby to choose from.

For those who don't know this area the easiest way to the start of this ride is to turn off the A286 Midhurst–Chichester road at Mid Lavant, where you take the West Stoke turning. Go past the few houses on the right which make up West Stoke, and when the road dips and bends left by the Old Rectory, turn right on to a narrow road by the car park, marked on the OS map, which is right ahead of you.

This is the ideal place to park – it leads directly to Kingley Vale to which it is unfortunately only connected by footpath. The bridleway we start on is about ½ mile (0.8 km) further down the road, leading off to the right just past a large house named Woodend. Here there is sufficient parking for a couple of cars, but no more.

If the weather has been dry the going should be OK, but if there has been rain a lot of mud is likely in places, stirred up by the horses that frequent the bridleways that criss-cross the area. The bridleway starts wide, but soon narrows to a horse width, which is madly irrational since the footpath from the car park is wide enough to take a car! It climbs gradually, passing woods on the right before breaking into the open with a narrow downhill section bounded on both sides by barbed wire. Here you get your first view of the Downs.

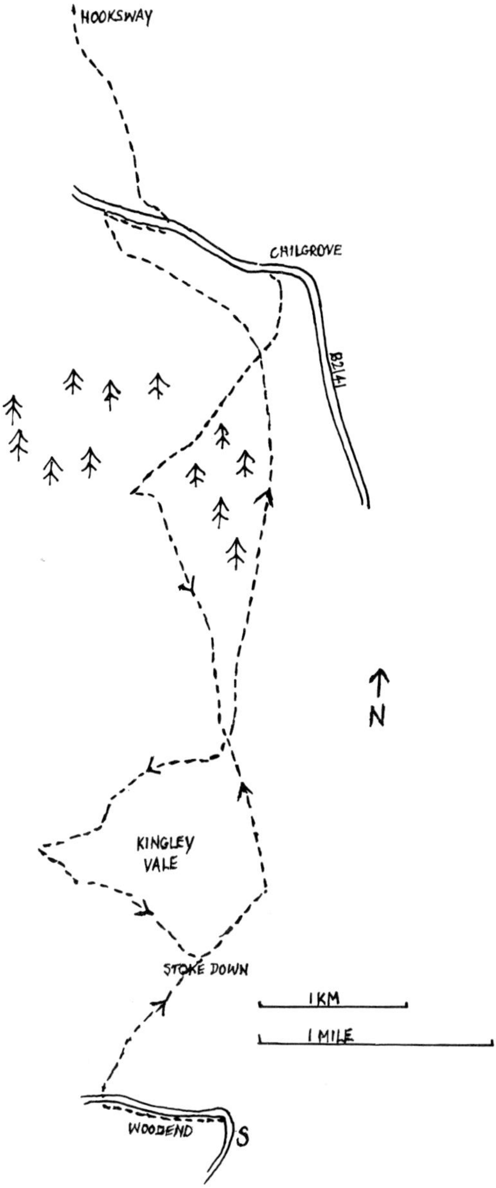

At the foot of the hill you will come to a junction where the car park footpath meets the bridleway. To the left is a wooden hut and a noticeboard explaining what you can hope to find in the Kingley Vale nature reserve, which also contains part of England's oldest yew forest. Carry straight on here and start to go up; you'll be lucky if you haven't already encountered some serious mud by now.

The bridleway takes you upwards and eastwards, until you come to a levelling of the ground and a crossroads of bridleways. You turn left, heading due north and up the hill. At first the going is narrow but easy, but when you come to another noticeboard (on your right) for the nature reserve (which is on your left), it suddenly becomes steeper, with much of the track worn away by the rain constantly eroding its chalk surface. You are now on 'Death Hill', rated as a hard ride and exceptionally difficult if the going is slippery. It is of course much easier on foot!

After ten minutes or so of climbing you will reach another bridleway crossroads – you are now at 694 ft (204 m) and should have pleasure in knowing that you are at the top of the hill. Turn right, and the track soon bears north, opening out into a wide, grassy 'road' with magnificent views to the right looking towards both West Dean with its fine gardens and Goodwood with its fine racecourse! Keep ahead ignoring all side turnings with the track running level along the top of the down.

At a point where the track ahead appears almost obliterated, just push on. In fact it narrows considerably and passes through dense trees (and sometimes thick mud), before skirting to the right of a single cottage which was used as a smallpox isolation hospital in the 19th century. Now it appears to act as someone's second home, and has been greatly spoilt by being surrounded by a Fort Knox-style fence that is well out of keeping with the surroundings.

The track from here on is a car's width, and you follow its twists and turns with woods on either side. After a time you will see a caravan parked in the trees to the right – the owner is apparently an artist, permitted to live there by the Edward Dean estate. Just after that pass through a gate, and after 50 yards (44 m) the bridleway signposts give you a choice of going straight ahead, or turning right or left. The right turn will take you down the hill to the White Hart pub. It's as fast as you like on the way down and as slow as you like coming back up, but if the weather's fine it's a pleasant pub to sit outside with good food. Inside it's fairly grand, better known for its wine list and smart restaurant than for catering to muddy riders!

Alternatively, cross straight over at the bridleway crossroads, head on across the field, and ride straight on until you pass farm buildings on your right. Here you head downhill on a made-up drive which joins the road. Turn right for a few hundred yards, and then take an acute left on to another bridleway which will if you keep left bring you to the Royal Oak pub at Hooksway, a hostelry well used to coping with muddy riders and walkers (it also has accommodation). From here you can extend the ride in a number of ways. One good loop is to ride up past Buriton Farm and on to the South Downs Way, heading east towards Beacon Hill before taking the track back down past Telegraph House which brings you out just above the pub.

Back to the bridleway crossroads. If you cut out the pubs, turn left down a long hill which passes through enchanting woodland which is at its finest in autumn. This is another very fast descent, but watch out for solid Land Rover ruts in freezing weather! Stay on this track as it passes a farm cottage on the right, levels out, opens out and turns grassy under your wheels, and then rises slightly to meet a gravel crossing track. Turn sharp left on to this track, and after about 100 yards (88 m) bear right on to another track straight up the hill. Here you're into the woods again, and will often see deer skipping away.

The track opens on to a clearing where there is sometimes an enormous pile of logs which acts as a handy seat for a rest after the hill. Push on and bear a little to the right, ignoring the sign which points straight ahead. The wide track drops down a little and then heads straight on up, eventually bringing you out on open ground with two humps or 'tumuli' ahead of you. Ride up and down them, and if it's clear you will get a magnificent view of Chichester and its cathedral to the south; Chichester Harbour and the Isle of Wight beyond to the south-west; and the course of the South Downs Way running from north-east to north-west.

On a still day this could be an idyllic place for a picnic. To continue, carry on past the tumuli and take the right-hand bridleway which carries straight on ahead. This passes through more woodland and a wide, grassy section before a T-junction with a left-hand turn – always look for the posts with the bridleway signs which are plentiful in this area.

Turn left for a fast descent with Kingley Vale on your left and open fields to the right, usually with a large population of pigs to watch you. Keep on down, bearing to the left rather than the right, and the going gets faster and faster. Eventually this bridleway brings you back about 50 yards (44 m) from the wooden hut you passed at the start of the ride. Turn right along the bridleway, which takes you up and down on the long track on which you started.

Ride 26 STANE STREET

Area: Stane Street, near Chichester, West Sussex.
Start: OS Landranger 197 grid ref 938108; near Eartham.
Nearest BR station: Chichester or Barnham.
Approx length: 21.5 miles (34.4 km).
Ride: Moderate.
Climbs: Plenty of steady climbs, but none rate as severe.
Conditions: Plenty of wide, dry tracks, though some sections become muddy with rain.
Difficulties: Very easy to get confused by the mass of tracks and bridleways around Stane Street; careful navigation is necessary.
High Points: Some easy, fast cruising; good views from the top of the downs.
R & R: Pub at Slindon.

Stane Street is one of those old Roman roads that cut a perfect straight line across the map. It starts at half the height of Burton Down, the highest point of the ride, which gives you a height advantage to start with. All around it there are countless trails – bridleways, footpaths, marked and unmarked tracks – which make it a great area for offroading, but one where it's very easy to get lost. Careful map reading is called for, and a compass becomes handy to check that you're pointing in the right direction.

The ride starts at the car park on a minor road that leads off the A285 to Eartham. Locate the rather faded Eartham Wood noticeboard (maybe they'll repaint it), and cross through newly-planted trees more or less parallel to the road. You soon come to a gravel track. Turn right here and go out on to the road, turning almost immediately left at the bridleway sign just past the first house you come to.

Head off downhill, keeping to the right and then heading uphill until you reach a bridleway crossroads (two of the signs were broken on our visit). Turn right up another hill; then right and uphill again at the next bridleway crossroads, and along a track which levels out through the woods, but can become mega muddy. Eventually you begin a long downhill, and as you go down so the track improves. The country opens out on either side, and you find yourself on a minor road with a turning for Slindon Bottom Hill just opposite. The track you have just come down is clearly marked with bridleway signs, despite the fact that it shows as a footpath on the OS map. Horses use it, so it's legal.

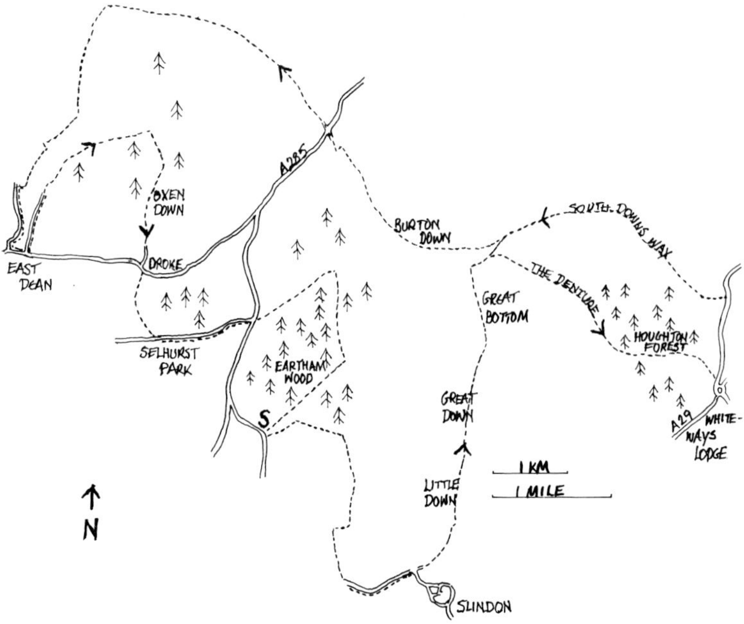

Turn left on the road and up the hill. Making height on-road is much easier than off, and besides this short stretch of road is not unpleasant. After about ½ mile (0.8 km) you come to Slindon College. The road bends round to the right; the bridleway which is unmarked runs straight ahead. For a drink, the village of Slindon is just round the corner with the pub on the other side past the two churches.

Head along the bridleway past a ruined barn which by the time you read this may well have been converted into a grand residence. Carry straight on and upwards, heading up Little Down towards Great Down with the top of the downs as your objective. The route here becomes much more convoluted than is shown on the map, with several diversions and 'No Horses' signs which may or may not be applicable. Keep on upwards, aiming for the radio masts on the top of Burton Down. You should come to a T-junction with a sign marked 'Blackjack' above Great Bottom.

Turn right here after what has been a long but fairly easy uphill, and ride along a good track running eastwards on level ground. To get to the top of the downs take the first fork left which will bring you up to the car park marked on the OS map by National Trust land at 707 ft (208 m). (Alternatively, if you want to put in an extra loop, fork right and then bear off down The Denture in a south-easterly direction. This is a great, wide track for riding with a good grass surface. Bear left through Houghton Forest and eventutually you come to the car park at Whiteways Lodge where in the summer there are usually refreshments available. A short ride up the busy A29 will take you back on to the South Downs Way, or try your luck on the forest tracks that connect to it but can be confusing.)

Back up at the 208m car park, head off west along the South Downs Way on a track below the radio masts, or make the short diversion and ride up to them if you wish. The track is good and level, eventually coming to an exhilarating downhill which gets steeper and steeper – great fun (but take care not to mow down walkers) until you see that you have to climb up the other side of the valley. Cross the A285 road at Littleton Farm, and bear right up the track on the other side of the road. After a short, steep hill you come to a gate; go right and left here across a field (not straight on), following the sign for the South Downs Way.

Halfway across and halfway up the hill you come to a gate. Push on following the signs, and when the South Downs Way levels out you will come to a bridleway crossroads with a large sign marked 'Tegleaze'. Carry straight on past two more bridleway crossroads (the second is another large sign situated in woods), and after what can be a particularly muddy section, turn left at the fourth bridleway crossroads this side of the A285 road.

This will take you down towards East Dean. First you cross a gravel track coming from the right after about 50 yards (44m); and then you descend through very pretty woods until you come down to a gate with a field beyond – excellent for a rest or picnic. From here head on down straight across the field, more or less due south. This is a really good fun descent on hard grass; there's a caravan to the left and the gate should be dead ahead of you.

Turn right down the made-up track, and after a short distance just before you come to a barn follow the bridleway sign and turn hard left up the hill, and then hard right through a gate and into trees. You then plug your way up the hill before heading down the other side (turn left on a marked bridleway here if you want to miss East Dean) into open country, and coming down to the road which goes up to Newhouse Farm on your right.

Turn left, keeping right for East Dean a few minutes' ride away along this quiet road. At the T-junction bear right and the Star & Garter is but a short way. It has a pleasant garden and serves food, though on our visit service had ceased at about 1.45 pm. When you've finished at the pub, retrace your tracks to the T-junction where the 12th century church may be worth a look. Carry straight on at the junction, and where the road bends right with some houses on the corner go left up an unmarked bridleway which starts alongside a footpath going up to the right. This will take you up to a Charlton Forest Sign which connects via a short bridleway with the route for those who cut out East Dean.

Head on up through Charlton Forest on a wide, hard track with a fairly easy ascent. You eventually come to a bridleway crossroads pointing left, straight ahead, and to the right. Take the latter course, bearing off right again when you see another bridleway sign after about 100 yards (88 m). This will take you down Oxen Down towards Droke, where you cross the minor road by a large house with a tennis court. Ignore the bridleway directly opposite, turning left and right on to the next bridleway that goes up by the side of the car park heading you towards Selhurst Park.

The hill that follows goes up through the woods endlessly, getting steeper and steeper and steeper. A full kit of medals for those who ride it all the way to the top! Here you hit another road, but you can almost immediately turn back off it and along an unmarked track that runs east parallel to the road, connecting the two car parks. It was at this point that we were overtaken by a pack of hounds and huntsmen going full bore after their quarry. They didn't seem to care where they went, for next they went down a footpath, scattering walkers left, right, and centre. It's the bikers who behave!

Go back on to the road for a short distance at the second car park, and approach the A285 which can be very busy. On this corner we found an ice-cream van on Easter Monday, so it's fair to assume it's there most weekends through the summer. Go straight over and on to a bridleway that runs between a couple of houses. This goes gradually uphill, and will eventually take you back up to the South Downs Way if you so wish. However to get back to the start point turn right at the first bridleway sign with a lot of fast downhill on hard, stony ground to follow. After a short uphill you come to a clearing with a large Stane Street signpost showing the Roman road and all the ways you can go; turn down Stane Street, which is clearly indicated, for the final big dipper ride, with more downs than ups, taking you to a point just south-east of the car park where you started.

Turn right back up the gravelled track for a few yards and then left through the newly-planted trees – and you've finished! Allow about five hours with a stop for this great ride in what is a great area for biking!

Ride 27 WEPHAM DOWN

Area: Wepham Down, near Arundel, West Sussex.
Start: OS Landranger 197 grid ref 070124; car park on top of the downs off the B2139.
Nearest BR station: Amberley.
Approx length: 16 miles (25.6 km).
Ride: Moderate.
Climbs: Three climbs, one of which is hard.
Conditions: Mainly dry and hard up on the Downs; severe mud in some lowland sections after rain.
Difficulties: Just mud.
High Points: Starting high; beautiful views; lots of variety.
R & R: Pub at Burpham.

The ride around Wepham Down starts from a car park which is right on the South Downs Way. The track that leads up to it is on the B2139. Going east from Amberley it's to the right about 500 yards (440 m) past a large farmstead (Springhead Farm) which advertises garden machinery repairs; if you are going west from Storrington then it's a similar distance past a solitary house on a left-hand bend.

Drive or ride your bike to the top, and turn right along the South Downs Way. Keep right when you see a bridleway to the left, and after just over a mile start a long downhill descent. The views here are magnificent on both sides, with the River Arun snaking its way across flat country to the north-west. There follows a splendid drop on a narrow track which is fenced on both sides – fast and safe on a very good grass surface. After a gate the track down becomes really steep with a good view of Amberley Castle, a large pile now converted to a country house hotel with a flag fluttering from its battlements.

Dead ahead is Downs Farm. Before you reach it, at the bottom of the hill follow the bridleway sign which points at an acute angle to the left, at first almost doubling back on your trail. A little further on keep right at another bridleway sign along the edge of a field on a pretty bumpy track,

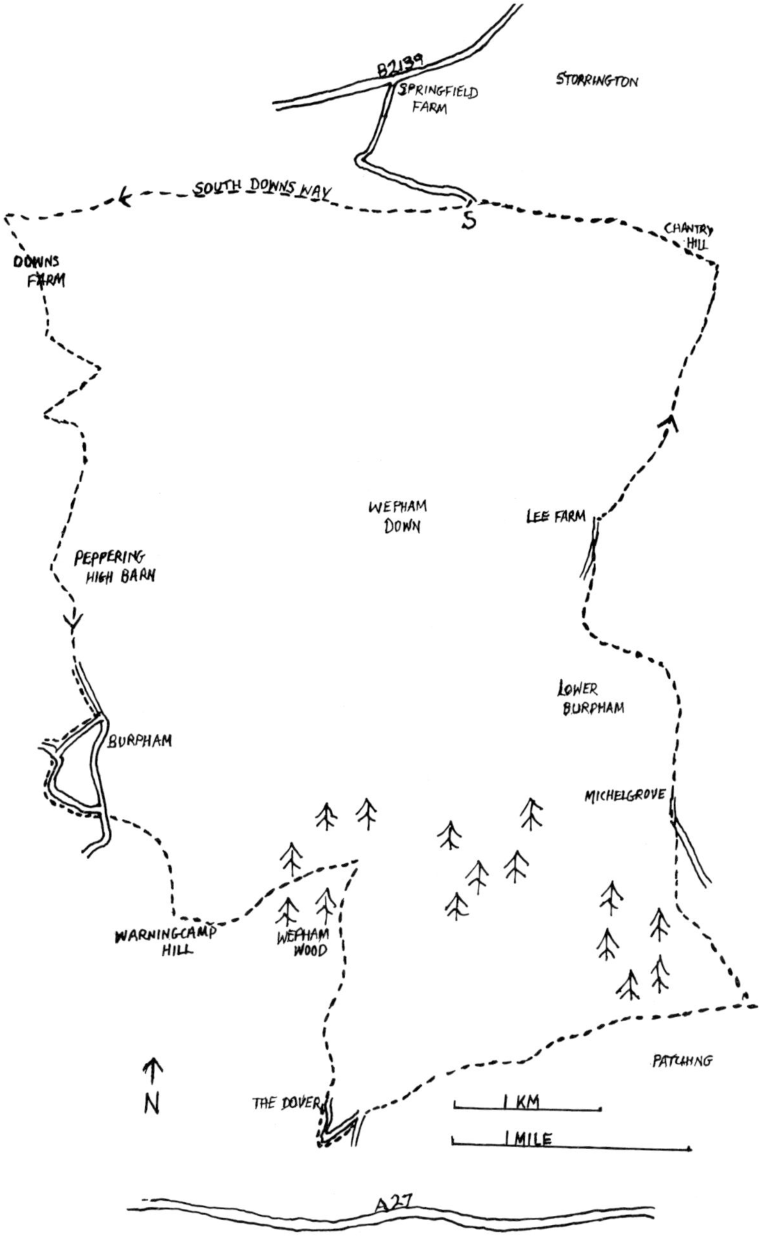

level with Downs Farm which is now on the other side of the valley.

In a short while you come down to a gate with a sign pointing straight ahead. Go through this field which on my visit was full of cows, and filled with a liquid cocktail of mud, cowpats and water in roughly equal proportions.

Riding through this lot was an extreme test of technical ability, with severe penalties if you fell off! Thankfully, it was not very far to push.

On the other side, the track goes down a muddy hill into a peaceful valley, taking you to a stile with a bridleway sign pointing right and up the first hard hill of the day. At the top, turn right at the four-way bridleway sign, heading downhill on a good track with fine views over open country. Before you come to a ruined barn (with a modern barn behind it), turn hard left following the bridleway sign, going down a short hill to another sign adorned with green and red blobs. Here you take the right-hand turn which will take you all the way down to Burpham.

The track heads south, passing Peppering High Barn which is a farm, and then changing to a tarmac surface which soon turns it into a minor road. Halfway down a steep hill you'll see the sign for Burpham; turn right into the village, past a few houses and a country house hotel, and then keep right for the Forge & Dragon which is a short way up the hill. This pub has outside tables and chairs in a rather nice and undeniably affluent setting, over the road from the very grand Burpham House with the church up behind it.

From the pub go down the hill keeping right, following the road round a long left-hand bend past a farm, before climbing up a steepish hill that leads to a road T-junction. Turn right here, and then almost immediately left on to a hard concrete bridleway which continues to climb, with views of Arundel Castle and Wildfowl Reserve behind you.

Where the concrete bends left, turn right down a mud track which is bumpy and becomes extra muddy at the bottom. Ahead you'll see a brown sign with white letters for the Angmering Park Estate, with a bridleway off to the left and then immediately up to the right. You toil up a difficult track through woods that leads out of this pleasant valley and away from Warningcamp Hill, carrying straight over at bridleway crossroads where the ground thankfully flattens out. Carry on through Wepham Wood, and a little further on there's a sign for a bridleway to the left, footpath to the right, and bridleway straight ahead which is the way that you go.

Here the track opens up and gives enjoyable riding, soon coming down to a dip in a big clearing with a bridleway crossroads where you turn right and head south through the woods. There follows an easy and very pleasant downhill, eventually arriving at a gate with a house on the left. Keep left along the track which then becomes a minor road, passing a couple more houses, one of which (The Dover) looks rather fine and had a paddock full of Shetland ponies when we passed it. The little-used road bends left as you come within earshot of the din of the A27, running between fields where we were surprised to see herds of Highland cattle!

Keep straight ahead, through a gate and on to another bridleway which starts as a hard track, crosses a minor road, and then degenerates into mud as it enters more woods. When the bridleway bends 90 degrees left, you turn right at the sign which also shows a bridleway ahead and footpath to the left. Carry on through the woods on what is likely to be a pretty muddy section, and unridable if it's been wet. The track breaks out into open country, but may well continue as hard going with the surface badly broken up by horses. To your right you'll see Patching church, and then a gate takes you on to grassland at Patching Hill with the downs laid out before you – this is an excellent place to stop for a picnic and a rest.

Follow the bridleway sign left and go through some old trees, heading for the gate which is set off to the right. This takes you into the woods once more, and on to mud which once again can be severe. Go past the first footpath sign, turning right at the bridleway crossroads and down the hill which eventually comes out onto a minor road.

Here you turn left up the hill, past Mitchelgrove, which is yet another smart farmhouse that appears to have been built on the site of an old manor with a walled kitchen garden opposite. Ignore the bridleway sign to the right which takes you to the east on to OS map 198 (and connects to No 29) in the direction of Findon and beyond, if you want to extend the ride. By this stage the road has become a private drive and bridleway going towards Lower Burpham, and where it bends left, you head straight on through a gate and on a bridleway that goes over a grassy field which was populated by sheep when we passed by. Keep straight ahead uphill, following the horse trails if you are unsure of the direction, and go through the gate on the other side. Then down a steep, fast hill, heading for Lee Farm at the bottom left corner of this large field.

A bridleway sign points right up the hill, but take care to take the left hand of the two tracks on offer. From here it's a steady plug on a good chalk surface back up to the South

Downs Way at the top of Chantry Hill where there's a car park; and finally a fast ride westwards back to your start point.

With these two car parks close together on top of the downs, this section of the South Downs Way can become clogged by walkers ambling along digesting Sunday lunches. If it looks like being a problem, go straight over when you reach the first car park, and then turn left along a bridleway which runs parallel to the South Downs Way a short way down the hill before climbing back up to your start car park.

Ride 28 COCKING

Area: Cocking, near Midhurst, West Sussex.
Start: OS Landranger 197 grid ref 879176; limited parking in Cocking, in pub car parks, or off the road just outside the village.
Nearest BR station: Chichester.
Approx length: 13 miles (20.8 km).
Ride: Moderate.
Climbs: Two hard climbs.
Conditions: Generally good going; some mud.
Difficulties: None.
High Points: Great views from the South Downs Way; a pleasant rural ride.
R & R: Cocking has two pubs, one right in the village and one on its northern outskirts. There is also a small village shop/post office where you can refuel with sweets.

Cocking is a village on the A286 between Midhurst and Chichester. It is situated just to the north of the South Downs Way, with Cocking Down and Westdean Woods to the west and Singleton Forest and Heyshott Down to the east. This is excellent biking country.

Seventy-five yards (66 m) or so south of the Potter & Vine, a metalled track bears off to the right away from the main road. This leads you gradually up alongside a stream and under a railway bridge until you pass Crypt Farm, a rather grand place typical of this area. Keep to the left until you see a bridleway sign pointing either straight ahead to take you up to the South Downs Way, or right to take you round via Cocking Down.

The latter takes you on a track which curves away to the

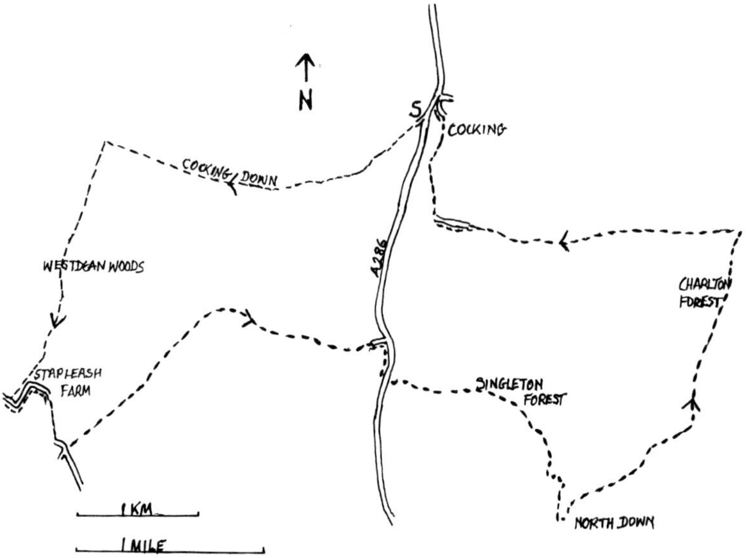

left up a fairly easy going hill. There's an L-shaped bench at the top of this first climb – have a sit-down here because the next part is hard! Toil on up the track to the top of the downs, taking in the optional loop round Bepton Down if you want to. At the top turn right along the South Downs Way, taking the next left at a bridleway crossroads sign near to a conspicuous ladder in a tree.

There follows a long and fun descent through Westdean Woods which will completely obliterate the pain of toiling up the other side. Keep straight on ignoring signs to right or left, first through woods, then through an area of flattened trees followed by a nature reserve where there are lots of primroses in spring – but don't stop to pick them! Carry on down a narrow track, through a gate and across a field where a solitary, grazing horse ignored the passing of my bike. In the bottom corner there's another gate, and beyond a minor metalled road which leads to Stapleash Farm. Turn left here for a short onroad section with a little uphill, a nice glide downhill, and on Easter Saturday not a car in sight.

The next bridleway is on the left at the bottom of the hill, just after a sign for West Dean Estate with a great electricity pylon off to the right, so you can't miss it. Go through the gate and on to the broad track, riding past a rather idyllically situated farmhouse to your right set in the midst of fields with a bridleway going down to it. Carry straight on into muddier territory with trees on either side. A moderately hard hill leads to a clearing with another bridleway sign where you turn right, bearing right off the gravelled forestry road after 50 yards (44 m) or so.

You then begin to descend on what is at first a really nice grass track, with more of those strange ladder affairs all round. The track soon becomes more difficult, chewed up by 4-wheel drive vehicles with broken branches all over the place. Eventually it leads on to a hard metalled section which goes steeply down to the busy A286 road. Turn right along the A286 for about 150 yards (132 m), passing a converted barn and then turning left where there is a large bridle road sign for Singleton Forest/Littlewood Common. Go straight up a short, steep, slippery track which makes a good technical section; across the metalled driveway; and straight on again through Singleton Forest.

The track here is variable – some is good and fast, while some is mud. Eventually you come down into a valley with Broadham House farmstead on the right – also rather idyllic. Here, there's a bridleway sign pointing left, right, and ahead to the right. Take the latter course, heading uphill round to the left on a hard track until you come to a major waymark sign at the top, a short distance later. This points you to Singleton, Goodwood, Cocking, Heyshott, and Charlton which is the direction you take, downhill on a hard driveway with a fast descent that has a sharp left-hand turn at the bottom – so take care!

At the bridleway T-junction turn left on a hard track that climbs away to the right, dropping down a bit before you come to a sign for Charlton Forest Forestry Commission with a small Nissen hut on the left. Carry straight on into the woods, and where the bridleway sign points left, turn left up a long hill which gets steeper, and steeper, and steeper. Eventually you cross a gravel forestry track with a bridleway sign where you carry straight on; a little further and you're back at the top of the downs on the South Downs Way.

Turn left here. Riding westwards along the South Downs Way you get the usual great views if the weather is clear, with England looking at its untouched, pastoral best. Ignore turnings to the left and right, and you'll eventually start to head down a fast, long hill with farm buildings ahead and the road beyond.

When you reach the farm, turn right through the yard as

indicated by the bridleway sign. If you're thirsty there's a tap on the left, put there in memory of a boy who died at the age of 14, and intended for the use of walkers. Unfortunately, when I passed by it was dripping, but refused to give up any water.

The ride through the farmyard can be extremely sludgy, but a good biker will get through OK. Head straight on and down a muddy hill, past a quarry and on down a hard track as Cocking comes into sight. You ride by a stream and the pretty church is ahead of you about 3 hours after starting. Now's the time maybe to try the Potter & Vine, a friendly pub with a few seats outside. They ask you to take your muddy boots off inside; serve good beer; the food looks good; they welcome children; and they also do B&Bs.

Ride 29 CHANCTONBURY

Area: Washington, due north of Worthing off A24, West Sussex.
Start: OS Landranger 198 grid ref 123128; parking in lay-by opposite pub. OS Landranger 197 will also be required.
Nearest BR station: Worthing or Pulborough.
Approx length: 18 miles (28.8 km).
Ride: Moderate.
Climbs: One hard climb up to Chanctonbury Ring; an easier climb to Cissbury Ring; two steady climbs west of A24.
Conditions: Plenty of hard chalk and grass; some sections could become very muddy after wet weather.
Difficulties: None, unless there's mud, or possibly horses blocking some of the narrow tracks.
High Points: Fine views; good South Downs Way fast cruising; Cissbury and Chanctonbury Rings both interesting archaeologically.
R & R: Frankland Arms at Washington does food, has a large garden, and is used to muddy walkers.

I did this ride on a fine weekday in mid-May after a long period of dry weather. All the ground was dried out and hard, making the going good and fast with the usual splendid views from the top of the downs. Just over 18 miles (29 km) took an easy three hours, but in wet weather, sections of this ride could turn very muddy and you'd need to allow quite a bit longer.

You can park in the lay-by just opposite the Frankland

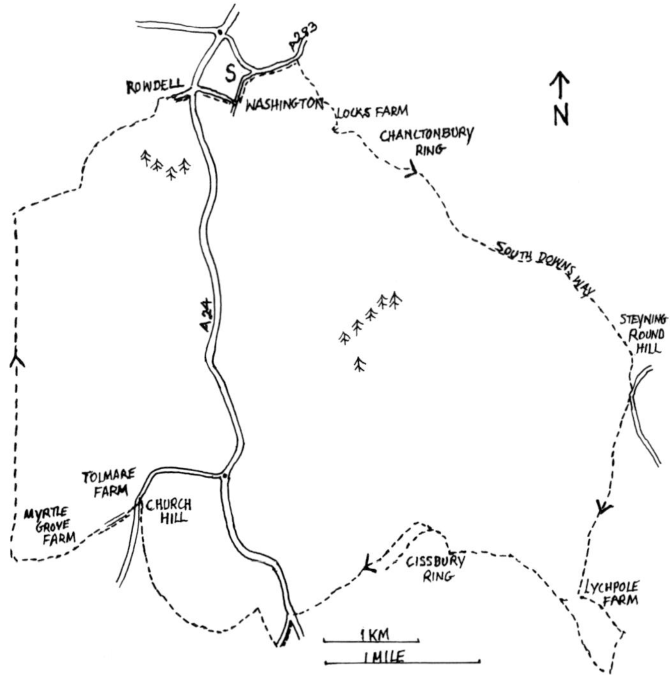

Arms at Washington, about a couple of hundred yards south of the A283. Head back on to this busy road and turn right along the verge for about ⅓ mile (0.5 km). You pass a few driveways on the right, and then, when the road bends left, there's a bridleway indicated to the right going up the drive to Locks Farm on the apex of the bend. You don't leave this short section of road a moment too soon! The cars and lorries seem to hurtle along it in a fashion which is as menacing as it is ridiculous. Why are they going so fast? What's the point of it all? It reminded me of a visit to Goodwood many years ago when we watched the likes of Jack Brabham and Jim Clark hurtling round corners in Ford Galaxies and Lotus Cortinas. At the time they seemed pretty incredible; but now drivers on the roads do exactly the same!

The driveway/bridleway leads up past Locks Farm and up the side of a field beyond. When you come to the woods at the base of the hill turn right at a bridleway sign, and a little further on follow the next bridleway sign uphill to the left into the trees. At first the track is steep; then it levels out; then it gets much steeper as you grind up slowly towards Chanctonbury Ring. In dry weather it is ridable all the way, but you have to be determined and fit – this is a real hill climb challenge!

After just over a mile of climbing you break into open ground with the circle of trees on Chanctonbury Ring before you. Go through the gate and ride over to the right to join a track which is part of the South Downs Way – or pause and inspect this strange edifice. Carry on along the South Downs Way on a good, fast chalk track. The way is clearly signposted, and most of it is downhill as you start to head south-west. After a time you'll see a Trig Point at Steyning Round Hill set in a field to your right; then the track goes through a gate by a memorial to a local farmer; before joining a narrow road about 50 yards (44 m) from the car park on top of Steyning Bowl – conspicuous since it is much favoured by hang-gliders as indicated on the car park noticeboard.

However, before you hit this road you leave the South Downs Way which continues along it. Don't go through the gate – turn right along the perimeter of the field towards a small blockhouse, where there's another gate and a bridleway sign showing you the way straight on along a good track just to the right of the blockhouse. Keep on mainly downhill until you come to Lychpole Farm where the track goes ahead through the farm buildings before bending left. The track, which is now tarmac, passes several barns before coming to a few houses at Beggars Bush where it meets the road. Just before the road when you come to a left-hand bend there's a bridleway indicated off to the right. This goes along a grassy track which bends left and then starts a steady uphill. When you come to another bridleway sign with trees up ahead, turn right uphill through the gate and then bear right following the bridleway direction.

The grassy track which follows takes you along the base of Lychpole Hill just above Lychpole Farm. Eventually there's a slight uphill as the track swings left, and another gate. Go through and ignore the bridleway track doubling back to the left. Keep on for a short distance, and at the National Trust notice for Cissbury Ring follow the bridleway sign bearing left uphill through the trees. There follows what is almost an enjoyable uphill on a very narrow track that takes you right up to Cissbury Ring – it's ridable all the way if the going is dry.

At Cissbury you can pause and rest, and look north to Chanctonbury which now seems a long way away. Leave your bike outside for the 'ring' is foot territory only. This would make a good place for a reflective picnic, and only the proximity of Worthing to the south spoils what seems like an English countryside idyll – you might wish that the downs could go on forever and had never been touched by the hand of man.

When you're ready to move on, bear round the right-hand side of the 'ring', heading downhill towards the car park. Where the track bends right downhill to the cars, keep straight on for a gate with a bridleway sign. This directs you left downhill, along the fenced perimeter of a field beneath Cissbury. At another bridleway sign keep on along the side of the field, until you eventually go through a gate and on to a narrow track edged with trees and bushes. This is a good ride, but you wouldn't want to meet horses coming the other way! Keep on until you come to a modern housing development where the track continues down the right side of the houses, becoming incredibly overgrown but ridable all the way to the road.

Here, head straight over the A24 on to a minor road which bears left uphill. You soon break into open ground where there's a car parking space and a bridleway indicated to the right. Take this track past a number of equestrian fields, and then at a bridleway/footpath crossroads turn 90 degrees left uphill. There follows another steady plug uphill through trees on a narrow track, before you join a wide crossing track at the top of the hill. Turn right here, and continue along a good, fast track with fine views to the west, which eventually brings you down Church Hill to the A280 above Tolmare Farm.

Cross over the road (watch out for cars speeding round what some may consider a fast bend) and go on to the track leading to the farm, but almost immediately take the first bridleway sign leading left downhill. This track heads down more or less parallel to the road, reaching a dip and then bearing right uphill on a section which promises to be viciously muddy when it's wet. You then come to a gate where the bridleway sign shows you the way straight ahead across a field. The track had been sown over when I rode this route, so it was a matter of cycling straight across.

On the far side you'll see a track continuing over to the left with a mild uphill on a concrete surface. This comes to a crossing track with yet another bridleway sign. Turn left here, and almost immediately turn right as indicated by another bridleway sign, following the tarmac track down through Myrtle Grove Farm with a very flashy house in the foreground. The track goes through the farmyard, and then bends left and right up through a gate past the left-hand side of a substantial house.

This takes you briefly on to OS Landranger 197, and at this point you might like to consider doing a mega figure-of-eight circuit by linking this ride to No 27 round Wepham Down. Go down and up on the narrow track which brings you up alongside an old walled garden, and then on to the minor road above the big house at Michelgrove. Here you turn right for a couple of hundred yards along the road, before bearing right offroad once again at the first bridleway sign.

Head down on another good track through fields, with a steep downhill on chalk before you bear left on a steady uphill past a row of ancient lime trees. In the hill on the far side of the valley there are apparently flint mines which you may care to reflect upon, and at about this point you'll be pleased to rejoin OS 198.

The bridleway is clearly indicated, becoming a narrow track crossing another large field with rolling agricultural land on all sides. At the far side of the field you come to a bridleway sign indicating a crossing track; turn left here downhill, go through the gate, and after a short uphill take the bridleway sign going 90 degrees to the right. This goes steeply down and uphill on the perimeter of a field, coming to a 90-degree left-hand turn with the track continuing up between two fields – on my ride the sign here was broken. Plug on uphill, and you'll soon come to the South Downs Way once again, after what has been a relatively painless long uphill.

Turn right along the South Downs Way, which in these parts is good and fast in dry weather. Go past a barn and bear left, ignoring the hard left which would take you down to Sullington. If you do wish to go that way it also leads on to a slightly longer route to Washington. Keep on along the South Downs Way with Chanctonbury Ring clear ahead of you, and after a short distance on a hard track turn 90 degrees left at the first bridleway sign. This takes you on a long downhill through fields, sweeping round to the right and then bearing left down a tarmac track towards the bijou residences of Rowdell – watch out for the sleeping policemen on the way down!

At the first house carry on straight ahead through a gate, then turn right on the second track which heads downhill on a quiet road, taking you over the A24 via a bridge and past the handsome church of Washington. Keep on down past houses until you come to a T-junction. Turn left here, and the Franklin Arms is about 500 yards (440 m) pedalling ahead.

As with all South Downs rides this one could be extended, most notably by adding it to the Wepham Down circuit (No 27) which would make a taxing 34 miles (54 km). It could also be easily shortened. If you want to take the quickest offroad way back to Washington from Cissbury Ring, there's a bridleway running due north from the car park which takes you direct to Chanctonbury Ring from where you can enjoy downhilling that first long haul up!

Ride 30 HARTING DOWNS

Area: West Marden, South Downs, West Sussex.
Start: OS Landranger 197 grid ref 773136; park by roadside.
Nearest BR station: Rowlands Castle.
Approx length: 18.5 miles (29.6 km).
Ride: Moderate.
Climbs: Several moderate climbs.
Conditions: Could be muddy and slippery in wet weather.
Difficulties: Only if it's muddy.
High Points: A good blast along the South Downs Way with lots of variety.
R & R: Pubs at West Marden and Hooksway.

Start at West Marden on the B2146 – there's a lay-by on the east side of this road which is convenient for parking, or, if not, try up by the pub. Ride through the village heading east with the pub on your right. Start heading uphill, and where the road bends left you'll see a bridleway track signposted to the right.

Go up this track, passing a large house on the right. You soon come to a crossing where you turn right, bearing right a little further on when you come to Horsley Farm. The bridleway along this route is very clearly signposted, and you take the next left and continue along the track until you come to the top end of Markwells Wood. Here the bridleway route turns right and then forks left, heading downhill on a fast track through the trees. This brings you to the bottom of the woods where you go through a gate and head straight down the track ahead to the road with fields on either side.

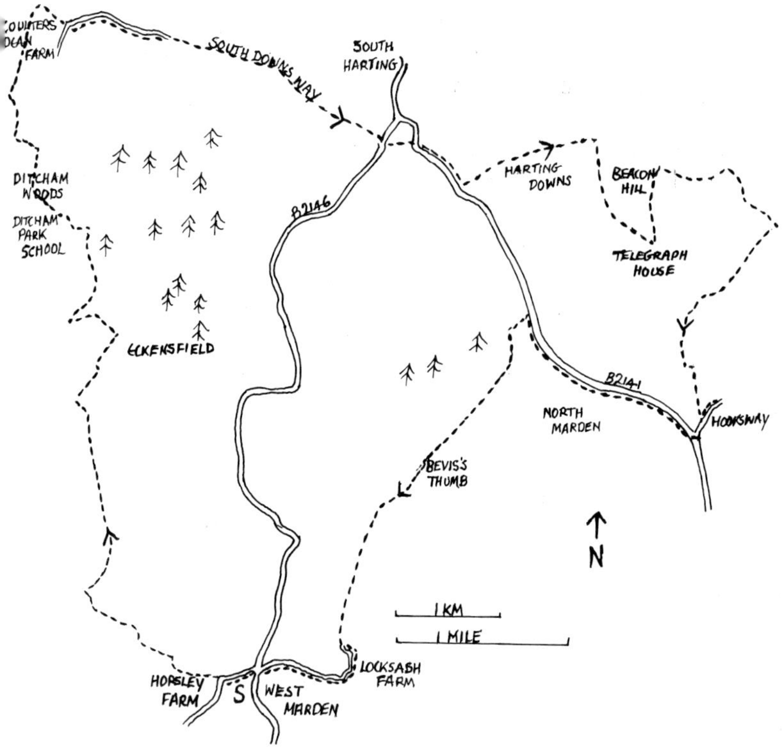

At the road turn right and then almost immediately left on another signposted bridleway track. This leads you through fields, crossing a track in a belt of trees. Continue straight on for the next belt of trees where the bridleway track goes through a gate and bears left across a field, passing a small copse with newly planted trees to the left by a well-hidden Trig Point. Pick up the next bridleway sign on the far side of this field, following the left-hand track on a slight downhill between fields. This soon brings you to a crossing track, with a couple of houses down to the right at Eckensfield and Ditcham Park School conspicuous up on the hill to the left.

Turn left here, following the track round to the left with woods on the right. Just before you come to the farmhouse at Ladyholt there's another bridleway sign immediately to the right with a hard right turn taking you down through the woods in a northerly direction. Bear left downhill on this track until you come to a grass crossing track where you turn right and continue in much the same direction.

Eventually the track comes out of the woods with a long and rather splendid valley ahead of you. Here it bends left and becomes very narrow on a short but very steep uphill, bearing right at the top with a fine view over the valley with the farm buildings at Downley tucked into the left-hand side below. The track then bears left past a strange red-brick building shaped like a conning tower, joining a tarmac lane.

Here you bear left towards Ditcham Park School which is more or less straight ahead. Just before the school follow the bridleway sign which indicates that you turn right along a wide tarmac lane. After a few hundred yards you reach a belt of trees on the left, with a bridleway sign showing a narrow track running alongside them. Turn off here, bearing right and passing a Forestry Commission sign for Ditcham Park Woods. To keep to the bridleway bear left on a narrow track after a short time, following it down through the woods to the minor road which you join just east of Coulters Dean Farm. This bridleway route through the woods is poorly signposted, and if you miss the turning you come out on the same road further to the east.

Turn right along this road, heading uphill and then picking up your first South Downs Way signpost at the top of the hill. Carry straight on a long downhill on the quiet road, which brings you to the large farmstead at Sunwood Farm. Here the road bears left between buildings, and on the far side you will see a South Downs Way sign pointing up a track to the right. Follow this uphill on chalk, and from here on keep following South Downs Way signs for the next few miles.

Past a crossing track you soon get glimpses of South Harting with its conspicuous church over to the left. Next you come to the B2146 going downhill to the left, with brown metal South Downs Way signs on both sides of the road. Cross straight over here, wheeling along the short, linking footpath which runs across towards the B2141 and then alongside it. This avoids having to ride down the B2146 and then back up the B2141, both of which are busy roads. When this footpath brings you out on to the B2141, cross straight over following the South Downs Way sign and you're back on bridleway.

After climbing past the car park by Harting Downs the track goes through a gate and then dives steeply downhill to Cross Dykes. At the bottom there is a five-way crossroads sign, near to a much larger old-fashioned signpost which when I passed by had lost all its arms! The South Downs Way is indicated as bearing right, though the direct route is straight ahead up Beacon Hill. This is a very steep and clearly unridable ascent, so it's better to follow the South Downs Way diversion up a lesser hill, which is nevertheless hard going if it's wet and slippery.

The track continues towards Telegraph House, with the South Downs Way turning hard left just before a gate. This turning is easy to miss, so watch out for it. After a short, level section heading north it bends downhill to the right, rejoining the direct route from Beacon Hill with fine views down the valley ahead over towards Buriton Farm. Follow the South Downs Way sign on a steep uphill – also hard going if it's wet – before following the track round the left-hand side of a field, heading downhill with views of the South Downs Way as it snakes up towards Linch Down well beyond this ride. You come down to a four-way cross-roads sign by a gate in trees on the left; keep straight on along the edge of the field here, following the track round to the right until it bends left round the perimeter of the woods. From here it joins a track running along between wire fences, which soon brings you down to a gate at a chalk crossing track.

The South Downs Way carries straight on here, but you turn right downhill past Buriton Farm buildings. The track gets worse further on as it goes down to the right before heading uphill to the left, but it continues to be easy to follow. After a time you will see a small building over to the right nearby a bridleway sign pointing back towards Telegraph House. Keep straight on here, bearing left by the foot-path sign and eventually joining the minor road that goes down to the Royal Oak at Hooksway. This is a pleasant pub to stop at, with food and plenty of outside seating; they also do B&B, and it would make an excellent centre for a biking weekend with ride No 25 possibly combined with this one for a long day's circuit.

When you've finished at the Royal Oak ride back up the hill to the B2141. Turn right along this road for just over a mile, passing the left-hand turning to North Marden. From here the road heads downhill and then goes up into trees. After a good climb you will see a track going left into the woods with a bridleway sign; don't mistake it for an unmarked track which you passed a short way back. Go along this track bearing left past the entrance to one of the Uppark gatehouses which has been converted into a 'desirable residence'. The bridleway track from here is clearly signposted, as it runs along between fields on a good surface. Keep on through trees, and then go straight over the minor road at Bevis's Thumb.

From here the track goes straight up the hill ahead, with fine views of the National Trust house at Uppark opening out to the north. The track then bears left past a smart, small pink house in the middle of nowhere on Telegraph Hill. Go past and carry on through a gateway at the bottom of the field where the track bears left, heading south on a fast surface and soon passing under overhead power cables, bearing left and right through woods before joining the road just below Locksash Farm. Turn right, and from here it's a short, mainly downhill ride along the road which leads back to West Marden.

Ride 31 ALFRISTON

Area: Alfriston, Friston Forest and East Dean, East Sussex.
Start: OS Landranger 199 grid ref 521033; two car parks on north side of Alfriston.
Nearest BR station: Berwick Station.
Approx length: 18.3 miles (29.28 km).
Ride: Moderate.
Climbs: Stiff climb out of Alfriston; other less taxing climbs en route.
Conditions: Mainly good going on chalk and grass.
Difficulties: Chalk can be slippery after rain.
High Points: Fine views; some very good downhills through Friston Forest.
R & R: Pub and tea house at Jevington; otherwise numerous places to refuel in Alfriston.

The downs looming above Alfriston look forbidding, but this is a fine ride and not too taxing. Allow about four hours, and if you want to do more, the ride can be extended in a number of directions – one obvious way is to follow the bridleway from Jevington to Folkington to Alfriston on the return loop, rather than taking the direct South Downs Way route.

Turn off the A27 on to the minor road that runs south through Alfriston and beyond. On the outskirts of Alfriston you will see a car park on the left; on my visit it cost 50p for four hours plus £1 for each hour thereafter, which would

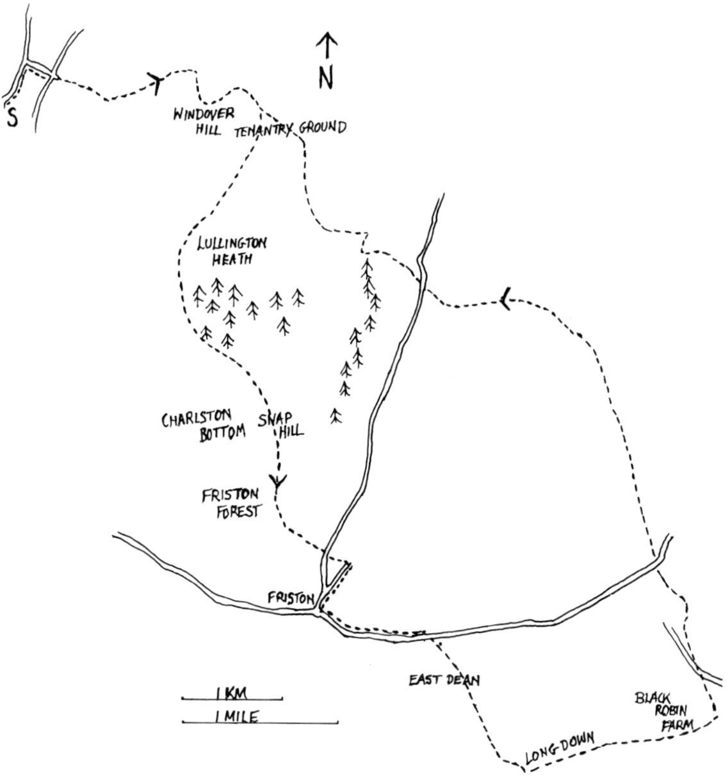

leave you tight for time on this ride. A little way on there's another car park on the right which is free, but get there early!

From the car park head back north for about 200 yards (176 m), turning right across a bridge and over the river. The bridleway goes straight ahead at a T-junction by the side of a house; this is a very blind bend and great care should be taken when crossing.

Head up the hard track, but take it easy as there's plenty of climbing ahead. It soon breaks out into open country, crossing a minor road and then going on up through a gate with a blue bridleway blob. From here the hard chalk track snakes up the side of the hill past a strange little building which has sprouted a TV aerial. Go through another gate, and follow the track round to the right with fine views over the immense bowl of Tenantry Ground below you.

At the top of Wendover Hill go through a gate and take the bridleway sign to the right, ignoring the sign pointing straight ahead. Fork right at the next sign about 75 yards

(66 m) on, and then follow the signs across fast, open fields heading south-west towards Lullington Heath. Go through the gate and on to the heath next to a brown information sign. Carry straight on, following the bridleway signs which are very clear. Fork left for Charlston Bottom which takes you on a long, fast downhill; and then follow the signs for Snap Hill uphill and down another fast hill which leads to a metalled crossing track.

Go straight over here, following the sign for Friston. The going is very good on hard, wide tracks despite the hoof marks of many horses. Carry straight on, and eventually you break into open ground with some horse-race style jumps to your right. Go down through the trees, ignoring the sign to Westdean and following the sign to Friston straight ahead. Here you join a bridleway which runs up the side of a long, straight lane with Friston Place over to the right.

When you reach the road, turn right and then left on to a signposted bridleway after about 50 yards (44 m). Follow it up a narrow track and across a field to the outskirts of Friston. (Here you could turn left and ride north-east up towards Willingdon Hill, turning left for Jevington to cut out the southern section of this route.)

To push on turn right to rejoin the road, and bear left on to the A259. Keep on the A259 downhill past Friston and East Dean, and near the top of the hill on the outskirts of the town turn right on to a bridleway just opposite the Eastbourne Heritage Coast sign. Follow this track up and down along the side of a field, passing a bridleway sign to the right and taking the footpath sign straight on which is marked as bridleway on the OS map.

When you come to a barn with views out over Beachy Head, go through the gate on its right side and head left on a long downhill by the side of a fence. After a short uphill this brings you to a bridleway crossing track with a house off to the left. Here you follow the bridleway sign straight ahead up the very steep, grassy hill, bearing left beyond the row of trees to find the next bridleway gate set in the row of trees beyond.

Turn left when you reach this gate, following a good track and keeping straight ahead for just over a mile until you hit the road with fine views out past Eastbourne over the sea. Bear left along the side of the road past Black Robin Farm, and where the B2103 joins it, cross over and head off to the right on a bridleway. Bear left at a junction marked by bridleway and footpath stones, and then bear left again up to a pond with a couple of benches where you might like to stop and recuperate awhile.

Head on until you reach the A259, where you cross straight over on to the South Downs Way. Ride past the golf club and head out into open country, following the South Downs Way on a long downhill which bears down left into Jevington where you can find both a pub and a tea and coffee house, though the latter was closed when I passed through. From the bridleway go right for a short way along the road, and then almost immediately bear left up past the church, still on the South Downs Way. This takes you up past a corral with some very upper-class horses (the mares wear headscarves!), and on up a difficult track which is criss-crossed with tree roots making a tricky uphill section.

Carry on following the signs for the South Downs Way, turning right on to open country and bearing left across a large field with tumuli and a strange garrison-style building over to the right. Continue to follow the South Downs Way signs, and you will eventually join up with your outward route at the top of Windover Hill. At this point I took a high speed fall on the chalk, so take care!

Cruise down towards Alfriston, but at the foot of the hill where you join the road just before the bridge, follow the bridleway sign through the gate to the left. Keep along the left side of the field parallel to the river, and you will reach a gate where you turn right. You immediately come to a small bridge leading on to the White Bridge which takes you across the Cuckmere into Alfriston. Here you may care to pause awhile on the fine church green, or follow the signs for horses round to the right, turning right when you reach the road which will take you back to the car parks.

Ride 32 FIRLE BEACON

Area: Firle Beacon and Alfriston, East Sussex.
Start: OS Landranger 198 grid ref 468059; good parking on the top of the downs. OS Landranger 199 also required.
Nearest BR station: Glynde.
Approx length: 14.3 miles (22.8 km).
Ride: Moderate.
Climbs: Several climbs; the longest of which is back up from Alfriston.
Conditions: Good going mainly on grass and chalk.
Difficulties: Some poor signposting on southern loop.

High Points: Fine views; visit to Alfriston.
R & R: Pubs, cafés, tea houses, etc in Alfriston; pub at West Firle.

This ride could start at Alfriston, although the car parking is much easier on the downs above West Firle and it's psychologically better to start high! It could also be combined with ride No 31 to make a grand 33-mile (53 km) route for those who can handle it.

From the A27 take the road running south to West Firle, bearing left for Firle Beacon. Drive or ride on up to the top of the downs where there is a large, free car parking area. Head west along the top of the down towards the radio masts on a good, grass track. Just past them, you will come to a cattle grid with a track coming up from the north and a bridleway sign pointing straight on. Don't go over the grid. There's no sign, but take the unmarked bridleway down to the left heading south across a field. Go past a barn, keeping on down and then forking left uphill at the foot of the hill.

Ride up a short way until you reach a field. Here you go straight across, following the barely discernible track across to a bridleway gate (no fence); then on a narrow, grassy track between two fields bending back round to the south as you head down to Gardeners Hill. The track bears right and then left downhill, eventually joining with a crossing track in a

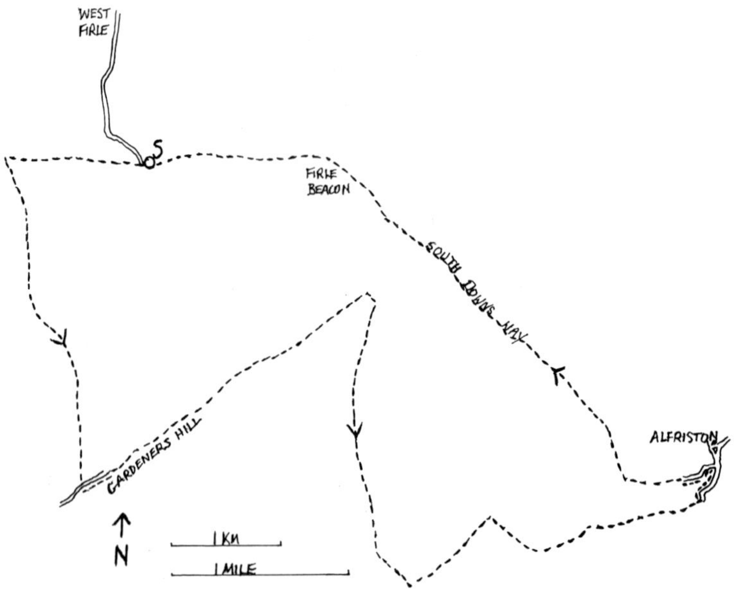

small valley with a clump of trees beyond. We found no signposting on this section, so careful map reading may be necessary here.

Turn left, heading north-east up the crossing track at Gardeners Hill to a bridleway gate. Follow the bridleway left around the edge of the next field, and along a narrow track on its northern edge still heading north-east. Go through a gate, and then up the side of another field until you reach a gate, where the bridleway sign points straight on to the left. A track joins from the right, and you have come almost 2 miles (3 km) from the turning at Gardeners Hill.

Turn right here and after 100 yards (88 m) bear left to join the crossing track. Turn right on to it, and head south on a fast surface with fine views over the downs to your left and out over the sea at Seaford ahead. Go through a gate, ride a short way uphill, and then through another gate. Keep straight on past a bridleway sign to the left, keeping left and then following a narrow bridleway track which is sign-posted downhill if you want a difficult technical section. The narrow track slithers down perilously close to a barbed wire fence, and an alternative and easier route is to ignore this turning and go straight on for The Comp where you can backtrack on another much wider bridle path. For those using an OS map this is where you ride off 198 on to 199.

Both tracks come down to a valley where you go through a gate marked with a bridleway blob and continue uphill. Go through the next gate, toiling up the side of a field before turning right along its perimeter at the top at a point marked by a stone. Go through another gate out of the field, and on a long, fenced track to the left which swoops down towards Alfriston with wonderful views out over Long Barrow.

Eventually you hit a hard track which takes you down into the centre of Alfriston which has plenty of pubs, shops, tea houses, souvenirs, etc, and is likely to be crowded in high summer. Bear right at the tourist sign for the National Trust's Alfriston Clergy House which brings you out by the church, which is a scenic place for a picnic. From there follow the horse track for 50 yards (44 m) parallel to the river, before turning left back up into the town where you can join the South Downs Way for the return trip. Alternatively you could make a longer return trip via Firle, or add on No 31 to make a grand circuit.

To get on to the South Downs Way turn left through

Alfriston and after about 25 yards (22 m) turn right on to a road with a South Downs Way sign. When the road forks, bear left up past modern houses, with the road becoming a hard track that gradually leads up on to the grassy downs. It's a long climb but not too taxing, and the way is very well signposted. As the view unfolds and you gain height you begin to catch glimpses of the radio masts, egging you on to your destination.

Keep on through the few buildings of Bopeep Farm where you go straight ahead through the gates, maybe seeing a few hang-gliders jumping off the hill on the right. Carry on to the Trig Point perched on top of the tumuli at Firle Beacon for a mega view on all sides, and from there it's a short ride to the car park.

Ride 33 DITCHLING BEACON

Area: Ditchling Beacon above Brighton.
Start: OS Landranger 198 grid ref 332132; small car park.
Nearest BR station: Hassocks.
Approx length: 10 miles (16 km).
Ride: Moderate.
Climbs: One long climb back up to Ditchling Beacon; otherwise minor climbs.
Conditions: Chalk, flint, grass, mud.
Difficulties: None.
High Points: Fine, short downland ride for views and variety.
R & R: Ice-cream van frequently in the car park.

This is a comparatively short ride within easy reach of Brighton which crams a lot of variety into its short length. It can easily be extended with an additional loop towards Clayton Windmills, and starts at the top of the most infamous hill of the London to Brighton bike ride.

The car park at Ditchling Beacon is right on the top of the downs, marked by a National Trust sign. Start off eastwards, and take great care in crossing the road on this dangerous bend which motorists appear to regard as a rally stage. Head straight on along the South Downs Way which is clearly marked. Cross over the track heading to Streathill Farm on the right, and continue past the bridleway sign to Ashcombe Bottom.

Ride past the Trig Point on your left at Blackcap and push

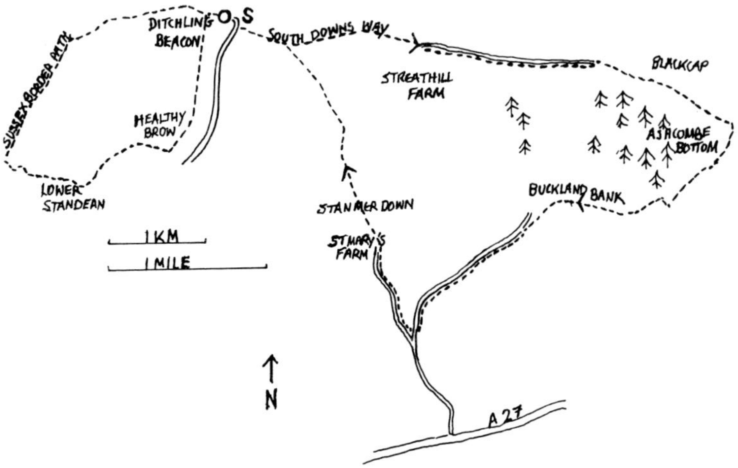

on up Mount Harry. The going is good and fast on chalk and firm earth, and you soon come to the end of this 3-mile (5 km) section along the South Downs Way. The turn-off is easily recognisable as the electricity pylon lines pass directly overhead as you pass through a gate near the start of a downhill. A few yards further on you turn right down a narrow bridleway that goes into woods and gives you a short, muddy section before you break out into open ground by a gate.

Go through the gate and head across the field to the next bridleway gate and the one after; then head left downhill across a big grass field. You can't see where you're heading because it's hidden by the brow of the hill, but you soon come down to the bottom left-hand corner of the field where the track goes on down a short 'bike severe' downhill with a very limited run-out at the end – not recommended for a fast descent!

At the bottom turn left and then immediately right through bridleway gates and a sheep pen, heading up the grassy hill and into woods. A short track through the woods leads to another gate where you cross a field following the bridleway sign, heading along a track running along the side of the next field with a hill sloping down to the right.

When you come to a bridleway crossing track head straight over. Although there was no clear indication on our visit, the correct bridleway route bears right across the field. Near the bottom right-hand corner you will see the next bridleway gate; go through it and uphill to the next gate some 200 yards (176 m) distant. Here you join a track where you turn right and ride up towards the pylons at Buckland Bank. Just before you reach them turn hard left on to another bridleway, taking you south-west along a deeply rutted track with views over St Mary's Farm in the valley.

Carry on for almost a mile, ignoring a bridleway sign to the right and keeping on past a couple of old barns (which might be executive-style homes by the time you read this!) before reaching a tarmac driveway. Here you turn hard right, following the bridleway signs uphill and then down on tarmac to St Mary's, a small and isolated settlement.

Just past the farm buildings the track bends round to the right. Take the bridleway sign straight ahead uphill along the side of a field. After a long plug up the track levels out, and then passes a bridleway gate on the left. Ignore this and carry straight on, going down a narrow, muddy hill to the valley bottom. What comes down must go up and there follows a short, stiff ride up over grass to a gate. Go through and into a field, pushing on uphill with Ditchling Beacon in sight to the left ahead of you. It's a long climb, but the going is good and eventually you reach a gate where you turn right through a few trees before rejoining the South Downs Way a few yards uphill. From here turn left back to the car park where Mr Whippy may be waiting for you, or if not you may find refreshment in Ditchling.

To extend the ride to the west, carry on through the car park and along the South Downs Way towards Clayton Windmills. Bear left on to the Sussex Border Path after about ¾ mile (1.2 km) and then left again heading for Lower Standean. From here bear left up Healthy Brow on a bridleway which brings you back to the car park. This circuit adds just under 4 miles (6 km).

Ride 34 THE SOUTH DOWNS WAY Stage 1: Queen Elizabeth Country Park to Steyning

Area: The South Downs, West Sussex.
Start: OS Landranger 197 grid ref 718185 (ride continues on to OS 198); car park at Queen Elizabeth Country Park.
Nearest BR station: Petersfield.
Approx length: 40 miles (64 km).

Ride: Long and energetic.
Climbs: Don't ask! Half a dozen long climbs to the top of the downs, some more strenuous than others.
Conditions: Very good in dry weather; can be muddy and very slippery in wet weather.
Difficulties: Just keep going – you'll certainly feel like you've done it when you get there.
High Points: On a clear day there are wonderful views all the way along.
R & R: Café at Queen Elizabeth Country Park; pub and café *en route* at Amberley; otherwise many pubs off route at South Harting, Elsted, Hooksway, Cocking, Graffham, Houghton, Washington and other places.

The South Downs Way is Britain's longest non-stop bridleway, stretching along the length of the downs from South Harting near Petersfield on the West Sussex/Hampshire border to Eastbourne some 75 miles (120 km) distant on the coast of East Sussex. It's a traditional favourite among long-distance walkers who generally take about a week, and if the going is dry it's a fine long distance offroad ride.

You can of course do it non-stop from end to end, but with its up-and-down nature and little chance to take it easy, the full length would be an exhausting marathon and little fun for those who like to enjoy the superlative views and maybe stop off at one or two of the fine pubs in the downland villages. For this reason I decided to break the ride into two sections, choosing Steyning as the halfway point, a pleasant small town with a choice of hotels, B&Bs, pubs, and cafés. The 40-mile (64 km) ride took me nearly six hours with a lunch break and a couple of rest stops, plus a puncture – and I wouldn't have cared to go any further.

Nor would I do it in wet weather. Many of the hills are chalk, and they become unridably slippery going up – your back wheel spins while *you* stand still. Some sections can also get muddy, but in dry weather it's excellent going most of the way. There will of course be walkers and maybe horseriders, and you should give them due consideration. Most of the walkers are concentrated round the South Downs Way car parks at Harting Downs, Bignor and above Storrington, so be prepared to take it easy in their vicinity, riding the South Downs Way on a weekday if you are able. Unless you go off route there is no café, pub or shop until you reach Amberley some 30 miles (48 km) from the start of the ride, so pack your victuals accordingly. Also take plenty

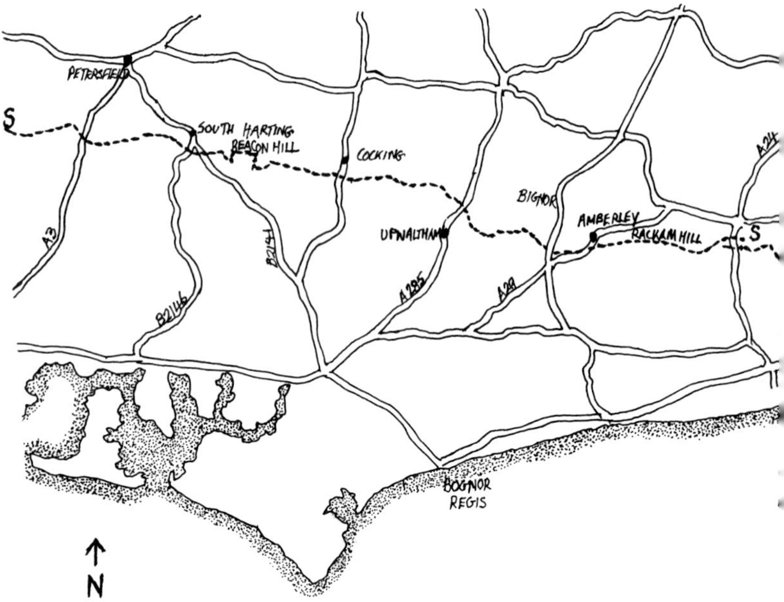

of liquid which is likewise unavailable apart from a tap on the side of the track by Hill Barn, just south of Cocking.

I started the ride from the Queen Elizabeth Country Park which is just off the A3 south of Petersfield. It's not the official start of the South Downs Way, but it has a large car park (for which there is a modest charge), the ride through the woods to link with the South Downs Way is excellent, and there's a shop and café which may be handy for those who do this ride with a car-borne support team. Those who arrive by train can easily reach here from Petersfield, and then pick up a train home at the end of Stage 2 at Eastbourne. If you're only doing Stage 1, Shoreham is the nearest BR to Steyning, a little over 4 miles (6 km) away onroad. You could of course do the whole ride in the reverse direction, but the only good reason for doing it this way is that the prevailing south-west wind will be behind you.

To start, follow the tarmac lane to the stables, heading round the right side of the main Country Park building parallel to the road. Just before the stables the track sweeps left towards the woods, and here you will pick up blue horseshoe bridleway signs on the trees going uphill. Head

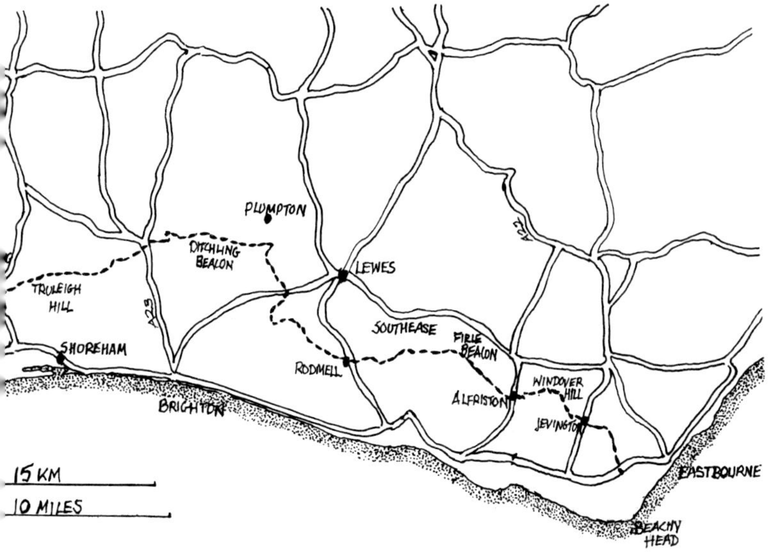

up here, and where you see red horseshoes follow that route which takes you gradually on the long uphill to the top of the down. At the top you unsurprisingly begin to go down, and then come up to a crossing track with the red track going right and the blue track left. Since you are now surrounded by woods it's easy to lose your bearings, and I took the red track which turned out to be the wrong track, but nevertheless gave a superb, fast ride down to the bottom of Holt Down where it comes to the road on a corner by a bijou cottage opposite a large barn. If you come down this way turn left and follow the quiet road past the signs for Buriton, coming to a large car park on the left at the bottom of War Down which is on the more direct route via the blue horseshoes.

Just by this car park (an optional start point for the South Downs Way) a narrow tarmac lane goes off to the right. Turn down here, ignoring a bridleway sign to the left and keeping on until you reach a narrow track going straight ahead. Keep on along this bridle track which winds its way due west, heading into woods at Coulters Dean Farm and then emerging on a tarmac lane on a bend. Keep on up a short uphill, bearing left on a long, straight downhill at the top where you pick up your first South Downs Way signpost. This takes you down to Sunwood Farm on a left-hand bend; just past here you turn right offroad and on to a track signposted as the South Downs Way.

From here on the South Downs Way is just a matter of following your nose, generally keeping on ahead. It traverses the B2146 and B2141 on a narrow track above South Harting, and from there goes on to the Harting Downs where it heads on a fast downhill to bridleway crossroads at the foot of Beacon Hill, a very steep climb on chalk ahead of you. Here you should follow the South Downs Way signpost, going off to the right on a diverted route which avoids Beacon Hill via a gentler slope, heading south and then turning sharp left to go north and get back on course just before a gate that leads on to Telegraph House.

A quick down and an up takes you to the top of Buriton Hill where you can see the big climb up to Linch Down ahead of you, but before you start going up you have to go down, crossing a track just above Buriton Farm. Once you're up the South Downs Way bears left around the back of Monkton House, the surrealist cottage which now has a wire fence around it worthy of a high security prison. After a ride along Cocking Down the South Downs Way drops on a fast downhill to the road just south of Cocking, crossing straight over and heading up to Heyshott and Graffham Down with a long ride through the woods before once again heading down to the road just above Upwaltham.

A long uphill takes you past the twin radio masts on Burton Down, passing a car park and then crossing the busy A29. Here you turn right and immediately left on to a fast downhill track towards Amberley with the River Arun snaking across the valley below. The track leads down to a lane where you turn right, joining the B2139 for a short onroad ride over the bridge and past the pub, shop and café. An overgrown track on the left says 'horses' which gets you offroad for 50 yards (44 m) and then you rejoin the road on a left bend, heading on a short uphill past a grey house behind a hedge before turning right onto a tarmac lane signposted as the South Downs Way.

This heads uphill past a large red-brick house in a wonderful position, and you then bear off on a short and very steep uphill which takes you offroad on to the South Downs Way once again, followed by a much longer steep climb from Downs Farm up to the top of Rackham Hill. Watch for the

Long, steady downhills and uphills characterise the first half of the South Downs Way.

two car parks along this stretch, for it's popular with those who like to take a walk after Sunday lunch. You're soon clear of them and into the last section, heading downhill to the A24 where you bear right, cross with care, and then bear left up the other side. There follows what is probably the most vicious climb of the ride, but it is also the last, taking you up to Chanctonbury Ring which is a fine place to stop for a final breather.

From here follow the track round to the right, heading south-east on a long, fast section with the sea ahead. Where the track joins a narrow road at a gate ride on as far as the car park on the left which is the 'Steyning Bowl'; and then unless you're possessed with a mad desire to carry on non-stop to Eastbourne, turn left down the bridleway that goes down by the far side of it. This is a fast concrete surface all the way, bringing you through a farmyard to the outskirts of Steyning where you turn left towards the town, joining the main road and following it all the way to the town centre at the end of this most excellent ride.

Ride 35 THE SOUTH DOWNS WAY
Stage 2: Steyning to Eastbourne

Area: The South Downs, East Sussex.
Start: OS Landranger 198 grid ref 176112 (ride continues on to OS 199); car park in centre of Steyning.

Nearest BR station: Shoreham.
Approx length: 42.5 miles (68 km).
Ride: Long and energetic.
Climbs: As with Stage 1 there are half a dozen long climbs to the top of the downs.
Conditions: As for Stage 1.
Difficulties: As for Stage 1.
High Points: The fine views continue, and when you get to the end you've achieved something!
R & R: Pubs, cafés, etc in Steyning and Eastbourne; pubs *en route* at Devil's Dyke, Clayton, Long Hill by the A27, Rodmell, Alfriston, Jevington; tea shop/café at Jevington.

The second half of the South Downs Way is no easier than the first. On the day I rode it there was a strong north-east headwind and there had been plenty of rain the night before, making the going more tough than it needed to be. Choose your weather carefully, for Stage 2 is much more open than Stage 1 with no protection from wind and rain on the top of the downs.

Leaving the car park in the centre of Steyning turn right down the main street, riding out of town and turning right when you come to Maudlin Lane. There's a bridleway sign at the first right turning after that – go along the lane that leads towards the downs, bearing left through a farm, and then heading up to Steyning Bowl on a concrete track, a distance of 2 miles (3 km) from the centre of town.

Once on the top turn left along the road, then left again after a few hundred yards, riding along the side of a field following the South Downs Way signpost. This takes you through a gate and then downhill to Annington Farm where you turn right on to a lane, following it ahead until you reach a right-hand bend where you go straight ahead on to a wide track – if you reach the church you've overshot. Cross the River Adur by the bridge, passing a free tap to fill your water bottle which so far as I know is one of only two along the whole length of the South Downs Way.

Once past the river you have to turn left along the busy A283 for a couple of hundred yards, before turning right on to a track signposted as the South Downs Way just before the roundabout. This takes you on a steady climb up Beeding Hill where you join a lane on a bend and continue straight ahead along it – there was no South Downs Way sign to put you on the right course here when I rode by. Carry on past a dead-end road sign, passing the YHA hostel by Tottington Barn on the left and coming to the radio masts at the top of Truleigh Hill in a fairly desolate situation.

From here the track goes down Edburton Hill and then heads up the Fulking Escarpment by a National Trust sign. At the top it bears to the right side of the pub on the top of the fort at Devil's Dyke where you may care to stop, crossing the lane that leads up to the pub and going on to a fast track through bushes. From here on the South Downs Way signposting deteriorates. The South Downs Way track bears left where it reaches the road ahead, turning north-east to run parallel to it before turning left to the north-west to head down to Saddlescombe.

Here you cross the road, and go through a gate on a narrow track going up to the left. This leads to a wider track passing a few farm houses, and then up a moderately steep narrow track before heading uphill across open downland. At the next road you cross straight over by the pub at Clayton, turning left up a lane and then right which brings you to the A273. A track runs along the side of this road, before you turn right up towards the golf club as signposted for the South Downs Way. The track heads on up through the middle of the golf course and can be muddy going, heading into open country and then turning left to join a much better track running along the top of the downs where you turn right.

Follow this track ahead which brings you past the small car park at Ditchling Beacon where you cross the road and continue on straight ahead. The going is good and fast, but watch out for the sharp right turning which appears a couple of miles on. When you've passed the lane to Streathill Farm you come down to a gate on a moderate downhill with a copse of trees over to the right. Here you turn right along a track without going through the gate – the way is indicated by the blue South Downs Way long distance acorn sign, but this can be easily missed.

Head down this track which takes you SSW across Plumpton Plain. Where it widens out you follow the South Downs Way sign left downhill, heading south-east and ignoring the bridleway that carries straight on ahead. This brings you down a long, fast track to a valley where you veer right up towards a belt of trees, heading through them on a narrow track and then bearing right on a final downhill to the busy A27 dual carriageway by Long Hill. How horses get across here I don't know – it's bad enough on a bike.

There's a pub on the other side where you may like to

stop, though not in the most attractive of positions. Ride round the side of the pub, and then head left on a track which steadily takes you up to the top of Newmarket Hill. Here the South Downs Way bears left and right along the top of this immense down which dominates the landscape above the River Ouse. Having passed a couple of dew ponds it turns right and left above Iford, joining a concrete track which speeds up progress as you zoom south-east along Front Hill. More downhill and a short uphill brings you to a narrow track passing between the two houses on the top of Mill Hill, and then you turn left downhill into Rodmell where another pub awaits you.

Turn right along the road here for about ½ mile (0.8 km), and take the left-hand turning at Southease, heading down a lane past a dead-end signpost, passing the church and crossing the River Ouse which runs down to Newhaven. A little further on you cross the railway line, coming up to the A26 where you turn right for a short distance before turning left on to a track that bears right uphill. It then bears left up a long grassy slope, taking you towards the two enormous radio masts on the top of Beddingham Hill. From here it's a steady ride along the top of the down, passing through the car park above Firle and coming to the tumuli at Firle Beacon where you get superb views.

By this stage you're on to OS 199 and on the last leg. The track starts to head downhill, getting steeper as it nears Alfriston in the valley, bearing left for the final downhill and bringing you into this picture postcard village. The quickest way to continue is to turn left along the main street, out of town, and then right across the road bridge which takes you to a narrow track heading uphill. If you want to stop awhile, turn right and then left for Alfriston's village green which is in a fine setting and a grand place for a picnic. From there you can wheel your bike over the narrow footbridge that crosses the Cuckmere River, keeping on ahead and then turning left along the signposted bridleway which runs along a tributary parallel to the lane beyond. This brings you to a gate at the end of the field, where you bear right and then turn right uphill on the same narrow track that heads up towards Windover Hill.

The South Downs Way crosses a lane, and then plugs on uphill on a wide, chalky track bringing you up to a fantastic view over Tenantry Ground on the right. Here the South Downs Way bears left across open grassland, with direction posts showing the way. Follow them round in a curve

Heading down the hard track towards Rodmell on the second stage of the South Downs Way.

which bears round to the right, eventually bringing you to a gate and then on to a track which runs down through the woods above Jevington. This is a good, fast ride, but don't miss the right turning which brings you down by the side of the church to the road.

Turn right here (or left for the pub), and then left by the side of a tea house which makes a good stopping place if it's open. The track heads uphill towards Wealdway – the last climb of the South Downs Way and ridable all the way up. On the top you get your first view of Eastbourne which looks most inviting after 40 miles (64 km) in the saddle, and then the track speeds up with a succession of downhills as it passes the golf course on the right. At the A259 go straight over on to a narrow track ahead, and follow the South Downs Way acorn signs down towards Eastbourne. The track bears left and gets faster and faster and better and better – the best downhill of the whole ride. Eventually and all too soon it comes down to a road, with a noticeboard informing you that this is the start/finish of the South Downs Way and you've done it.

Unless you aim to ride home or happen to have a chauffeur waiting, you'll probably want the railway station where you can ship your body and bike to a final destination. Turn right along the road, and then keep bearing left, turning left at a T-junction which will bring you to the station.

The Yorkshire Dales

The Yorkshire Dales have a character all of their own and must vie for the title of the best offroad area in the UK. The uphill riding is tough going, but once you're up you stay up, and the downhills tend to go on for ever. The northern part of this area is particularly well laced with tracks and bridleways that are for the most part on hard ground and fast going as they cut through the unforgiving terrain. Much of the riding is exposed to the elements and care should be taken accordingly; there is no point going up on the hills for a famous view when the landscape is lost from sight in the murk and rain.

Ride 36 GAYLES

Area: Gayles, north of Swaledale in the Yorkshire Dales.
Start: OS Outdoor Leisure 30 grid ref 124075; limited parking in village.
Nearest BR station: Darlington.
Approx length: 12 miles (19.2 km).
Ride: Easy/Moderate.
Climbs: None.
Conditions: Could be muddy; some sections overgrown.
Difficulties: No bridleway signposting; bridleways in various states of disuse.
High Points: An enjoyable countryside ramble.
R & R: Pubs in Gayles and Dalton.

This ride should be easy. However there are virtually no bridleway (or footpath) signs, and some of the bridleways are in a severe state of disuse and badly in need of clearing. Wet weather permitting, the route should be ridable all the way, and it's easy going through fine, mainly flat country to the north of the Yorkshire Dales.

Start by the pub in Gayles which is a small North Yorkshire hamlet. The pub has a large garden, does food, and also advertises 'afternoon teas'. Just east of the pub you'll find Long Lane which is a bridleway track (with no sign) running NNE, taking you gently downhill on a good

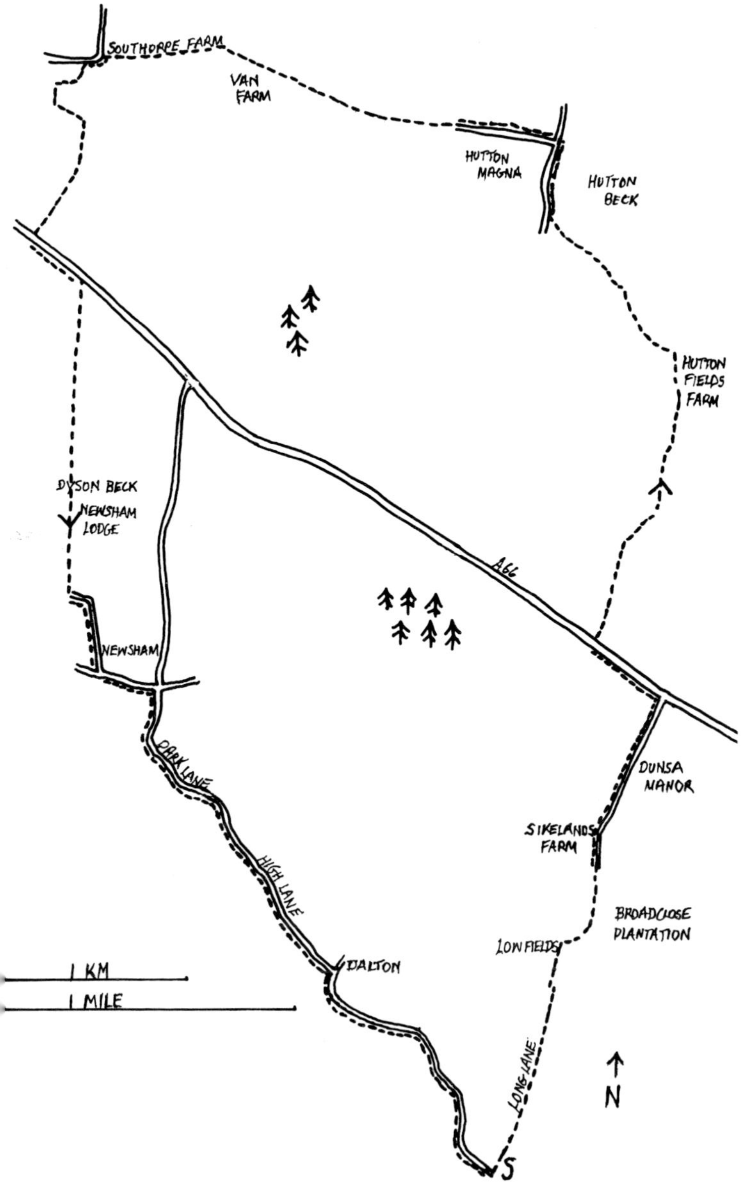

surface towards Low Fields farmhouse. About 100 yards before the farmhouse the bridleway route bears off to the right on a more indistinct track, which takes you to a gate by the left side of a barn. Go through, straight ahead, and on through the next gate.

Keep straight ahead across a field. By this stage any

semblance of a track has disappeared, but the going was easy when I rode it in June. At the bottom of the field you have to cross a ditch and a fence – this is the bridleway route as marked on the map, and there is no obvious alternative. Go across the next field to a belt of trees with Broadclose Plantation some distance off to the right. Ride along the side of these trees, and then cross the beck at a bridge which is very overgrown and in a poor state of repair. Go straight ahead across the next field with Sikelands Farm ahead of you. This will lead you down to the road on a 90 degree bend.

Ride on up the road past Dunsa Manor until you come to the busy A66. Cross straight over, and on the other side turn left along the disused road running alongside it. Just before this leads you back down to the A66, turn right into a field with a hedge running up the left side which is the bridleway route. Ride up the side of this field which was hard going when I did it, due to it being overgrown with no discernible track. You then come to a gate which you go through – or sling your bike over as most of these gates are only movable with difficulty. Ride on across grass with a wall on your right, and then join a good track which soon brings you down to Hutton Fields Farm.

Keep left through the farm and go straight up to the tarmac crossing track. For the bridleway turn left, then after about 20 yards go over what was once a gate and follow the line of trees across the field to another 'what was once a gate', beyond which the track was severely overgrown on my visit. The farmer recommended a small detour on the right to circumvent this, joining the official bridleway about 75 yards (66m) further on. Due to the loss of a discernible track and no signposting this section is confusing, but if you keep more or less north-west the track soon reasserts itself. After crossing several gates you come to the road at Hutton Magna, a short way to the right of Hutton Farm.

Hutton is a pretty enough place with a small pub if you wish to stop. To carry on, turn right along the quiet road, going over the bridge crossing Hutton Beck, and then take the first left by the imposing vicarage. Keep straight ahead on this road which makes for pleasant riding with fine views across the valley. Where it bends right, go straight ahead on a tarmac lane with a sign saying 'No Vehicles Except For Van Farm'. The track is tarmac all the way to Van Farm which comes into sight on your left. Where the track bends left down to the farm, you go straight ahead on a much less obvious track along the top of a field. This brings you down through a couple of gates to the road on a 90 degree corner by Southorpe farm, the only place on this ride where I found a bridleway sign.

Go ahead along the road for about 50 yards (44 m), then turn left through a gate with a well-defined track heading down a field towards a clump of trees. The track crosses 'Main Stell', a sort of farmers' canal, and then bears right along the edge of the field and the canal towards the trees, bearing round their east side towards a gate. Go through this gate, and immediately turn left along the edge of the field. Turn right along its far side, go through a gate, and join a track which takes you back up to the busy A66.

Turn left along this road for a hundred yards or so until you pass what was the old railway line, indicated by white fences on the sides of the road. Go past a modern barn on the right, and 50 yards (44 m) further on, cross the road to turn right through a gate and ride along by the hedge on the left-hand side of the field. This takes you due south on good ground, through a gate, and on to a track which leads over a bridge at Dyson Beck, past the very pretty Newsham Lodge farmstead, and on to a tarmac track which bears left and right before rejoining the road.

From here turn left into Newsham, and then take the second right as indicated for Gayles. This quiet country road leads via Dark Lane and High Lane to Dalton where you may like to stop at the Travellers' Rest. Bear left up the hill here, and you soon come back to Gayles on what I found to be a virtually car-free road.

Ride 37 MALHAM

Area: South Yorkshire Dales.
Start: OS Outdoor Leisure 10 grid ref 901627; Pay & Display car park by Information Centre in Malham.
Nearest BR station: Hellifield.
Approx length: 16 miles (25.6 km).
Ride: Moderate.
Climbs: Stiff climb out of Malham onroad, and out of Kilnsey offroad.
Conditions: Mainly good tracks; some riding on grass; can be muddy along western end of Mastiles Lane.
Difficulties: None.

High Points: Fine riding on moorland tracks and trails; Malham Cove and Kilnsey Crag are worth seeing.
R & R: Pub, café, tea houses in Malham; pub in Kilnsey.

This ride takes you on a criss-cross route from Malham to Kilnsey where Kilnsey Crag is a famous sight; and then back along Mastiles Lane, a superb long track that runs virtually straight all the way to Malham Tarn, the second largest tarn in Yorkshire.

Start from the car park next to the Information Centre in Malham where parking is 50p all day. From here turn left through Malham which is a pleasant, though popular village, forking right at the end of the main street. Keep on up Gordale Lane past a dead-end road sign, ignoring a turning to the left. The road drops down to Gordale Bridge where it's worth jumping off your bike to see two of the local sights.

To the right a footpath goes down the short way to Janet's Foss, a spectacular waterfall; and a little further on the second footpath to the left leads up to Gordale Scar, an even more spectacular geological fault which is well worth a 30-minute detour – but be prepared for a little climbing to get to the top! Carry on up the hill past a building on the left. From here it's a long haul up Hawthorns Lane and Smearbottoms Lane, passing a bridleway and footpath turning to the right near the top. When you start to go downhill you will see the Middle Laithe farmstead ahead, marking the end of the road where you take to the moors.

Go straight ahead up a grassy track towards a gate as

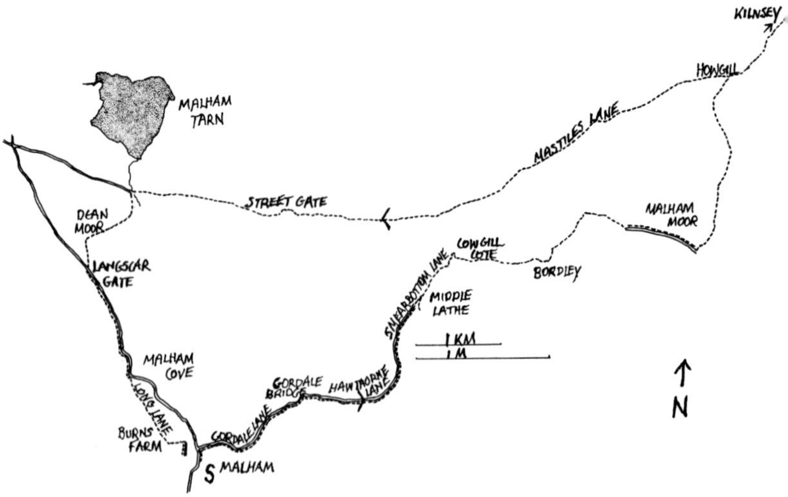

indicated by a bridleway sign. Once through the gate, bear over and join the right-hand track, heading for a gate set in a wall. Carry on along this track which is a rough, rocky ride, heading downhill with a barn on the hillside to the right ahead. Follow the track down to Cow Gill Cote, turning hard right up the other side before bearing left along the side of a wall which you follow until you head downhill for Bordley House Farm in the valley.

Go through the gate and on through the farmyard here, ignoring a bridleway turning to the right. Head straight up the hill ahead, following the tarmac track round to the right and then on a long downhill where it comes to a wall with a bridleway crossroads. Here you take the right-hand turning to Threshfield which is in effect straight on, going on a short uphill and then bearing left through a gate along Malham Moor Lane. You come to a bridleway crossing track after a few hundred yards of fast downhill. Turn left here, bearing right uphill on grass over Malham Moor, and then bearing left downhill as you follow the bridleway stakes which mark the route. Keep on down through a gate in a stone wall, and where the track gets bumpy and lumpy bear to the right, heading over to the walled crossing track ahead which is Mastiles Lane.

You join Mastiles Lane by a gate at Howgill. Here you can turn left and start the journey back, or take the long downhill into Kilnsey where you bear left for the Tennants Arms pub in the lee of Kilnsey Crag, an infamous rock overhang which was only climbed for the first time in 1988. From Kilnsey you have to grind back up the hill, ignoring the right fork and taking the left fork with a bridleway sign for Malham. Keep on along this track which is Mastiles Lane, running all the way to Malham Tarn in a more or less straight line. At first it heads up on a long, long uphill on a good track with stone walls on either side; then at the top it continues in much the same direction, following a wall on the right on a track which can be lumpy and muddy.

At a gate follow the bridleway sign straight on for Street Gate, eventually dropping down to cross the ford at Gordale Beck and heading up to leave Mastiles Lane at Street Gate. Go through the gate in the wall here, heading straight ahead along the quiet road ahead and ignoring the bridleway sign to the right. After a few hundred yards you cross Tarn Foot which is the stream running down from Malham Tarn, and go through a wall with a bridleway sign about 10 yards further on to the left.

Turn through the gate here, and follow the bridleway stakes up the hill on a clear, grassy track that bears right across Dean Moor, going through a gate, and then bearing left up to the road at Langscar Gate. Turn left here, crossing the cattlegrid for a fast downhill into Malham with fine views of Malham Cove where the streaks of sooty black are said to have inspired Charles Kingsley's *Water Babies*. You pass a bridleway sign pointing right to Settle, and then if you fancy a final mile offroad there's a bridleway sign pointing straight ahead for Malham on a sharp, left-hand bend about halfway down the hill. The track here goes down to a rickety old gate where you follow an old, bumpy lane between stone walls. The bumps and lumps smooth out as you join a crossing track by Burns Farm, and a little further on you turn right at the T-junction which takes you directly back to the car park over some final bumps.

Ride 38 GRASSINGTON

Area: South Yorkshire Dales.
Start: OS Outdoor Leisure 10 grid ref 002638; Pay & Display car park by Information Centre in Grassington.
Nearest BR station: Skipton.
Approx length: 13 miles (20.8 km).
Ride: Moderate.
Climbs: A few steady climbs.
Conditions: Mainly good tracks; some sections rocky and some on open moorland.
Difficulties: None.
High Points: An excellent, short moorland circuit with a choice of four pubs on the way.
R & R: Pubs, cafés, tea shops, etc in Grassington; pubs in Linton, Cracoe, Hetton and Threshfield.

The area between Grassington and Malham is well laced by bridleways that give excellent moorland riding. As such this ride could easily be customised to fit in with the Malham ride which follows, thus extending the distance considerably.

The ride begins with about 1.5 miles (2.4 km) on quiet roads, goes offroad for 10 miles (16 km) and then finishes onroad with a final 1.5 mile (2.4 km) stretch. Start from the large car park on the south side of Grassington which is an interesting, though fairly touristy old Yorkshire village;

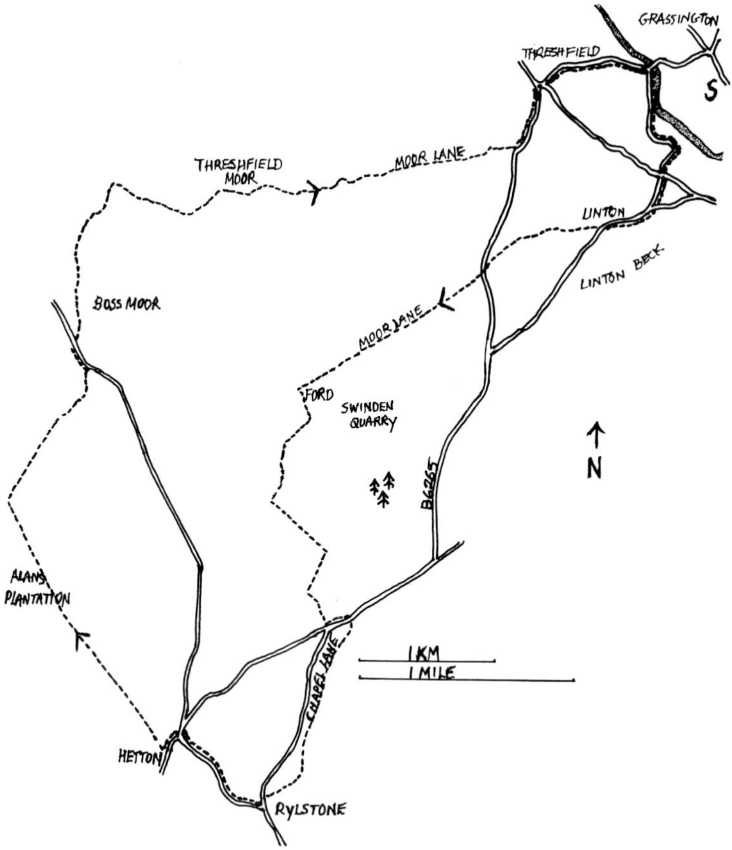

parking is 50p all day, and there's a Yorkshire Dales Information Centre there.

Turn left out of the car park, and bear left along the main road and down the hill, crossing the bridge that goes over the River Wharfe. Here take the first turning left for Linton, and follow the minor road round to the left and right uphill, crossing over another road and soon coming to the hamlet of Linton. Ride across the bridge over Linton Beck here, passing the pub on your left which is in a beautiful setting. A couple of hundred yards further on where the road bears left you will see a bridleway track going off to the right which is where you then go offroad.

The track runs straight between fields, before heading down to the road at Tarns Lane where you cross straight over on to Moor Lane. This continues straight ahead into more open country with Swinden limestone quarry over to the left. After a time the track appears to peter out ahead and bear right uphill. However, keep straight on ahead, heading for the right side of a clump of trees which you can clearly see in the distance at the point marked 'Ford' on the OS map. The track here is marked by blue bridleway posts and soon reasserts itself.

At the trees bear left downhill and cross Eller Beck stream, going up through a gate in the left-hand corner of the woods. From here head on across an open grassy field, heading for a hole in the wall with a disused barn up to the right. Go through this wall and the next, and then you'll pick up a bridleway post in the middle of the field ahead, where you bear diagonally left to the gate in the bottom corner which is marked by a bridleway blob of blue paint. Follow the track to the right which runs straight between stone walls, passing behind a copse of trees and then turning 90 degrees left down Swinden Lane. From here it turns right and left again before passing under the old railway, going through a gate, and coming up to the road by a farmhouse on the corner.

Turn left here and join the main road. After about 100 yards (88 m) a signposted track goes off to the right, just opposite the first building you come to. Head along this track which is called 'Chapel Lane', running parallel to the road with no cars to hassle you! Follow it through a narrow gate and on through the next gate behind the farm. From here bear right down a lane running past the church, and you soon come down to the road at Rylstone.

Turn left and right for Hetton here, passing the duckpond and then going down under the railway bridge. On the other side of the bridge the OS map shows a bridleway going to Hetton, but the signpost marks it as a footpath. It is in fact so narrow that you'll have to dismount if you meet any walkers, so it's sensible policy to leave it to pedestrians. The road soon comes up to Hetton where you turn left into the village, and after about 75 yards (66 m) go right on to a signposted bridleway track a short distance before you come to the pub.

This bridleway is the continuation of Moor Lane, heading across the moor in a dead straight line between stone walls as it slowly gains height. After a time it passes a copse of trees to the left which is Alans Plantation, and it then comes to a gate where you take the right-hand turning signposted for Kilnsey. This is an indistinct track heading across grass and peat. In places it fades to nothing, but the riding is comparatively easy with wild moorland and fine views to the left. Keep in the same direction and the track soon reasserts itself again after passing a sheepfold on the hill to the right. From here it drops down by the side of a stone wall and goes through a gate, heading up a much rougher walled track to join again at the top of Boss Moor Lane.

Turn left up to the top of the hill here, and then follow the signposted bridleway track off to the right. This heads out on a sandy track which weaves and twists its way across Boss Moor, skirting the left side of a hillock and then coming to a gate in the wall ahead. Here you follow the right-hand signpost for Threshfield, following a track which is reinforced by railway sleepers as it heads mainly downhill across Threshfield Moor. It passes grouse butts with views of the limestone quarry ahead, and it would be a very quick downhill if it weren't for the occasional rocky sections which demand some care.

Keep on following the track down, with Grassington in sight on the other side of the valley. Eventually it comes down to a gate on the left, with footpath signs pointing right across the moor. Go through this gate and follow the track which is still Moor Lane downhill, eventually joining the road at Tarns Lane about ½ mile (0.8 km) from where you crossed it on the way out. From here it's a fast ride onroad back to Grassington. Turn left downhill and ride through Threshfield past the pub on your left. Take the right turn for Grassington, heading down over the bridge and back up to your start place.

Ride 39 MARSKE

Area: Swaledale, Yorkshire Dales.
Start: OS Outdoor Leisure 30 grid ref 105006 at Marske; limited parking near post office.
Nearest BR station: Northallerton.
Approx length: 10 miles (16 km).
Ride: Moderate.
Climbs: One hard climb; one moderate.
Conditions: Mainly hard tracks; some sections overgrown; some could be muddy.
Difficulties: Care needed to find the bridleway route from Low Oxque to Shaw Bank.
High Points: Fine views; plenty of variety in a short ride.
R & R: Pub at Marrick.

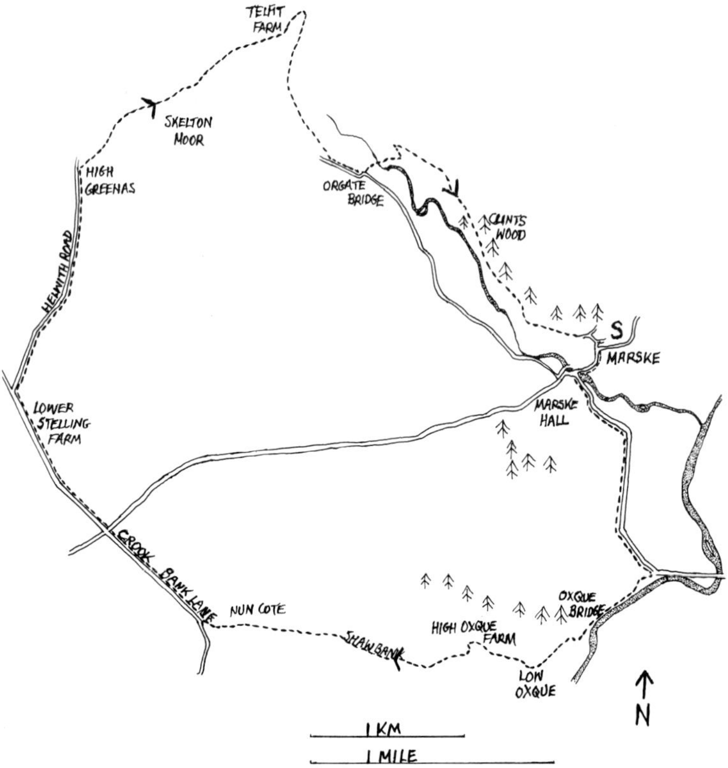

Start from Marske by the post office where there is limited parking on the roadside. Ride downhill, and then bear left and uphill past Marske Hall which looks fairly splendid. Ride on up the road which bends right and then start a long downhill towards the River Swale.

Ignore the first bridleway sign on the right, and turn off the road at the second bridleway sign about 50 yards (44 m) further down the hill – it's on a left-hand bend close to the river, and is about a mile from Marske. Ride along a good track with the beautiful river on your left. The track takes you past the woods at Oxque Bridge and you soon come to the farmstead at Low Oxque. Here the bridleway turn is easy to miss, turning right on an indistinct track uphill (no signs) towards old, disused farm buildings, well before you reach the farmhouse and its modern barns. When I rode up, the way was also very overgrown, and it may be easier to do it during a hard spell in winter. Keep on up the hill heading ENE, going over an old gate which takes you on to a track that is in a poor state but improves as you gain height.

After a time High Oxque farmhouse comes into sight ahead. Before the gate the bridleway bears left round the side of the hill on an old, indistinct track leaving the more obvious track which runs down to the farmhouse. This brings you up to the top of Shaw Bank with fine views over to the north. Ride alongside a stone wall on top of the world, and when you're well past High Oxque bear downhill on a track which leads back down to join up with the farmhouse track in the valley. The track down is easily missed, in which case you can take a 'bike extreme' down the grassy hillside.

Keep along the track and through a few gates which eventually brings you out on to Crook Bank Lane by Nun Cote Nook farmstead. From here you can turn left to the White Horse at Marrick if you feel in need of refreshment. If not, turn right and ride along this dead straight road which soon leads up to a crossroads. Cross over and carry straight on, passing the driveway to Lower Stelling Farm. A few hundred yards further on Helwith Road leads clearly off to the right with a signpost for High Greenas Farm.

Take the 30mph plus downhill on this tarmac track which becomes greener as it heads towards the moor, and then goes uphill to where it joins a crossing track with High Greenas farm off to the left. Turn right through the gate here, and then bear diagonally left across the open moorland, following the clearly defined track. You soon pass the Trig Point for Skelton Moor on the right, and then the track starts to head downhill. Go straight over a crossing track, and on through a gate following a wall downhill on the left side. This leads down to another gate, and then the track zig-zags left and right on its way down past Telfit Farm.

Go through the gate at the bottom and keep on past the barn. The bridleway as shown on the map inexplicably ends here, but the track carries on bearing left round the side of the valley on a good surface. If in doubt ask the farmer if it's OK to use this track; in case of any problem you could push across the footpath route which links with the bridleway by Orgate Farm.

The Telfit Bank track soon leads down to a large modern barn above Orgate Bridge. Go straight on here, passing the left-hand side of the barn and going down through a gate on a concrete track which leads down over the bridge, before bearing right and left uphill to Orgate Farm on the hillside. By the farmhouse bear right on a crossing track which leads on through a gate on a good grassy surface, heading down into Clints Wood. Ride on through the woods on this fast track, and you're soon back down by the post office in Marske.

Ride 40 NIDDERDALE

Area: Nidderdale, Yorkshire Dales.
Start: OS Outdoor Leisure 30 grid ref 089735; parking is available near the How Stean Gorge.
Nearest BR station: Knaresborough.
Approx length: 12 miles (19.2 km)
Ride: Moderate
Climbs: Long climb from How Stean Gorge and up past Middlesmoor.
Conditions: Some rough going and open moorland.
Difficulties: None.
High Points: Wonderful ridge ride; How Stean Gorge is an added bonus.
R & R: Pubs in Middlesmoor and Lofthouse; How Stean Gorge café.

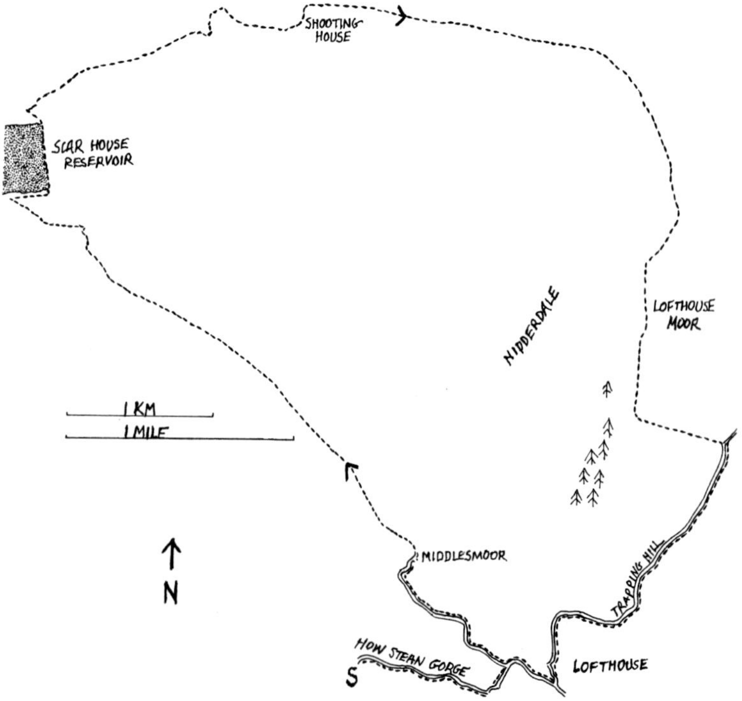

This is an excellent ride with fine views, which is energetic, but by no means difficult. Start at How Stean Gorge, about a mile west of Lofthouse. There is one car park just before you reach the gorge (paying in season), and another for patrons of the excellent How Stean Gorge Café. This wonderful place does very good food at most reasonable prices, is open all year round, and baked the wedding cake for Charles and Di – what more can you ask! It is sited right on top of the gorge which is also well worth exploring, though not on a bike! Take a torch to get through the underground section; you can also hire them from the café.

From How Stean Gorge ride back up to the main road – which is extremely minor – and turn left for Middlesmoor. There follows a long and serious plug uphill to this charming, small Yorkshire village, perched on the hillside with old stone streets intact by the church and a pub called The Crown. Carry on uphill and the road soon turns to a rough track, taking you steadily up into open country with fine views opening out all around.

Carry straight along this track on a surface which improves once it levels out. Pass grouse butts, like small towers, on the right; then keep on for another mile or so on a gradual downhill which becomes steeper and the track looser and rougher as it zig-zags its way down to the side of Scar House Reservoir. At the bottom it meets a tarmac track running along the side of the reservoir; turn right here, and then left over the magnificent Victorian dam (they don't build them like that anymore!) which takes you to the north-east corner of the reservoir.

On the far side go immediately 45 degrees left uphill on a rough track, and after about 75 yards (66 m) take the sign pointing to the right along the Carle Fell Road. This initially heads up on grass, after which the track is variable but remains ridable. Continue following the track along the side of a wall and into open country. It soon bears left downhill and then swings down to the left on a loose rock track, crossing a ford and going steeply left and right uphill – your first technical ascent of the day with plenty of loose stone. The track immediately dives down again, crosses another ford, and bears steeply right uphill – your second technical ascent!

This track soon brings you to a lonely shooting house. Looking through the windows we saw rows of empty wine bottles on the shelves, indicating that it's wise to keep well clear of the shooters when they're at work! Bear left slightly uphill on a wide, peat track here, which brings you up to a good crossing track where you turn right. From here it's a good, fast ridge ride along the dale edge which swings round to the right ahead of you. The track has a few ups and downs, but nothing severe and the views are of course magnificent. It swings to the right to run due south down the side of Lofthouse Moor, and then after a second shooting house you follow the track round 90 degrees to the left which soon brings you down to a road.

If you want to extend the ride from here, turn left and then almost immediately right on a good track which will take you south down to Ramsgill from where you can ride back to How Stean Gorge along the road which is by no means unpleasant. To take the short 12-mile (19.2 km) route back, turn right down Trapping Hill which will soon bring you into Lofthouse where there is a pub also called The Crown. Bear right at the T-junction just opposite a craft shop, and then take the next left which will take you back down to your start point.

Ride 41 NORTH OF REETH

Area: Reeth, Swaledale, Yorkshire Dales.
Start: OS Outdoor Leisure 30 grid ref 038993; roadside parking in Reeth.
Nearest BR station: Knaresborough.
Approx length: 11.5 miles (18.4 km).
Ride: Moderate.
Climbs: Hard climb up to Fremington Edge.
Conditions: Mainly hard tracks and good going; some soft grass and heather riding across Reeth Low Moor
Difficulties: None
High Points: Magnificent views; two good descents.
R & R: Pubs, tea houses, etc in Reeth; pub in Langthwaite.

This is a moderate but energetic ride in the hills above Reeth. Ideally start from the top of the village green – it's a pleasant enough place and there's a selection of pubs, tea shops and other stores close to hand.

Head down the hill out of Reeth on the B6270. Go over the bridge and continue along the road. When you pass the village sign for Fremington, take the next left turn past a road island enclosed by a low stone wall with a higher wall behind it. This starts the long uphill which will take you on

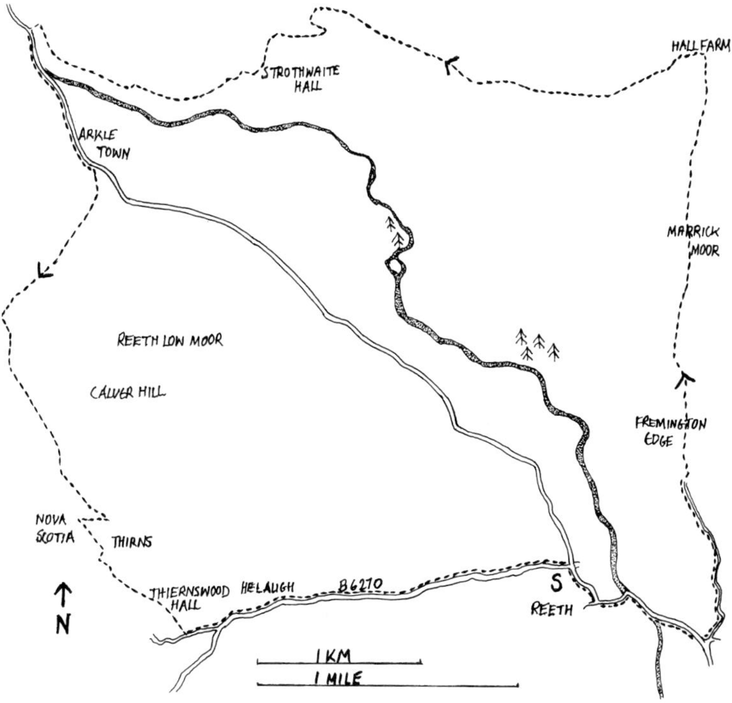

to Fremington Edge. After a short time climbing leave the tarmac road to go straight ahead on a rough track which cuts a corner. Continue on up the very minor road, ignoring a bridleway sign to the left. Eventually the tarmac peters out as the track heads up into open moorland, still climbing up the easily followed track.

When you reach the top there are fine views behind you, looking out over Reeth. From here go straight ahead through a gateway in a wall, and follow the track which continues over Marrick Moor and is easy riding. After a time you come down to a gate with an old chimney ahead and Hall Farm beyond it. Carry on down to the farm, and then bear left on the bridleway track through a gate and across an area of disused tips, pits and shafts. The track is easy to follow, but the bridleway leaves it where it bears off to the right at the top of a hill with views over the valley. Here you turn left towards the stone wall which should be about 75 yards (66 m) away; bear left along this wall, and then turn down to the right through a gateway.

From here the track heads on in an ENE direction, gradually losing height over an area with yet more disused mine workings with the occasional cairn marking the way. After a short time you will see two conspicuous cairns on a hillock over to the left, from where you get a magnificent view over Strothwaite Hall in the valley straight ahead of you. The bridleway track heads downhill well to the right of these two cairns, before snaking left and right down the edge of the hill beneath them. The going becomes good, grassy, fast downhill riding, with the track bearing left down the side of a wall and passing through a couple of gates before emerging by the side of Strothwaite Hall.

Turn right along the track here, crossing a ford, and bearing left uphill on a rough track past a bridleway sign pointing up to the north which is not the way you are going. The track soon bears down through trees, and then follows the side of Arkle Beck all the way to Langthwaite where the Red Lion is a well-known hostelry. They serve good food in pleasant surroundings, and sell a range of local maps and guide books.

From Langthwaite go over the bridge, and then left on to the road signposted for Reeth. Head along this road through the small hamlet of Arkle Town where the road crosses the Fore Gill stream and then goes uphill. Just past the cattle-grid a bridleway sign indicates a grassy track turning right on to Reeth Low Moor. Ride along this track, keeping right as it heads gradually uphill, though not enough to be hard going. After a time the track levels out, and then bears right and heads slightly downhill towards a conspicuous tip on the hillside ahead.

Bear off to the left here about 100 yards (88 m) before these mine tips, taking a grassy track which heads up between Calver Hill and Cringley Hill. The track comes and goes with some riding on grass and some on heather, but the going is not too bad and you soon come round the side of Calver Hill and begin to head downhill, still following what there is of a track in a more or less direct line.

Carry straight over at a grass crossing track near to a corrugated iron shack, and then bear downhill to the right, taking the shortest possible route through the heather to join the conspicuous track ahead which runs along the side of a wall. Turn left on to this hard track and head downhill above the farm building named Nova Scotia, but just before you reach the next farm building named Thirns, turn hard right on to a track which takes you back towards Nova Scotia.

About 25 yards (22 m) from Nova Scotia bear left downhill on a grassy track which runs down the left side of a wall. Follow the track down on a fast and very enjoyable descent towards woods, going through a gate at the bottom, and then straight up the short hill ahead and out through a narrow bridleway gate. From here turn left past Thiernswood Hall and follow the tarmac drive down to a minor road. Turn left and rejoin the B6270 at Healaugh, from where it's about 1.5 miles (2.4 km) back along the road into Reeth.

Ride 42 SOUTH OF REETH

Area: Reeth, Swaledale, Yorkshire Dales.
Start: OS Outdoor Leisure 30 grid ref 038993; roadside parking in Reeth.
Nearest BR station: Knaresborough.
Approx length: 14.5 miles (23.2 km).
Ride: Moderate.
Climbs: Long climb on road from Grinton to Ridley Hush.
Conditions: Rough miners' tracks and narrow moorland tracks through heather; last section along river could be very muddy.
Difficulties: Careful navigation needed on moorland section beyond Morley's Folly.
High Points: Good technical riding through heather; fast descent from moor; good riverside ride.
R & R: Pubs, tea houses, etc in Reeth.

After the ride north of Reeth you might want some more; this makes a suitable complementary ride, and both can easily be completed in a day with a good break for lunch in between.

Head downhill out of Reeth on the B6270 again, crossing the bridge and continuing past Fremington. After crossing the next bridge over the River Swale, keep straight ahead through Grinton, up the hill on the road for Bellerby and Castle Bolton. Plug on uphill, and when the country starts to open out take the next right turning signposted to Castle Bolton.

There follows a long and quite hard uphill, with moorland on either side. Every time you think you're near the top you find that there's more climbing ahead of you! About 2.5 miles (4 km) from Reeth there's a straight, level section which crosses a stream called Ridley Hush where

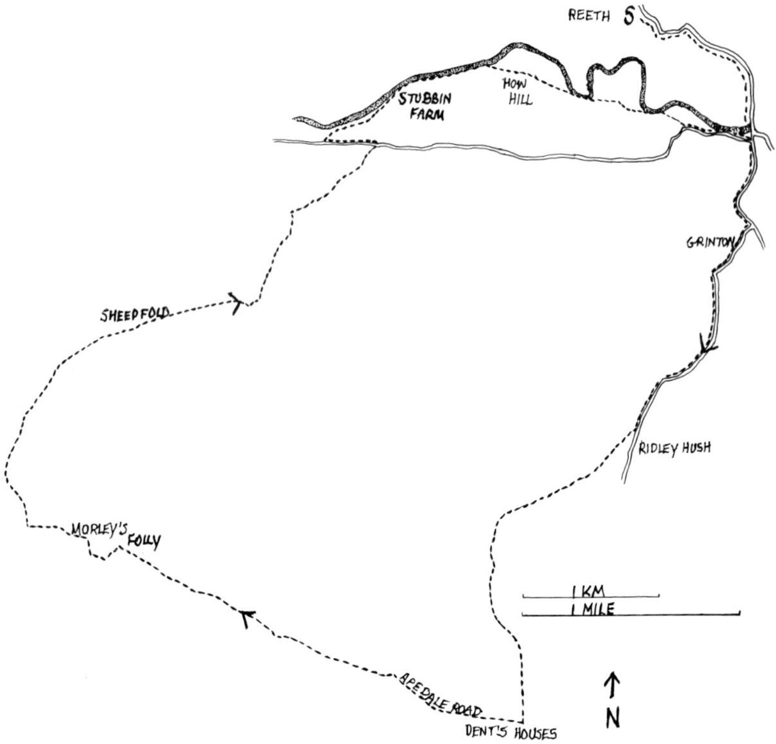

the ground has been badly eroded by the force of the water – it is an easily-spotted landmark. On the right there's a bridleway sign pointing out across the moor and in the far distance two cairns on the top of the hill which you are heading for.

Leave the road and follow the bridleway sign's general direction on a track which comes and goes through disused mineworks, but is easily followed and the riding is not overhard. The track eventually heads steeply up to the two cairns, with a fence running across beyond. Turn left along the fence and ride along to another fence where you go through a gate, following the clear, hard and very bumpy track which takes you south on a fast downhill towards Dent's Houses. You'll know you're there when you see a barn on the left, a track going on ahead up the hill past a lonely building, and the Apedale Road turning right which is the route that you take.

At first this is a good, fast track. After about a mile there's a tricky technical uphill on loose gravel, and then the track becomes less obvious as it passes a lonely railway carriage and heads on into the wilderness. The track bears left and goes through a gateway in a fence past a large crater, before bearing right and following a wiggly course over strange ground disfigured by mineworkings. You pass Morley's Folly with the remains of a small building on a hillock to the left, and then come down to a conspicuous pile of shale by a cairn with a pole stuck in it.

Turn right – due south – on a shale track which becomes grassy and enters a gully after about 100 yards (88 m), heading down past grouse butts looking like mini turrets. A short way on the track continues south out of the gully, and heads along a narrow track through the heather which is interspersed by grassy sections. The riding from here on is technical, but good fun!

A cairn over to the left indicates another bridleway heading down to the road at Sheepfold. You keep to the right, following the track round to the east with fine views over Swaledale as you negotiate the way past a large crater. Continue on along the track which becomes easier to ride as it heads down to a lonely footbridge. Cross this bridge, and ride on past the back of a timber building. Ignore the track off to the right, and follow the more obvious track which starts a fast, winding descent, bringing you down to the road above Stubbin Farm in record time.

Turn left down the hill here, and after a couple of hundred yards take the bridleway to the right, signposted to Grinton. This starts on a grassy track which heads downhill, and then follows a stone wall before dropping down to the river. From there on you have an excellent riverside ride along the Swale, though in some places the bank has been washed away by floodwater where carrying becomes necessary.

Go through several bridleway gates/stiles which are all marked with blue blobs, continuing along the riverside until the river bends left and you come to the end of the trees. Here you head diagonally right across an open field, going through a gate on the far right-hand side where you turn immediately right and left on to a well-worn track. This bears right uphill through a gate, and then keeps to the left along the side of trees, going through another gate and continuing in a more or less easterly direction. The track remains easy to follow, passing through several more gates on a variable surface and passing below a couple of farm buildings. Eventually it comes alongside the Swale for one last time, and then rejoins the road on a bend by Swale Hall.

Turn left here and ride along the road to Grinton, passing the church and taking the next left back to Reeth.

Ride 43 KEXWITH and BARNINGHAM MOOR

Area: Barningham, north of Swaledale, Yorkshire Dales.
Start: OS Outdoor Leisure 30 grid ref 084103; roadside parking in Barningham.
Nearest BR station: Knaresborough.
Approx length: 23.5 miles (37.6 km).
Ride: Moderate.
Climbs: Hard climb from Langthwaite to Peat Moor Green.
Conditions: Some good tracks; some hard going on open moorland.
Difficulties: Gill Wood bridleway very overgrown; navigation from Gill Wood to Stang Top is tricky.
High Points: Good ride over Kexwith Moor; a testing and fairly long circuit.
R & R: Pubs at Barningham and Langthwaite.

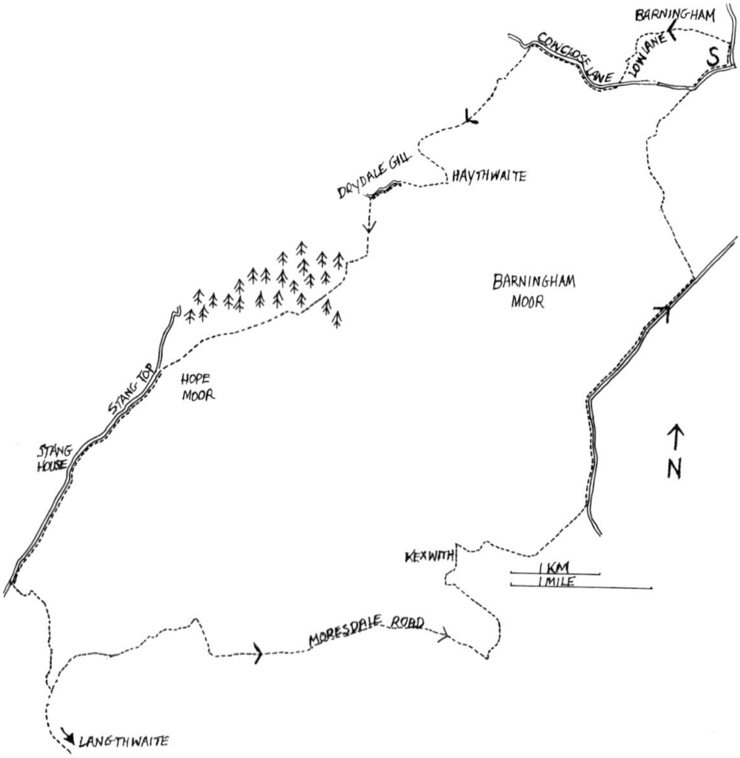

This is a good, moderately hard ride which is only suitable for fine weather. Start from the large village green at Barningham which is a model village with fine buildings reflecting the former prosperity in these parts. The smart pub is on the corner as you go into the village, opposite 'the manse'.

Head out on the Greta Bridge road, going downhill. Pass a gate on the left, and about 300 yards (265 m) outside the village some way past the church turn left on to a track running between walls – you can't miss it, as it's opposite a track on the right-hand side. This is called Low Lane and it's a pleasant ride which eventually comes up to the road. Turn right here and go down Cowclose Lane and into Gill Wood. Cross the bridge at the bottom of the hill and turn immediately left through a gate – more like a movable fence – which is the start of the bridleway track leading through the woods, following the course of Gill Beck and crossing it several times.

The narrow track comes and goes as it snakes through the grass and undergrowth, but is reasonably easy to follow and is ridable 60–70 per cent of the time. However, be warned that crossing the beck in winter could be a cold and wet business. Eventually the track bears uphill to the right and comes out of the woods by a gate. Turn left along the edge of the woods towards another gate, and then ride around the left-hand perimeter of the next field – all grass and sheep – with the valley falling steeply away to your left and the beck at the bottom of it.

Ahead you will see a large expanse of Forestry Commission woods, and to the left a small clump of trees on the other side of the valley. Go down and cross the beck here, going through a gate and bearing round the right side of the clump of trees to bring you up on to Barningham Moor at Cowclose Gill. From here there is no semblance of a track, and riding over the moorland grass is hard going. Head more or less straight uphill, and then bear along the right side of a ravine which soon brings you to a hard crossing track running down from Haythwaite farmstead.

Turn right along this track into the woods to link up with the Forestry bridleway. Shortly after the track enters the woods, take a left turn before Drydale Gill and head south. From here keep more or less south-west. Finding the bridleway marked on the map is well-nigh impossible as most of the forestry area is flattened and it looks as if there's been a war here! The correct route should bring you out on the Stang Road just beyond the forestry, but the best I could do was emerge on a track which hit the road some way down the hill after a lot of riding over hard shale, mainly uphill. The object is then to get to the top of the hill, past the forestry and into open moorland.

At Stang Top you'll pass the County Durham/North Yorkshire border sign. The road from there on is as pleasant as any you'll cycle on, taking you on a long and very fast downhill with great scenery on both sides. About a mile from the forestry you pass Stang House over to the right by a pond, and some way on Shaw Farm on the same side of the road next to a conspicuous bridge crossing Shaw Beck. A few hundred yards further on you'll see a bridleway sign pointing off to the left up a well-defined track which is where you turn offroad.

Head uphill on the track which bends round to the left and then the right as it gains height, winding its way past the rock face below Windegg Vein which appears to be a popular place for climbing. The track continues past mine workings and tips, and then doubles back in a U-bend to the left. Ignore this bend and keep straight on, heading south on a much less well-defined track. Keep your course and it will eventually bring you down to a stone wall by Peat Moor Green.

Go through the metal gate here, and then ride down the field by the left-hand wall where a gully marks the bridleway track. At the bottom go through another gate, and then head left down the gully which continues bearing ESE – it was once a walled track, but the walls have fallen in and this short section is consequently mainly unridable. It brings you down to a gate by a ruined building with a farmstead up the hill to the left. Turn right down Scotty Hill here, following the track round to the right past a few buildings and then on a steeper downhill into Langthwaite. This is a picture postcard place with an incredibly narrow main street, single village store, and the Red Lion pub where you can sit outside and enjoy the food. The ride thus far is about 11.5 miles (18.4 km).

From Langthwaite retrace your route back up the hill, rejoining the track on to Peat Moor Green. This time when you reach the U-bend by the tips, bear right uphill through the old mine workings. The track is good, and soon bends round to the west heading past a gully towards a wooden building. Keep along the track past this building until you come to a clear right-hand turning after a few hundred yards. This drops you back down on to the bridleway route which was lost in the heather, bearing left on a track which continues as good, fast riding. You will see the Stony Man boundary stone on your right, and then the Moresdale Road continues downhill across the fine open spaces of Kexwith Moor.

When you reach some grouse butts look over to the left – you will see the farm buildings at Kexwith, and the track going up the hill behind them is the route you are making for. Keep on past the grouse butts until the present track reaches a stone wall with farm buildings at Schoolmaster Pasture some way ahead. Bear left around this wall on a much less well-defined track which heads north and then swings north-west along the left side of a wall. When you are opposite the barn on the hill above Kexwith, ride by the first gate set at right angles in the wall and look for the second gate which is about 200 yards (176 m) further on. Go through, and follow the track downhill and over the stream. Ride up to the farm buildings and cross the bridge, going past a modern barn and bearing left on the track which takes you up the hillside. This track bears right and left before going through a gate, taking you across Holgate Moor on a good surface until it reaches a minor road ahead.

Turn left on the road on a fast downhill. The road then bears right and uphill, passing a cattle grid by the entrance to Long Green Farm with its large buildings over to the right. Less than a mile further on you pass Byers Hill Farm away to the left, after which the road goes down and up, levelling out past a small, disused quarry. Ride past the next field, looking for a gateway on the left with a track running down the right-hand side of the field past a couple of old barns at Carter House. This ½ mile (0.8 km) track is not a bridleway or footpath, but a sign indicates that it is used by walkers and it's the only way of connecting with the bridleway ahead.

Go through the next gate and follow the track which is now a bridleway round to the right. It's easy to follow as it winds mainly downhill, crossing a ford by a footbridge and then bearing left towards buildings. Cross the cattlegrid and join the road, riding down the hill ahead which soon brings you to the green at Barningham, hopefully in time to try the pub.

Ride 44 GUNNERSIDE

Area: Gunnerside, Swaledale, Yorkshire Dales.
Start: OS Outdoor Leisure 30 grid ref 951982; limited parking area in Gunnerside.
Nearest BR station: Knaresborough.
Approx length: 14.7 miles (23.5 km).
Ride: Moderate.
Climbs: Stiff climbs out of Gunnerside and Feetham.
Conditions: Mainly rocky moorland tracks.
Difficulties: None, but the bridleway turning away from Melbecks Moor up Gunnerside Gill is easily missed.
High Points: Fantastic scenery and some very good riding along Gunnerside Gill.
R & R: Pubs in Gunnerside and Feetham; Le Routier at Peat Gate Head.

This is a good ride made great by the spectacular views down Gunnerside Gill, but be prepared for lots of climbing! In Gunnerside you can park by the wall on a dead-end lane

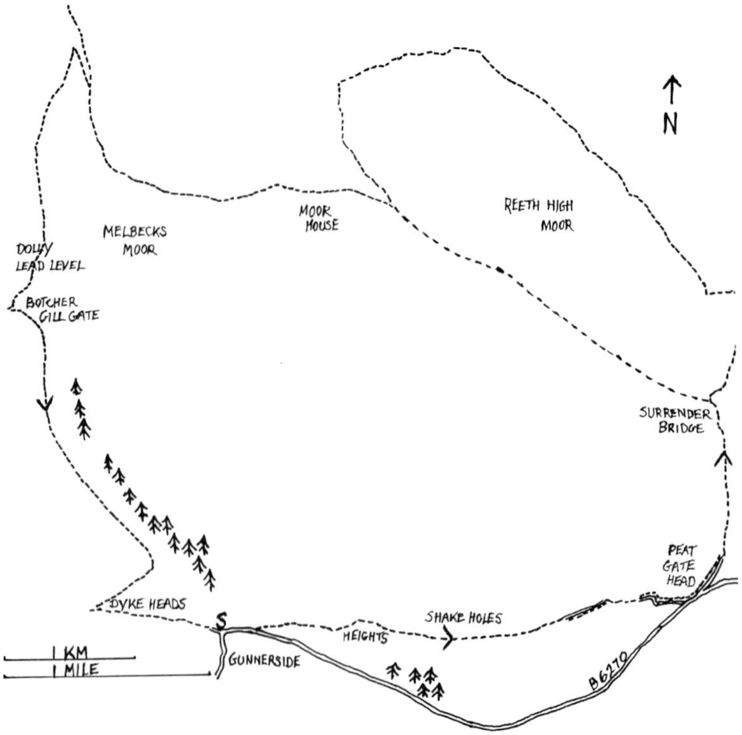

going north, just over the bridge from the pub. Ride back through Gunnerside in the direction of Reeth, and just past the last house on the right turn off on to the track which goes steeply up to the left.

Follow it uphill, and where it bends left continue straight ahead on a rougher track past the back of a farm building. Follow this track due east, steadily gaining height up the hillside – it's easy to follow, but is quite hard riding. After a while you will see the farm building at Heights ahead with a barn on the hillside above you. Bear left round the back of Heights on the grassy track which continues past 'Shake Holes' shown on the map until the track becomes tarmac.

Carry on along this track with good views across the valley, dropping down past the attractive small cluster of houses at Blades. From here the track drops rapidly down to Feetham where it rejoins the B6270 road. Bear left past the hotel/pub, or stop there for sustenance for the hill ahead, and take the next road turning to the left uphill signposted for Langthwaite. Grind on up past Le Routier at Peat Gate Head, gradually gaining height on the road as you pass the farm at Gallows Top over to the right. Pass a footpath sign to the left and then head downhill for Surrender Bridge. Cross over, and ignore the first bridleway sign to the left, or take it if you want to make the route shorter and on a better surface than the top track offers. Continue uphill on the road, and after about ½ mile (0.8 km) you will see a track to the left with a second bridleway sign.

Head offroad here, steadily gaining height on an easy uphill. Keep on the track which is easily followed on level ground, but of variable quality passing over a couple of boggy sections. Evenutally it passes a large sheep pen on the right, with an old, abandoned van on the left. Keep straight on here, heading for the tips ahead which are marked by a conspicuous pair of cairns with posts in. When you reach the cairns, bear left to head for the next single cairn through old mine workings. The track becomes somewhat vague here; just bear left riding parallel with the wall on your right, heading downhill and towards the line of mine workings which leave a long scar up the hill on the far side of the valley.

The track heads down and then bears left through a gate, entering another area of mine workings at the spot marked Ford. Keep left here as the track goes down and up, ignoring a track which appears to go off to the right. Some way on you

Enjoy the view at this lonely cairn, high up on the Gunnerside ride.

pass a ruined mine building just below Level House where the track improves; take the track going off to the right here, well before you come to the next gate.

The new track leads uphill along Old Rake Hush, passing a crossing bridle track to the ruined buildings at Moor House which you can glimpse to the left. Keep on along this track which bends left and right before going into an area of more mine workings, with big tips all around and Melbecks Moor to the south. Here it's easy to miss the right-hand bridleway fork which turns off through the tips where the track levels out and starts to bear left downhill. If you come to a cairn with a fine view of a track snaking up the hillside on the opposite side of the valley, you will have overshot the right turning by about 150 yards (132 m), just as I did.

The bridleway bears downhill to the right past a footpath sign, and runs along the east side of Gunnerside Gill. Keep on this great downhill track with fine views opening out on the left. Stop when you reach a lonely hut – it's barred and bolted, but makes a fine place to stop for a picnic if the weather is OK, with wonderful grandstand views down Gunnerside Gill and up Blakethwaite Gill as far as the dam.

Looking south from here you will see a track meandering down the east side of the gill. This is the bridleway track that leads to the bottom, joining a clear track which goes up the other side. Finding your way on to it is not easy – ride back uphill from the hut, searching for a suitable spot from where you can start downhill to join it. Having gone over the handlebars I resorted to a steep scramble which took me more or less directly to the bottom, carrying the bike most of the way. Here you'll find strange, ruined mine buildings in an unforgettable setting just above a waterfall.

Start up the track on the other side of the gill. At first it is barely ridable – narrow and rocky, with a vertiginous drop on the left side. It leads you along to more splendid old mine buildings below Lownathwaite Mea, and the track then greatly improves and becomes easily ridable as it heads steadily uphill passing Lownathwaite Lead Mines and Dolly Lead Level. Soon after it bears right and then heads on a short downhill to join an easily spotted crossing track at a T-junction at Botcher Gill Gate. Turn left here and ride uphill through a gate, following the track round to the right after which it becomes a long, fast downhill on a moderately rocky surface. You shoot down past Jingle Pot Edge, and the track then bears right downhill to join the tarmac road above the houses at Dyke Heads.

Turn left here, and it's a fast downhill all the way into Gunnerside. The pub is highly recommended for beer and food – and they were still happily serving the latter at 2 p.m.!

Ride 45 KISDON FORCE

Area: Gunnerside, Swaledale, Yorkshire Dales.
Start: OS Outdoor Leisure grid ref 951982; parking area in Gunnerside.
Nearest BR station: Knaresborough.
Approx length: 13 miles (20.8 km).
Ride: Moderate.
Climbs: Hard climb up from Muker; other minor climbs.
Conditions: Mainly good going on grass and hard tracks.
Difficulties: None.
High Points: Beautiful scenery and some good riding along the upper reaches of the Swale.
R & R: Pub in Reeth; pub and teashop in Muker.

Having sorted out Gunnerside Gill and spent some time at the pub, you will no doubt be looking for an afternoon ride out of Gunnerside. Here's an equally enjoyable jaunt of similar length which is memorable for a very hard climb out of Muker, followed by an even more memorable descent to Kisdon Force waterfall and a magnificent ride along the upper reaches of the Swale.

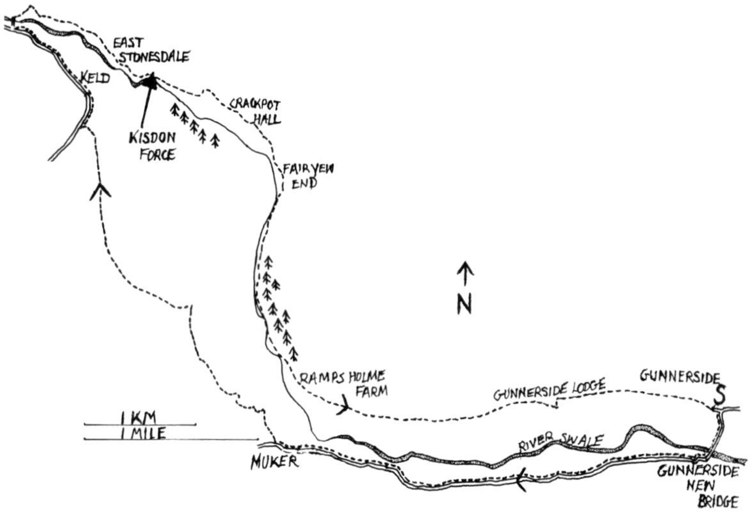

Head downhill on the road out of Gunnerside, bound for Muker. The road crosses the Swale at Gunnerside New Bridge, and then climbs for a short while before following the contours on the south side of the dale with fine views over the valley. Follow the road down in to Muker and cross the bridge. This tiny village has a pub, tea shop and craft shop to tempt you, and is popular with tourists.

Turn right uphill just before the pub on a narrow road which goes up past the church. When you see the post office bear left round the back of the houses and go on to a track with a footpath signpost – it's also a bridleway. This starts to head up, passing a hotel on the left and a modern small house on the right, and soon coming to a gate just past a barn. Go through the gate, and after about 50 yards (44 m) follow the track round to the left, leaving the footpath which continues straight ahead.

There follows a stiff, uphill zig-zag on tarmac as you rapidly gain height. The tarmac then peters out, and the track continues up ahead between two walls as directed by a bridleway sign. At the top of the walls, past a building to the right and Kisdon farmstead down to the left, there are two sets of footpath and bridleway signs. Ignore the right-hand signs which point along the Pennine Way, and head for the left-hand signs where you follow the bridleway direction directly up the hill. This becomes seriously steep, climbing up with a wall on the left – all but a few true heroes would have to push this section!

Stop and enjoy the waterfall at Kisdon Force before riding on along the River Swale.

The track remains easy to follow as it levels out and bears left through a gate before leaving the stone walls behind. Head downhill across grass to the next gate set in a wall by a sheepfold, going through and bearing right downhill on the hard, grassy surface with more fine views to the left. Keep on down this hill on the easily followed track which starts to turn rubbly and becomes tricky to ride near the bottom, by which time you've had your descent slowed by several gates. From here the track bears left across a ford at Skeb Skeugh, before heading uphill and joining the road by Thorns Farm.

Turn right along the road, and ignore the two signs for 'Keld Only' as you pass the World War I memorial with the names of the four unfortunate local boys who gave their lives. A little further on turn right over Park Bridge from where you get a fine view of Wain Wath Force waterfalls upstream which is a popular picnic spot and no doubt at its most dramatic in winter. Over the bridge the road bears right uphill. Where it bends left go straight ahead through a gate and then on to a track signposted to East Stonesdale Farm.

The track goes left downhill past Carrack Force waterfalls, and then bears uphill to the right. After passing through several gates it comes down to East Stonesdale Farm where you turn right with the farmhouse on your right and a barn on your left, going through a gate and then steeply downhill on a rocky track. This bears left down to the magnificent waterfalls at Kisdon Force in a fine setting which is perfect for a rest stop, although it is likely to be popular as it lies along the Pennine Way.

Follow the track through a gate above the falls and continue along it uphill, bearing left and right and following the course of the River Swale in a most beautiful setting. Ignore the track off to the left which goes up to Crackpot Hall, and you soon follow the track downhill to the footbridge and ford at Fair Yew End at a curve in the river. From here the track drops down to follow level ground by the side of the river, and gives splendid, easy riding. Follow the bridle track past the woods on your left and on through a gate with Ramps Holme Bridge ahead. When the track divides before the bridge, take the main track uphill to the left. Walkers will carry on and take the narrower track ahead.

As the track climbs above Ramps Holme Farm a sign informs you that 'the road' bears left. This is a tarmac track which plugs uphill with the occasional down, steadily gaining height on the hillside as it heads east past Calvert Houses and Ivelet Heads. At Gunnerside Lodge it heads down to the right where it meets a T-junction. Turn left down to the bridge here, following the road round to the right uphill past Shoregill Head and then on past the houses at Dyke Heads from where it's the same fast descent into Gunnerside as the previous ride.

Ride 46 SCAR HOUSE RESERVOIR

Area: Scar House Reservoir and Coverdale, Yorkshire Dales.
Start: OS Outdoor Leisure 30 grid ref 069766; car park near to Scar House dam.
Nearest BR station: Knaresborough.
Approx length: 14.5 miles (23.2 km).
Ride: Hard.
Climbs: Hard climb up Shaw Gill; long climb up from West Scrafton.
Conditions: Hard tracks; grass; open moorland.
Difficulties: Bikes must be carried from Little Haw to South Haw; careful navigation needed throughout ride.
High Points: Fine views and the crossing of a wild, wild area.
R & R: None along the way.

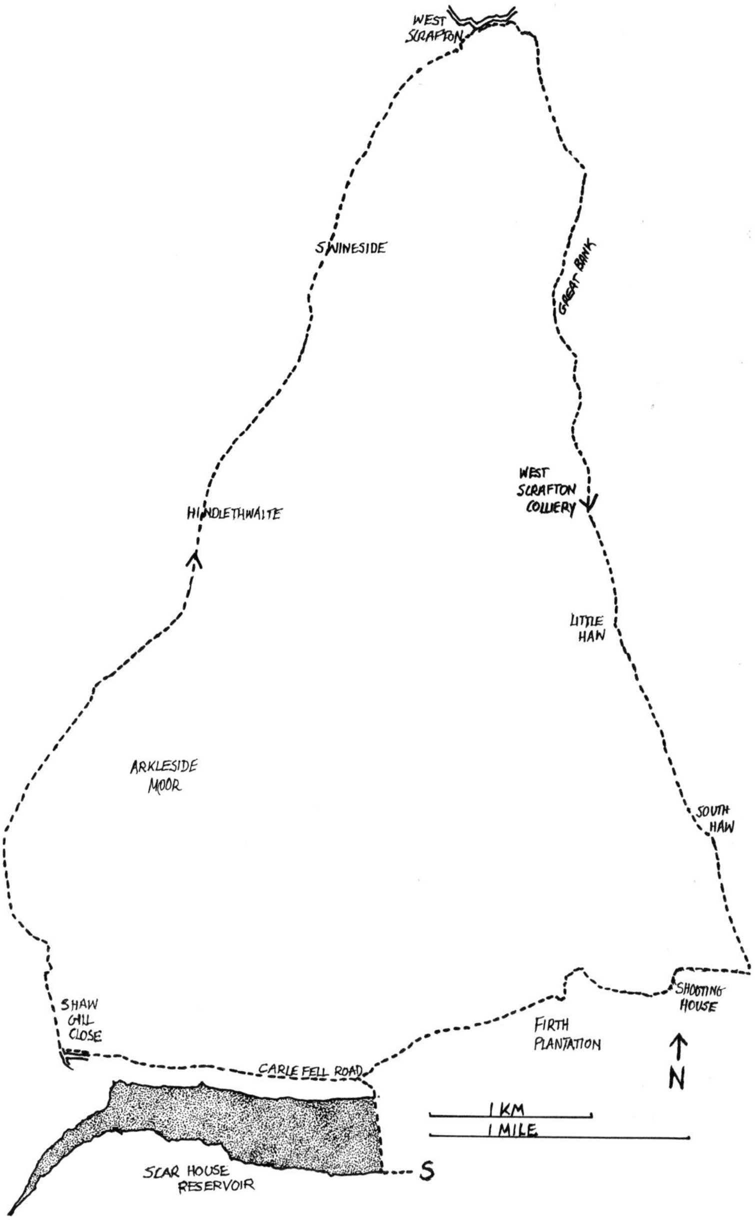

This is a hard ride, but interesting and quite rewarding. It's only for a fine day and you must be confident of your stamina. You should also take a compass and the relevant OS map.

Start at the Scar House Reservoir car park (50p). This is reached along a tarmac track that leaves the road just over the River Nidd from Lofthouse, where it is clearly signposted. From the car park, cross the dam and then bear 45 degrees left and uphill on the same track as ride No 40. This time keep on up, and bear left along the Carle Fell Road which follows the side of the reservoir.

When you pass a ruined lodge and come to a T-junction crossing track with a wall running alongside it, turn right uphill past Shaw Gill Close on a deteriorating 'road' which is badly worn. The track bears right and then meanders uphill to the left – in places it's properly made up with rock and is in good condition; in others it's in a terrible state and unridable. With no repairs it's getting worse every day.

As the track levels out it improves greatly, starting a long and fast descent that runs all the way down to Arkleside. However, you don't go all the way. At the first gate where the track bears left, look for a bridleway gate on the right side of the corner – this is about 300 yards (265 m) before a second gate further down the hill. Go through this bridleway gate, leaving the easy trackside riding behind, and plunge down a steep gully and then up the other side – it's unridable, but isn't too deep.

From there on the bridleway continues across open grassy fields in the shadow of Carle Fell, and is easy to follow and quite easy to ride as it passes through several gates. After a time you will come to a series of holes and bumps in the ground which are signs of old mine workings, with the woods of Hindlethwaite Plantation down the hill to the left. Bear left here and then turn right into the ravine which is Hindlethwaite Gill, following its side and crossing where you can to ride up the other side. The track then continues in much the same direction, following to the right of a wall for some distance.

After a time the wall peters out and so does the track, but just keep on ahead. Eventually you will see a couple of barns and a white gate. Go through this gate, ignoring the track which bears left downhill to Swineside. You then join a tarmac road which takes you rapidly downhill to West Scrafton, a picture postcard place which unhappily has no pub or shop and gives the appearance of being mainly full of holiday homes. Ride through this hamlet, cross the stream, and turn right through the gate following the footpath and bridleway sign which points up the hill in the direction of Nidderdale.

There follows a long, steady ascent, with the track bearing round to the right on a reasonable, grassy surface. When you pass the disused tips on the hillside at Great Bank things start to get more difficult. Bear left here, heading up the hill with little sign of a track until you come to a long since disused mineshaft at West Scrafton Colliery with a barbed wire fence around it. From here carry on to the fence ahead where you will see a stile with a blue bridleway blob. Cross over and carry on following the stakes with blue blobs up the side of Little Haw, where any semblance of a ridable track then disappears.

Look to the south-east and you will see the hump of South Haw (confusingly also called Little Haw) approximately a mile away. It looks a long way, and the only way to get to it on this 'bridleway' is walk, carrying and pushing your bike which is hard going through heather and lumpy grass – not at all for the fainthearted! When you reach South Haw, go through the gate on the right and then join the grassy track that runs round its side. The track comes and goes as you head across more open moorland keeping SSE, but eventually becomes 100 per cent ridable, though still tricky as you start to head downhill.

Just past another disused mineshaft you come to a clear crossing track. Turn right here, and retrace the outward leg of ride No 40 which feels and looks surprisingly different in reverse. Follow the track, and after a few hundred yards – immediately before a gate – take care to bear left downhill off it on to a grassy, peat track which brings you down to the Shooting House. Bear right through the gate here and then continue along the track, following a rough downhill section which bears left over a ford, uphill on more rough ground, downhill and over another ford, and then uphill bearing right. Here you bear right again on to a wide peat track, leaving the rough stone track which bears off to the left along the side of a wall heading down to Firth Plantation.

Follow the new track with the reservoir dam getting closer ahead of you, and after a couple of short bog crossings you reach the final downhill bringing you down to Castle Fell Road above the dam. Turn sharp left by the signpost, to cross the dam and ride back to the car park.

The Lake District

The Lake District is of course the best-known part of England for beauty, and is a favourite among walkers. Surprisingly it's not that well endowed with bridleways and other offroad thoroughfares that are legal to cycles, but here are three rides ranging from a simple ride through the woods to a hyper-energetic ride up towards the mighty Helvellyn that goes up, up and up.

Ride 47 GRIZEDALE

Area: The south-east Lake District.
Start: OS outdoor Leisure 7 grid ref 336944; car park at Grizedale Forest Centre.
Nearest BR station: Windermere.
Approx. length: 11 miles (17.6 km).
Ride: Easy.
Climbs: Plenty of moderate ups and downs.
Conditions: Virtually all hard forest tracks.
Difficulties: None.
High Points: Easy, fast ride through the woods – good introduction to offroading.
R & R: Refreshment van at Forest Centre; pub nearby and at Satterthwaite; tea at Force Mills.

This is an easy ride on forestry roads – good as a prelude to offroading, or if you are looking for a fast training session, in which case you can do it three times over!

Start from the Grizedale Forest Centre on the road between Hawkshead and Satterthwaite. This has a 'Forest Theatre', various displays, a large shop, and an incredibly original children's playground designed and made by a sculptor in wood. What it does not have is a café, although a mobile refreshment van is there in season, which is sometimes open and sometimes not. If you find it's the latter, there's a hotel/pub a short way up the road to the north, or a couple of possible stopping places en route.

The Forestry Commission have marked out four cycle trails which are colour coded with very good signposting.

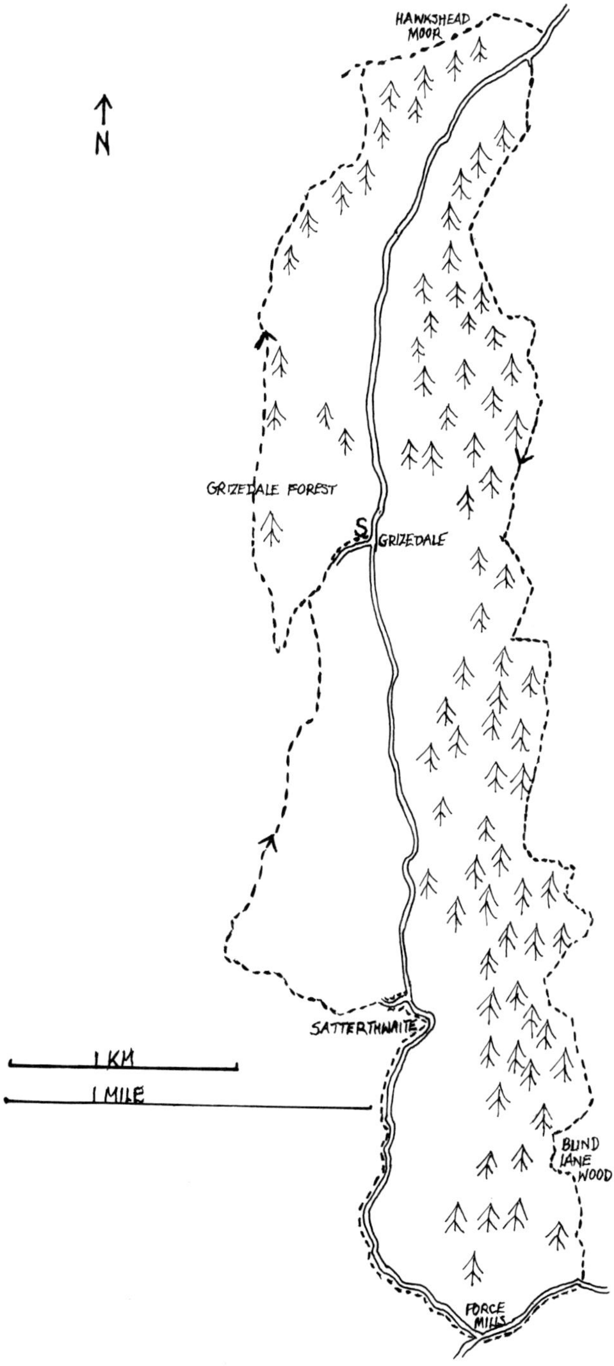
HAWKSHEAD MOOR
N
GRIZEDALE FOREST
S
GRIZEDALE
SATTERTHWAITE
1 KM
1 MILE
BLIND LANE WOOD
FORCE MILLS

You can't miss the woodman by the car park at the Grizedale Forest Centre.

However, they are all pretty tame since they run along hard-surfaced wide boulevards, and you still have to watch out for walkers and their dogs when doing a 30 mph plus downhill – they do have a tendency to string right out across the way and all you can do is slow down and be polite when passing. This route uses three of the trails coupled with a little roadwork and a bridleway to make a fast circuit which should take little more than an hour.

From the Forest Centre ride out on to the road, and then turn right down by the farm just past the post-box. Ride past the large woodshed on the right, and from there on you will pick up the first of the blue route cycle track signposts taking you left over a cattlegrid. Follow the signs uphill and round to the north, until after a couple of miles you come to red signs pointing left and blue pointing right. The red route heads up to High Cross which is a dead end, but it could be extended into a magnificent circuit via Hawkshead, heading east on bridleways and then turning south on a lovely track past Moss Eccles Tarn to Near Sawrey and on to Satterthwaite. This was a route I intended to ride, but I was defeated by lack of time . . .

Back to the blue cycle route which takes you to High Barn where you hit the road. Turn right here, ignoring the first track to the left which is a footpath and taking the second which is marked by a white cycle route sign. This route will take you rapidly south down past the Forest Centre, until above Bogle Crag you pick up the first yellow cycle route sign and turn left to follow it on what is probably the best part of the circuit for fast downhills.

The yellow route brings you down to the road at Blind Lane. Turn right here and then right again at Force Mills where there's a farmhouse tearoom on the corner. Follow the road up past a spectacular waterfall to Satterthwaite where there is a small pub and post office, then ride on between the two tiny churches and look for a bridleway turning left on a right-hand bend. Go down the track here, following it past a children's playground and along the side of a stream. Go through a gate and follow the track ahead, bearing round to the right and going through another gate on the track which is far more offroad than those through the forestry.

Eventually you will come up to a T-junction at the bottom of the woods where you turn right – the other way goes to Coniston. Further on, the bridleway is indicated as bearing right off the track for a few hundred yards, but this is not at all obvious and by carrying on you soon rejoin the outward blue route and head back down to your start point. Try getting round in under 60 minutes . . .

Ride 48 ULLSWATER

Area: The north-east Lake District.
Start: OS Outdoor Leisure 5 grid ref 473243; car park at Pooley Bridge.
Nearest BR station: Penrith.
Approx length: 9.25 miles (14.8 km).
Ride: Easy.

Climbs: Moderate climb up from Pooley Bridge.
Conditions: Hard track to start with; grassy track and the long downhill can be muddy in places.
Difficulties: None.
High Points: A great introduction to Lakeland offroading with an endless downhill.
R & R: Pub, café, etc in Pooley Bridge; pub at Howtown.

This is a simple ride with all that's best in Lakeland offroad riding without going into it too deeply – a moderate uphill, and then a long, long downhill with beautiful views of Ullswater, followed by 4 pleasant miles (6.4 km) back along the lakeside road.

Start from Pooley Bridge at the head of Ullswater. If you have a car there's a large car park on the west side of the village, though for this ride it's more convenient to pull into the limited roadside parking space as you go out of the village on the west side. From here fork right off the B5320 on the Howtown road, going up past the small church. Go straight over at the crossroads, heading up a lane with a dead-end road sign. This takes you up past a small caravan park (maybe not in winter) to a gate and on to a track leading out over the fells.

Ride up this track on a steady uphill with the might of Arthur's Pike over to the right in the distance. When you come to a bridleway crossroads by a large cairn less than a mile on, take the right-hand turn to Howtown. Follow the left-hand fork ahead – it's a little rocky and boggy in places, but generally easy riding. Not far on you come to a strange circle of stones known as 'The Cockpit' on the left; bear right with the main track here, and a little further on ignore a dead-straight track forking uphill to the left which is High Street, the old Roman road.

Head towards the top of the woods at Barton Park. Just before you reach them the track drops down into a gully, going left downhill and then climbing steeply right up the other side – this is a good technical section which requires a low gear. From here on it follows a wall along the side of the woods, coming out into open ground and continuing in much the same direction beneath the crags above. You get fine views down the length of Ullswater from here, looking as far as Helvellyn on a fine day.

The track passes over a reservoir pumping station which is like a grass table-top, and then follows on downhill, passsing close by Auterstone Wood and continuing to lose

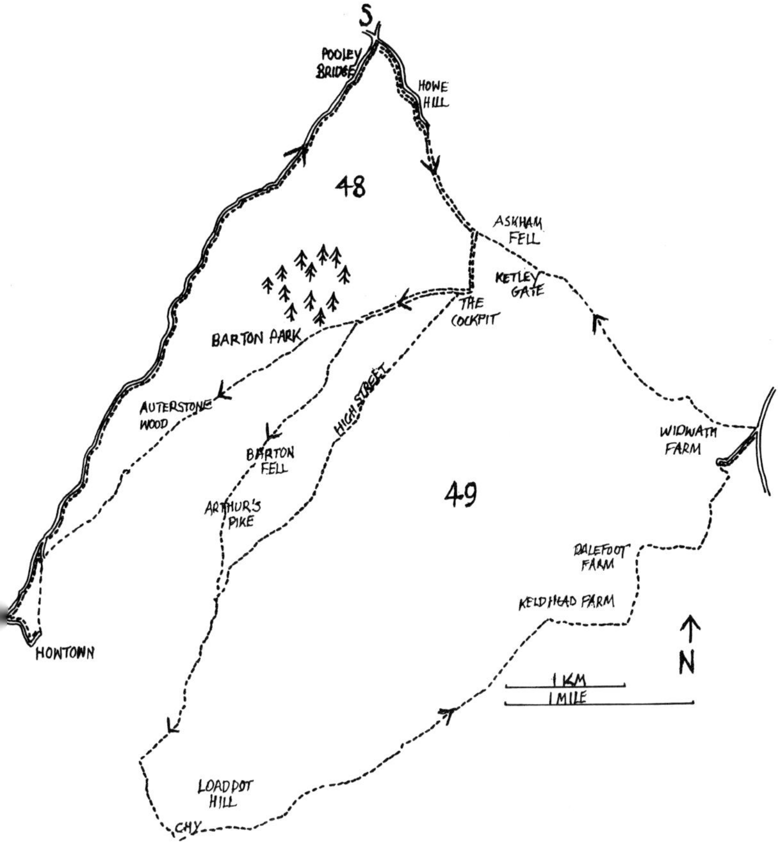

height with occasional small uphills, running along the side of walls until you come to a gate just above Howtown. Go through and turn right down the gravel track, and you will find the Howtown Hotel which has a 'Climbers' Bar' at the back which is well known for its good food. Carry on from here, forking right and joining the road from where it's an easy and not unpleasant 4-mile (6.4 km) ride along the lakeside back to Pooley Bridge.

Ride 49 LOADPOT HILL

Area: The north-east Lake District.
Start: OS Outdoor Leisure 5 grid ref 473243; car park at Pooley Bridge.
Nearest BR station: Penrith.

Approx length: 14 miles (22.4 km).
Ride: Moderate.
Climbs: Long, steady climb up to Loadpot Hill at 671 m (2,281 ft).
Difficulties: Finding the way down from Loadpot Hill.
High Points: A fine circular ride over the fells with magnificent views from Loadpot Hill.
R & R: Pub, café, etc in Pooley Bridge.

This ride is an extension of the previous Ullswater ride – a considerable extension, for although only 5 miles (8 km) longer it's all offroad going a lot higher and into altogether wilder territory. It breaks down into three sections: a long ride up to the top of Loadpot Hill; a long downhill where navigation becomes tricky and a compass is necessary; and finally an easy ride back across Askham Fell.

Leave Pooley Bridge in the same direction as ride No 48, forking towards Howtown at the small church, crossing straight over at the crossroads, and following the dead-end road up past Howe Hill to the gate that leads out on to the fells. Plug on uphill on the track, and once again turn right at the bridleway crossroads for Howtown, forking left and then bearing right at The Cockpit.

A little further on you will see High Street going straight up to the left. This is the way that you would go, except that what starts as a good track peters out to nothing and is lost amidst the moorland, only reasserting itself much further up the hill. Therefore keep on past High Street, and when you come to the gully by the edge of Barton Park woods look out for a track going off to the left just past it which will take you up the hillside.

Keep on up the main left-hand track towards the top of Barton Fell, ignoring the narrower track which bears off to the right along the top of Long Crag with its steep face above Ullswater. Keep on the track which starts to bear south, eventually coming up to Arthur's Pike which is a distinctive rock outcrop sticking up on the right. A little further on go straight over at a crossing track, keeping on uphill ahead. Some way on you come to High Street once again, which by this stage is once again a distinctive track coming from the left. Bear right along it, following the track which bears right and then left, steadily gaining height as you approach the top of Loadpot Hill (671 m) (2,281 ft) with a Trig Point over to the left. I am reliably informed that the views are stupendous from here! However, when *I* reached the top it was raining and visibility was about 20 yards (17m), so choose your weather with care!

At the top you soon come to the chimney marked 'Chy' on the map, which is in fact no more than a square-shaped ruin about 8ft (2.3m) high, offering reasonable shelter if the weather is being unreasonable. From here head straight on along the track ahead riding due east, cutting the corner shown by the bridleways on the map. The narrow track is easily followed downhill for a while, but soon becomes increasingly difficult to find as it disappears into the grass which is bumpy but easy downhill riding.

Keep ENE and take care that you are heading to the right side of the two big ravines – Red Gutter and Inkern Beck – that come into sight ahead. The correct route is along the right side of Inkern Beck where the track becomes roughly discernible about 75 yards (66m) below the top of the hill where there is a conspicuous cairn, the only one in the area. From here keep on riding ENE, heading well to the left of a line of trees sheltering a barn and the farmhouse at Howe which come into view ahead. Bear over to the left towards a smaller clump of trees with the farmstead at Keldhead beyond, and when you come to stone walls follow them round to a small stone barn near to the trees.

Here you turn right on to a good, hard track which runs due east past Rough Hill Tarn to the road. This is an extremely quiet road leading to the farms, and you are unlikely to meet much in the way of traffic as it weaves downhill giving 30mph plus cruising. Follow it round to the right past Dalefoot Farm, and then round to the left, passing a barn next to a footpath sign and bearing right over a cattle-grid past a ruined building where there's a short uphill.

A short way on you come to the road running up to Askham. Turn immediately left here, following the bridleway sign up a lane towards Widwath Farm. Ride on uphill past the farm which is down to the left, and at a gate in a wall go straight ahead towards open country. A few yards on you fork right up towards a bridleway sign which can be clearly seen ahead. Cross a tarmac lane here, carrying on straight ahead on a good, wide grassy track that takes you across Askham Fell on level ground, passing Moor Divock on the way. Go straight ahead at the first bridleway crossroads at Ketley Gate, and a short way on you come to the next bridleway crossroads by the large cairn where you turned right on your way out. From here you retrace your wheeltracks, bombing downhill bound for Pooley Bridge.

Ride 50 HELVELLYN

Area: The north-east Lake District.
Start: OS Outdoor Leisure 5 grid ref 401201; car park at Aira Force waterfalls (National Trust).
Nearest BR station: Penrith.
Approx length: 14.75 miles (23.6 km).
Ride: Hard.
Climbs: Don't ask! This is one long, serious climb.
Conditions: Some soft, grassy section on the way up; very rocky track on the way down.
Difficulties: It's a long climb up, and it's technically tricky on the way down.
High Points: A fine high ride – you can't get much higher.
R & R: Pub, cafés, shops in Glenridding.

This is a fine circuit, heading up towards the mighty Helvellyn with views that get more fantastic by the mile. It is predictably a hard ride going up and up and up to its highest point of 3,000 ft (883 m)! It's ridable all the way bar about 50 yards up the final rocky slope at Raise, but to keep on riding you need to be good, fit, and motivated! Nor is it too bad if you choose to push since the landscape is so fine. With that in mind only go for it on a clear day. The ground is very exposed and the usual precautions should be taken – ride in company and don't attempt it in winter. The first half of the ride down is also very rocky, so take it easy.

Start from the Aira Force waterfalls car park towards the western end of the north shore of Ullswater on the A592 lakeside road, just east of the A5091 turning to Dockray. Turn right out of the car park, and right again up the A5091 which takes you on a long climb uphill from base camp at 510 ft (150 m). Follow the road up into open country, and after just over a mile you come to Dockray. Turn left by the inn on the corner – stop if you like, but there's still a long way to go – and head up a narrower lane towards Gill Edge. Follow it for about ¾ mile (1.2 km), and where the road bends right around the edge of the woods at Red Moss carry straight on ahead through a gate, joining a track which heads along the left hand side of the woods.

Beyond the woods the track heads out into open country with a hill ahead, and then turns right across a footbridge over Groove Beck at Groovebeck Fold. A few yards further on a much rougher track bears off uphill to the left off the main track; follow it, and keep following it as it turns round

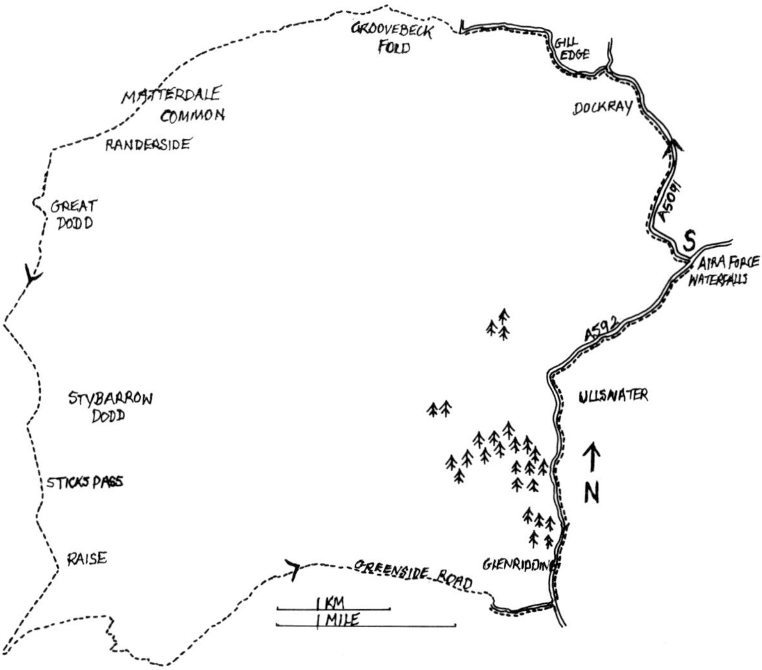

into a WSW direction heading across Matterdale Common. The going is uphill but not too steep, riding on a variable surface that sometimes becomes boggy with soft grass to slow you down. However, it's easy to follow, cutting a narrow path across the moor with big hills up ahead.

Keep on and you will come to a small plateau by the side of Randerside, a rock-strewn outcrop to the left. Ahead is Great Dodd with the track heading straight up its steep side over to the right – a fairly awesome sight. Head on up, and at the top you come to a conspicuous cairn, while over to the left there's a shelter cairn which will give you protection from the prevailing south-westerly winds. From here you can see the track snaking up and down the hillsides ahead in a southerly direction. First it heads down Millgill Head, before bearing right to Watson's Dodd where it starts to head up again along the side of Stybarrow Dodd with intermittent cairns showing the way. It then drops steeply downhill to Sticks Pass, before the last great climb up a particularly severe hill called Raise. To ride up you need to bear over to the right where the going is easiest, and only the last 50 yards (44 m) or so become unridable due to loose rocks and a very steep angle.

The long descent on the Helvellyn ride, a rough and quite difficult track.

On the far side the full magnificence of Helvellyn is revealed, bearing round to the left ahead of you and frequently looking like a dark, brooding mass. To the right is Thirlmere and to the left Ullswater as you survey the view from pretty near the top of the world. Head downhill on the track ahead, coming to a cairn at the bottom where the track starts to go up Whiteside Bank. The top of Helvellyn is about a mile distant, but the going gets harder and it makes better sense to leave your bike and walk it if you want to see what the summit is like. Beyond it a bridleway goes down to Glenridding via Dollywagon Pike, but this is so steep and rocky that it's not recommended for biking.

Looking east from the cairn at Whiteside there is a clear track running down along the left side of the valley above Red Screes and Keppel Cove. This will take you down to Glenridding in fairly quick time, but the track which zig-zags its way down the hillside is covered in loose rock and requires careful riding – if in doubt walk it. At the bottom of the zig-zags it straightens out and improves as it drops lower in the valley, crossing a footbridge where it bears right before coming down in a short series of more graceful zig-zags to the mountain rescue/outdoor pursuits centre below old mine workings.

From here the track heads straight down the Greenside Road on a good surface, passing over a cattlegrid with cottages on the left as it joins a tarmac road. Keep left downhill, and you soon come into Glenridding where there are plenty of tea shops and cafés. For the final section you travel just over 2 miles (3.2 km) along the A592 lakeside road back to your start point at Aira Force, a total of 14.75 fairly tiring miles (23.6 km) on a ride you can be proud of!

Useful Addresses

The Mountain Bike Club, Santon House, Santon Downham, Suffolk IP27 0TT (tel: 0842 812359/0273 696054).

The Mountain Bike Club is run for mountain bikers by mountain bikers. Started by Max Glaskin and Jeremy Torr, it is involved with organising offroad events, races, disseminating information, and protecting mountain bike interests. Membership brings with it a witty regular newsletter which makes the subscription worthwhile.

The Cyclists Touring Club, 69 Meadrow, Godalming, Surrey GU7 3HS (tel: 04868 7217).

The CTC is primarily an onroad cycling club. It has a long-established history of fighting for the rights of cyclists, and produces a regular magazine and a wide range of useful publications. It advises its members on all kinds of problems, and appears to look benevolently on offroaders.